RESILIENCE OF A NATION

ABOUT THE AUTHORS

Frank K. Rusagara

Brig. Gen. Frank Rusagara was born in Rwanda, but exiled to Uganda at the age of six where he lived, studied and worked, before a brief sojourn in Kenya where he taught for a while. He was involved in the RPF struggle and has held several portfolios in policy formulation and implementation with Rwanda's Ministry of Defense. He is currently the Military Historian with the Rwanda Defense Forces (RDF).

Gérard Nyirimanzi

Captain Gérard Nyirimanzi hails from the family of Court Poets of Kiruri, Nyaruguru, in Southern Province. He was initiated into traditional Rwandan poetry at a young age while living with his grandfather, who was born under King Kigeri IV Rwabugiri. He then joined his uncle, Bernardin Muzungu (OP), and was involved in the development of the *Cahiers Lumière et Société*, which translated and serialized traditional Rwandan poems collected by Abbé Alexis Kagame in the 1940s. His particular area of interest is the Rwandan conflict, which finds its genesis in the nation's history as distorted by colonialists and their sympathizers.

Gitura Mwaura

Gitura Mwaura is a Kenyan author and development journalist. His interest in the history of Rwanda arose from being involved in various Rwandan development projects while still in Kenya, which eventually led to his involvement in this book project. Also a poet and short story writer, his first work, *Portraits of the Heart*, was published in 2001.

Resilience of a Nation

A History of the Military in Rwanda

Frank K. Rusagara

with Gitura Mwaura and Gérard Nyirimanzi

FOUNTAIN PUBLISHERS RWANDA
Kigali

Fountain Publishers Rwanda Ltd
P. O. Box 6567
Kigali - Rwanda
E-mail: fountainpublishers.rwanda@gmail.com

Distributed in Europe and Commonwealth countries outside Africa by:
African Books Collective Ltd,
P. O. Box 721,
Oxford OX1 9EN, UK.
Tel/Fax: +44(0) 1869 349110
E-mail: orders@africanbookscollective.com
Website: www.africanbookscollective.com

Distributed in North America by:
Michigan State University Press
1405 South Harrison Road
25 Manly Miles Building
East Lansing, MI 48823-5245
E-mail: msupress@msu.edu
Website: www.msupress.msu.edu

ISBN 978-9970-19-001-0

A moment comes, which comes but rarely in history,
when we step out from the old to the new, when an age ends,
and when the sound of a nation, long suppressed, finds utterance.

Jawaharlal Nehru

Dedication

To the nation and people of Rwanda

Contents

Acknowledgements

I am for ever indebted to the late Major General Fred Gisa Rwigema and other martyrs of the Rwandan nation who died in the struggle to liberate Rwanda. Your gallant sacrifice to the Rwandan cause has not been in vain.

Special thanks go to Father Bernardin Muzungu for his generosity in allowing the authors to access his vast and treasured collection of Alexis Kagame's works (published and unpublished) on the Rwandan nation. Hopefully, through this modest contribution, the nation of Rwanda, long suppressed, finds its utterance; a dream he shares with the authors.

I also recognize the Rwandan historian José Kagabo for his insightful ideas on the history of Rwanda, Professor Josias Semujanga, Pierre Karemera, Rose-Marie Mukarutabana, and so many others for their encouragement and intellectual debates that were an inspiration in putting together the book.

I, on behalf of my co-authors, especially acknowledge our families for their patience and understanding for the lengthy period of time we had to be away while working on the project.

I would also wish to acknowledge my late father, Yohana S. Kanyambo, whose occasional talks and discussions while in exile spurred me to the interest in *Rwandanicity* and hence this project; my wife Christine Mukankanza for her resilience and commitment, and my children Veronica Shandari, Ernesto Che Guevera Rwatambuga, Steve "Gift" Rubanzambuga, Isabella Barakagwira and Ezra Kanyambo; this project hopefully encourages you to aspire to the Rwandan ideal.

Prologue

As Bernardin Muzungu once put it, "The history of Rwanda is the history of its military."[1] This may be said of any traditional society, but it rings particularly true of Rwanda. In the traditional Rwandan society, the military was the main institution of socialization with its commanders, mainly drawn from elite families, playing a prominent role in the politics of the nation through the generations.

It is the aim of this inquiry to examine the role the military has played throughout the history of Rwanda to date. We look at the different phases the Rwandan military has undergone, from the traditional, the colonial and immediate post-independence military to the present.

It is the premise of this inquiry that, not precluding any political expediencies, it is the military that has had the most central socio-political role to play in what became of Rwanda during its heydays when no slave trader[2] could tread its soil, to its lowest moment during the 1994 genocide. It is also our premise that it took the military to lead the way in re-uniting a shattered people and their country on Rwanda's journey to becoming a democratic country of reputable international standing.

This history of Rwanda to date covers almost a thousand years, and all through it the military has had a hand in influencing the socio-political life of its people, whether positively or negatively. As we shall demonstrate, traditional Rwandan society was organized around the military, which defined each individual and his or her place in the society.

Under the monarchy before the advent of colonialism, it is in the military that Rwanda found its unity. On their advent, the

Belgian colonialists not only divided Rwandans along "racial" lines as Tutsi "Caucasians" and Hutu "Bantu", but introduced the brutality that characterized the Belgian-Congolese military, *Force Publique,* which would inform the post-independence military leading to the 1994 genocide.

Much of what we know today of traditional Rwanda and its military is in the customs that were practised and handed down through folklore, and more especially through poetry. Rwandan history in general was expressed through poems *(Ibisigo)* composed by court poets, who mainly derived from the Abasinga clan. The court poets, much like the *griots* of West Africa, were the "keepers" of history, with the pioneer being the poetess Queen Mother Nyiraruganzu II Nyirarumaga in the 16th Century during the reign of King Ruganzu II Ndoli.[3]

The Queen Mother is credited with the establishment of the institution of court poets, *Intebe y'Abasizi,* which saw its end with the overthrow of King Kigeri V Ndahindurwa in 1960. Beginning with her first known poem, *Umunsi ameza imiryango yose* (i.e. The day of the birth of the Rwandan families),[4] Nyirarumaga speaks of Rwandan history as akin to a string of beads, which adorned the Rwandan women. She sees each bead as encapsulating an epoch or chapter in Rwandan history, and in her case, beginning with the reign of King Ruganzu I Bwimba in the 14th Century. Her poems, which summarized the major deeds of each reigning king, started with the first known monarch of the Banyiginya dynasty, King Gihanga Ngomijana, and have traditionally been referred to as *Ibisigo by'impakanizi* (epic poems).

In their pristine form, it is these poems[5] that we have resorted to glean our military history and offer a Rwandan perspective. As has been observed by Ki-Zerbo, "Oral tradition is the only path that can lead us right into the history and spirit of the African peoples. [...] Knowledge in African oral societies is not something abstract and separate from life; it is bound up with Man's tangible social behaviour. Through the divine Word, it is connected both with the present-day world and with the origin of all knowledge."[6]

It is our endeavour in this book to demonstrate the continuing cultural heritage from traditional Rwanda to the present as derived from the "Word". Drawing from our oral history, therefore, we dwell on the process of *ku-aanda* (from which Rwanda derives its name) which bore many heroes in the expansion of Rwanda from the original locality of Gasabo. As we shall see, many of their heroic deeds will be recalled centuries later and, such as with *Ingando,* harnessed for Rwanda's current socio-political, cultural and economic development.

One of the foremost heroes in this process of *ku-aanda* is King Kigeri II Nyamuheshera in the 16th Century who remains one of the greatest of Rwandan expansionists, conquering the "furthest lands" that included Masisi and Rucuro in today's eastern Democratic Republic of Congo and Bufumbira as far as Lake Edward in Uganda. His military exploits and heroism are attested by the traditional military award, *Umudende,* the foremost recognition in a system of ascending numbers of seven to the highest honour of 21. In this system of honouring bravery, a soldier who had killed seven enemy combatants would be awarded the *Umudende,* while the second highest honour called the *Impotore* was awarded to the one who had killed 14. The highest honour was of the award, *Gucana-Uruti* that was granted to a general who had killed 21 enemies.

In the case of King Kigeri II Nyamuheshera, his revered award was in recognition of his having killed or ousted seven foreign kings and annexed their kingdoms. Nyamuheshera's "medal of honour", a fashioned metal brace that was worn like a necklace, remained hanging in his *Ikigabiro* (official residence) in Bumbogo near Gutamba in the District of Kigoma until the 1960s.[7]

To have developed such a system of awarding "medals"[8] is remarkable and points to the importance placed on the individual's military contribution. It is thus that, in the process of *ku-aanda,* Rwanda found its "soul" with the military as the social organizing institution. Each man and his male descendants had to belong to a particular military regiment which gave them their social identity.

It was also incumbent upon the society as a whole to play its part, with religion playing a central role. Before any military expedition, Rwandans led by the king asked their God, *Imana,* for blessings and permission to go ahead in elaborate rituals *(kuraguza).* There had to be a sure sign of God's blessings *(imana zeze)* as divined by the high priests, *Abanyamihango b'Ibwami,* otherwise the expedition would not take place.

Fortified by religion, therefore, all able-bodied men and women participated in one way or another. Those not directly engaged on the frontline were either busy providing the required logistics and support, such as evacuating the dead and casualties or performing various war rituals.

Hence, there existed different categories of people involved in war. These included the actual combatants *(Ingabo zirwana),* their bodyguards *(abagaragu),* logisticians *(Ibitsimbanyi)* and a special troop of raiders *(Abakoni),* who were charged with gathering war booty, especially cattle which were the more cherished spoils of battle. Women and children were also involved in various war rituals at the royal court *(Abatangampumbya).*

Gutanga impumbya, for instance, was a war ritual that kept the society symbolically mobilized and focused on the battlefront. This was signified by the royal bull, Rusanga, which was ritualized to stand for the king in his royal residence while he was away at the war front. Such bulls held the symbolism of the patriarch of the nation. A special fire would therefore be lit to keep away the "nuisance flies" from that bull. As their contribution, the women and children would ensure the bull was undisturbed by collecting special plants to build a smoky fire. It was believed that with Rusanga calm and unperturbed, the outcome of the war would be in favour of Rwanda.

To further demonstrate the deep social involvement in a military campaign, elder women whose sons were headed for war would hold their right breast and shower it with saliva *(Gufata iry'iburyo)* while uttering words of encouragement, or offer a prayer to win the war and bring prosperity. Weddings were not allowed during military campaigns. Young, unmarried and married women abstained from sex when their husbands were at war. This was believed to offer a protective shield to their present and future husbands. It was also believed that any act of engaging in extra-marital sex would expose their husbands to fatal danger on the frontline.

Upon the war ending and annexation of new territories, the conquered communities were integrated into the Rwandan society. This was through the highly evolved socio-economic categorisation of cattle herders who were described as Tutsi[9], the agriculturalists described as Hutu and the artisans, the Twa. Depending on the socio-economic activity of the individuals in the conquered community, they were assimilated taking on a Rwandan identity according to their economic vocations.

Examples abound of such integrated communities. For instance, the invading Abanyoro, initially from the Bunyoro-Kitara Empire in present-day Uganda, who could not go back home after their defeat by Prince Forongo during the reign of King Mibambwe I Mutabazi-Sekarongoro, were assimilated as Hutu or Tutsi depending on their economic vocation in the Indara[10] region, in present-day Gisagara District. Many of Abanyoro were of the Abashambo clan, the ruling clan of Mpororo and Ndorwa kingdoms, which remains today as one of Rwandan clans.

Another example is provided by the Bahunde from North Kivu fleeing the invasion of the aggressive Barega during the reign of King Cyilima II Rujugira in the 17th Century. They installed themselves in Gisenyi (Nyamyumba-Rubavu) and got assimilated as Hutu, as their main socio-economic activity was agriculture.

A last and more recent example is that of the Bashi and Bahavu who in the early 1920s migrated to Cyangugu fleeing the expropriation of their land by the colonial Bukavu Urban Authorities in the Eastern Congo. The majority became Hutu. It is from this community that the first president of Rwanda, Grégoire Kayibanda, hailed from.[11]

From the above, it is demonstrable that Rwanda was highly organized with the military, as observed, being the core socializing institution. The Abanyoro who remained, for instance, were instituted as the Indara military regiment during the reign of King Yuhi III Mazimpaka in the 17th Century so that they could better fit in the society.

Nevertheless, how traditional Rwanda and its all encompassing military as a social institution would decline and succumb to a combined colonial and Christian onslaught, as we shall delve into in the book, can be demonstrated in the fortunes of many prominent elite families, of which one stands out.

Indeed, the family of Nturo ya Nyilimigabo *(Abanana)* best illustrates the decline of the larger family of Rwanda in the Belgo-Roman Catholic Church conspiracy to subdue a nation. Chief Nturo was among the first important army chiefs to embrace Christianity, and took on the name Paul upon becoming a Christian in the 1920s. Nturo descended from an illustrious family of Rwandan heroism, only to seem to throw away this legacy when he took up Christianity.

His father, Nyilimigabo ya Marara, was the celebrated commander of the *Intaganzwa,* that had been formed under King Yuhi IV Gahindiro (1746 – 1802) and commanded by Nturo's great grandfather, Munana wa Gihana. Gihana was the devoted son of King Cyilima II Rujugira (1675 – 1708) who sacrificed himself in Burundi as Umucengeri to preserve Rwanda's sovereignty. He was also the commander of the elite military formation, Abalima, under his father's reign.

Marara ya Munana was the powerful commander of Intaganzwa, who, under King Gahindiro, was always in competition with the de facto prime minister and army commander, Rugaju rwa Mutimbo, to see who was more powerful. Marara was grandson and confidant of the queen mother, Nyirayuhi IV Nyiratunga, while Rugaju was a close friend and confidant of King Gahindiro which brought about their perpetual rivalries.

Taking over Abataganzwa from his father, Nyilimigabo ya Marara would later die in battle around 1881 in Bunyabungo (Congo) under King Kigeri IV Rwabugiri. That he died on the frontline was considered an act of heroism, comparable to that of his grandfather, Gihana, who died as Umucengeli in Burundi, as we shall see in a later chapter.

On his part, his son, Nturo ya Nyilimigabo, commanded the company *Imbabazabahizi* around 1910 and, before converting to Catholicism, had fought alongside the Germans to quell the Ndungutse-Basebya rebellion in the north, also discussed later in the book.

Nturo's conversion to Christianity best symbolises the beginning of the deconstruction of traditional Rwanda and its military. His chiding of his Commander-in-Chief, King Musinga, as being "old fashioned" made Nturo one of the most important proponents of Christianity in its march towards the destruction of the Rwandan heritage.

Yet it would also leave a lasting mark on his family. Just like Rwanda would lose its identity, in his zeal, Nturo so adored the white man that he named one of his sons "Bwanakweri" (the-whiteman-is-always-right) after Leenaerts, the Principal of Nyanza School of Chiefs' Sons in the 1930s.

Prosper Bwanakweri attended the Groupe Scholaire of Astrida *(Indatwa)* and became an evolué (modernist) who seemed to have little respect for traditional Rwandan ideals, taking up from his father. It is said that Bwanakweri would mockingly greet King Mutara III Rudahigwa with a derogatory *"Bonjour le Mwami* (Hello King)", in contempt of the monarchy.[12] The Rwandan monarch was traditionally greeted with applause and handclaps accompanied by the greeting *amohoro nyagasani* (peace be with you, your majesty).

Bwanakweli would go on to form the political party, *Rassemblement Démocratique Rwandais* (RADER) in 1959 under the auspices of the Résidence claiming to push for a constitutional monarchy.[13] Nturo's other son, Frederic Butera, became a celebrated performing artist *(Intore)* who even graced the one hundred Rwandan Francs bill with his image, and appeared in Coca Cola commercials in the 1950s and 60s.

The two sons of Nturo and their descendants represent many Rwandans who, unwillingly, ended up becoming colonial "constructs"—not the *Intore* nationalists of the Intaganzwa regiment of their forefathers—by denying themselves their heritage as Rwandans with a common socio-cultural thread leading to the "ethnic" divisionism that ensued.

It is in this situation that the "1959 Hutu Revolution" would come and go, resulting in many exiles who, living in difficult conditions and xenophobia in the diaspora, would henceforth continually seek for ways, military or otherwise, to return home. But home was not rosy either for those who had remained, as the military regime was ever more oppressive in every sphere of life within the country.

The oppressive military regime was a direct result of the Belgian colonists. The decline of the Rwandan state and the unity of its people leading to the 1959 exiles and the 1994 genocide began with the advent of colonialism, further deteriorating during the post-colonial period in the First and Second Republics. The military was at the forefront of the destruction of the state of Rwanda during these periods.

The colonial and neo-colonial occupation of Rwanda, which took a century, from 1894 to 1994, ensured the desecration of the original Rwandan state and the military institution. In the colonial period, it was, first, the Congo-Belge *Force Publique* and the *Garde Territoriale du Rwanda-Urundi*. In the post-independence period, it was the sectarian and Hutu-nised *Garde*

Nationale du Rwanda in the First Republic, and then the *Forces Armées Rwandaises* in the Second Republic. None of these armed forces propagated a national ideology or character. They were sectarian and overtly divisive leading to the 1994 genocide.

We take stock of this history and how this gave rise to the *Inyenzi* guerrilla movement in the 1960s and then the Rwanda Patriotic Front and Army (RPF/A) in the late 1980s and early 90s, leading to the pragmatism of the current Rwanda Defense Forces (RDF). Borrowing from the *Ingabo z'u Rwanda* of old, the RDF today not only ensures security for all, but provides a model of national unity and integration that continues to inform Rwanda's socio-political and economic development.

As Achebe has observed, "The African past, with all its imperfections, was not one long night of savagery from which the first Europeans acting on God's behalf delivered the Africans."[14] In Rwanda, the *Ingabo* delivered the "Africans"

Notes

1   B. Muzungu, *Histoire du Rwanda Pré-colonial*, L'Harmattan, Paris, 2003, p.354.
2   Henry Morton Stanley, *Through the Dark Continent*, London, 1878, Vol.1, p.455; Ian Linden, *Church and Revolution in Rwanda*. Manchester, 1977, p.21.
3   A. Kagame, *Un abrégé de l'ethno-histoire du Rwanda*, Editions universitaires du Rwanda, Butare, 1972, pp.12-15.
4   B. Muzungu (ed), *Cahiers Lumière et Société*, No.21, Dec., 2002, pp.6-11.
5   Most of the repertoire of the oral Rwandan traditional poems were collected and transcribed in the 1940s by Alexis Kagame (some of which are found in, *La Poésie dynastique au Rwanda* (IRCB, Bruxelles, 1951) from various court poets of the time, led by Karera ka Bamenya. Later (since 2003), Father B. Muzungu serialised them all in his review, *Cahiers Lumière et Société*, from No. 21 to 32.

6   J. Ki-Zerbo (ed), *General History of Africa Part I*, UNESCO, 1981, p.62; Ki-Zerbo observes that "We still have among us some of the great depositories of this tradition, who can be said to be the living memory of Africa, but theirs will probably be the last generation. Oral tradition is a fragment of the cultural heritage of mankind that has been miraculously preserved by a combination of circumstances."

7   A. Kagame (1972), op. cit., p.122.

8   A similar system of awarding medals has been adopted by the Rwanda Defence Forces to recognize the contribution of individual military achievement with the presentation of *impeta* (as the traditional medals were called).

9   Simon Sebagabo in *Dialogue* No.178, of April-June 2004 (p.22) observes that *gutuuka* means to "adorn" or "ornament" with jewels or bracelets *(Indinga n'Indirira)*. By this he implies that the term "Tutsi" was derived from gutuuka. Hence "Tutsi" referred to "the rich" or the "well-off" who could afford such ornaments to denote their high social status.

10   *Indara* in Kinyarwanda means "remnants", which was used in south Rwanda to describe the Abanyoro who are also referred to as *Abasigari* in northern Rwanda, meaning the same thing - those who remained.

11   Laurent Gakuba, *Rwanda 1959-1994,* Coetquen Editions, 2007, p.24.

12   Interview with ex-chief Chrisostome Rwangombwa rwa Muterahejuru in January 2006 in Kigali.

13   G. Logiest, *Mission au Rwanda: Un blanc dans la bagarre Tutsi-Hutu,* Didier Hatier, Bruxelles, 1988, p.101; Gakuba (2007), op. cit., p.46.

14   C. Achebe: "Africa's genius", *The Daily Monitor,* 17 June 2007; http://www.monitor.co.ug/artman/publish/insights/Achebe_Africa.

1

Ku-aanda: The Formation and Growth of the Rwandan Pre-colonial State

It is a historical truism that the rise and fall of nations has always coincided with, and been complemented by, the strengthening or weakening of the military institution. As a consequence, therefore, nations, depending on the fortunes of their military might vis-à-vis their stronger or weaker neighbours have seen the expansion and waning of their territories through time in the hegemonic concept of realism. Realism articulates power relations between nations and states through the use of force to pursue national interests.[1]

In traditional Rwanda, this hegemonic notion of realism manifested itself in the process of *ku-aanda*. In its literal meaning *ku-aanda* means expansion or spreading out from the centre.[2] The principle of *ku-aanda*, which involved annexation and subsequent integration of neighbouring territories, informed the continued expansion and growth of pre-colonial Rwanda. In this process, the military played the central role as a vehicle not only of protection, but also of socio-political organization and prosperity throughout its history as a pre-colonial nation.

To trace this history, Rwanda is believed to have emerged around the 10th or 11th century AD[3] under "King Gihanga, the founder of the prosperous and sovereign nation" (in

1

Kinyarwanda we say, *Gihanga cyahanze inka n'ingoma*).[4] It may seem that Gihanga was destined to bear a heavy burden. His "founding mission" as bidden by the "Lord", and recalled by Poetess Nyirarumaga, was "Go forth and forge the great nation".[5]

Urya ni wo munsi ihamagara	That day He beckoned [our]
ba so ba mbere	ancestors,
Rugira rwo ku ruzi rwa	The Lord of Lake Muhazi,
Nyirarubuga	
Ijya kubereka imigisha	In His blessings to them said,
Ngo: haguruka mujye kubaka	Go forth and forge the Great
Kiyebe	Nation

In the same poem, in affirming realism, she also notes that *Bahera aho bararima bareza* ([line of kings] started from "Gasabo" and went on to "till" [forcefully expand] Rwanda).

Bahinga aho badasaturiwe	They conquer the lands
Abami b'i Saduka-mirwa	The kings of Rwanda
Ryarenga bagacyuka	And at glorious sunset
Bacyuye imigisha benda[6]	Return with booty

The line of kings *(Abami b'umushumi)*[77] that took the throne after Gihanga would lead to the reign of Ruganzu I Bwimba (1312-1345), hailed to be among the greatest of Rwandan monarchs. It was during his reign that Rwanda began to consolidate into a coherent political entity and thrive within a confederation of clanic principalities[8] that had politically existed by mutual respect of their individual sovereignties. It was also during this period that there emerged military institutions in loose and unstable formations, essentially for family and clan protection in the principalities. Being in close proximity, each principality therefore had almost a similar[9] leadership structure with a king, a dynastic drum and a military structure to protect its sovereignty.

Initially, these military "structures" played more of a social role, with their main concern being the preservation of the means of subsistence, other than securing territorial influence. King Gihanga's military formations, for instance, were meant for the security of his family and his economic assets, with the *Abanyansanga* and *Inyangakugoma* formations, protecting his cows *Insanga* and *Ingizi*, respectively, while the *Abahiza* and *Gakondo* were responsible for food provisions, either for the court or the extended family. The *Inshyama* and *Abakaraza* took care of the royal drums. These would form the first military formations in Rwanda.[10]

The society continued with its evolution along with its nascent family and clan military units and, by the time of King Ruganzu I Bwimba, the capital of Rwanda had moved from Nyamilembe ya Humure to Gasabo Hill (near Lake Muhazi), which is today recognised as the cradle of the state of Rwanda.[11]

By the time of Bwimba's reign[12] therefore, nearly three hundred years after Gihanga, the society had greatly matured given the increase in the number of its population. Along with this was the growth and emergence of Rwanda as a complex social structure, which necessarily required a profound change in the psychological basis of the people's social relationship within the now much larger community. The aggregation of this increased number of people into a complex society required that they refocus their allegiances away from the extended family and clan toward a larger social entity of the state.

In theory, as may be observed in similar societies,[13] this psychological change was facilitated by the rise of the national religion, which worshipped *Imana y'i Rwanda* (God of Rwanda) thus giving meaning to the individual's life beyond the narrowness of the family or clan. As may be presumed with similar nascent societies, an organized belief system was integrated into the social order and given institutional expression through public rituals that linked religious worship to political and military objectives that were national in scope and definition.

Thus, the Rwandan Mwami (king) became divine, and military achievements of great Rwandan monarchs were perceived as divinely ordained or inspired. In this manner the propulsive power of religion was placed at the service of the state and its military as we shall presently see with the inception of the institution of *Ubucengeri* that demanded personal sacrifice for country and therefore God's favour to win a war in the inevitable quest of *Ku-aanda*.

At the head of the military in this quest, and with divine blessings, therefore, it was up to each king, especially those bearing warrior names — such as Kigeri, Mibambwe and Ruganzu — to enlarge their inherited territory through military conquests or diplomatic integration of incoming clans. This form of integration was the case with clans such as *Abanyakarama* from Burundi, *Abashambo* from Ndorwa and Mpororo, *Abaha* from Buha, and *Abahinda* from Karagwe.[14]

Ku-aanda or the inclusiveness and expansion of Rwanda would be entrenched in oral tradition, which generation after generation would continually speak of the legacy of the monarch to enlarge the Rwandan territory through conquests or integration. For instance, in the poem *Ukwibyara*[15] (Self procreation) by Nyakayonga ka Musare, he extols this legacy during the enthronement of King Mutara II Rwogera noting, "The horizon stands yours to overreach."

Nimugarishye mwaraganje	Hail Rwandan conquerors
Mwagagaze mukuze uruharo	The horizon stands yours to overreach
Umwami uhawe uruharo	As the royal throne abides you
arwigiza imbere[16]	to

Similarly, in the poem *Umwami si Umuntu*[17] (The King is not a man, i.e., divine) Semidogoro ya Gasegege during the reign of King Mibambwe III Sentabyo explains Rwanda's largesse in the process of *ku-aanda* to accommodate all comers, conquered or otherwise, with the observation, "The calving cow/Satiates one and all".

Abyaza imwe ikaba ishimwe	The calving cow
Inshungu ya twese	Satiates one and all
N'abavuye imuhana irabahaza	Even those from afar.
na bo.	
(...)	*(...)*
Akamwa wenyine akagihaza	The king provides for all
Agahaza n'abamucikira	Even those who seek refuge
N'abamusaba imuhira	And those that seek abode
Akabemeza akabahagiriza rimwe[18]	And satisfies all and sundry

Through oral tradition, especially poetry, history was recorded and succeeding generations learnt the heroics of the great Rwandan military leaders, the most significant of which we shall now look at, beginning with King Ruganzu I Bwimba.

King Ruganzu I Bwimba (ca. 1312-1345) and the Institution of Ubucengeri

Along with the continuing socio-psychological progress in Rwanda early in the second millennium, the first stirrings of a collective feeling of Rwandanness or Rwandanicity began to take hold. This was helped by the development of the central state institutions and a supporting administrative apparatus, which inevitably gave form and stability to military structures. The result was the expansion and stabilization of the formerly loose and unstable family and clan military formations that would lead to a fully articulated military structure by the reign of King Ruganzu I Bwimba, under the military formations Inyangakugoma and Gakondo.

Bwimba is significant in the process of *ku-aanda*,[19] as he is credited with the popularization and establishment of the ideal of Ubucengeri as one of Rwanda's most peculiar and enduring hallmarks of traditional courage and heroism. This would hence form the pillar for patriotism in the survival and continued growth of Rwanda. In effect, the establishment of Ubucengeri laid the foundation for the initiation of the process of *ku-aanda* by Bwimba's grandson, Prince Mukobanya, who followed in his footsteps.

Ubucengeri can be defined as martyrdom for the nation or the act of "offensive liberation" whereby it was regarded as an honour to offer oneself, shed blood or die for Rwanda to become recognized as *Umucengeri*. An act of Ubucengeri was believed to be divinely ordained and blessed to succeed by *Imana* (God), for the selfless act in essence meant the preservation of the sanctity of God's own home (Rwanda). It was therefore believed that the life sacrificed and the blood thus spilled was special and would ensure victory in war.

Failing in this sacrifice, the saying was that *Wima igihugu amaraso, imbwa zikayanywera ubusa* (when you deny Rwanda your blood, then the dogs may take it for free). As a call to patriotism (much like Kennedy's 'Ask not what your country can do for you, but what you can do for your country'[20]) the Rwandan saying is interpreted to mean that you may not demand of Rwanda, but that it would be honourable to give it your all, as King Ruganzu I Bwimba would ultimately exemplify.

During his reign, Rwanda neighboured the powerful principalities or kingdoms of Bugesera under King Nsoro I Bihembe, and Gisaka under King Kimenyi I Musaya in former Kibungo in today's Eastern Province. While Rwanda was on good terms with Bugesera, it was at odds with Gisaka whose king harboured hegemonic ambitions in the existing confederation of small kingdoms and wanted to annex Rwanda.

As told in the poem, *Nigire inama nanoga*[21] (literally translated, Let me humble myself) by Muguta in the 17th Century, Kimenyi's ambitions were fed by his diviners' predictions that if he married the Rwandan princess, Robwa, sister to King Ruganzu I Bwimba, the resulting son would be the future conqueror of Rwanda. So, King Kimenyi I demanded the hand of Princess Robwa. Knowing from his father what the marriage portended, Bwimba opposed the obvious conspiracy in the marriage, but was overruled by his Queen Mother, Nyiraruganzu Nyakanga, and her influential brother, Nkurukumbi, who naively held the view that the marriage would serve to strengthen the friendship between Gisaka and Rwanda.

Kimenyi therefore went on to marry the reluctant Robwa who, before leaving, swore to her brother-king that she would never give birth to a future conqueror of Rwanda. During her stay in Gisaka, however, it may seem that there was a change of mind as the full implication of the marriage came to be realized by the Queen Mother and her brother. So when Robwa announced her pregnancy, the Rwandan court designated Nkurukumbi, the Queen Mother's brother, to become Umucengeri against Gisaka. When Nkurukumbi declined the honour, the oracles revealed that it would have to be the king himself for the supreme sacrifice.

Ndoba yitanze	Robwa sacrificed herself for Rwanda
Yanze guhozwa na Ndazi	Rejecting Kimenyi's amorous consolations
(...)	*(...)*
Bugiri ni we Bugingo	[And] Bwimba, Rwanda's saviour
Bwatabara i Buganza	Started offensive liberation from Buganza
Nyiri umugogo wagomera ubuhatsi	Whose royal remains pre-empted occupation
Ngo butajya i Bukobwa	Of Rwanda by Gisaka
Ngo atabatoya musaza we	And in that sacrifice equaled his sister
Mushiki wa Mugabwa-busarasi na Samayebe	So that Robwa's off-spring
Ngo Robwa atabwirongoranya[22]	Would not reign over Rwanda

The "supreme sacrifice" began with King Ruganzu I opening hostilities with Gisaka, while pretending to be on a hunting expedition where he killed a leopard *(ingwe)*. Having left his wife pregnant with his child, he sent instructions that if a boy, and therefore his heir, he should be named Rugwe in memory of the leopard he killed. Then he confidently went forth and subjected himself to the spears of Gisaka's warriors in his ordained sacrifice, knowing that there was continuation of the dynasty.

With the death and shedding of her brother's royal blood, Princess Robwa also chose to do the same and die with her unborn child. Legend has it that the princess died by hurling her heavy body on to the Rukurura, the Gisaka royal drum, presented to her by Kimenyi I in fulfilling the rites of enthroning her as the future Queen Mother to her unborn child. It was thus that the Rwanda, symbolized by its royal drum, Rwoga, was saved.

With this selfless sacrifice for the country, Ruganzu I Bwimba served as an ideal to concretize and firmly establish a sense of patriotism in Rwandan lore, hence the saying, *urugumye rugomba nyirarwo* (ultimate responsibility rests with the king), perhaps best echoed by Truman's "the buck stops here"[23].

With the institution of *ubucengeri* firmly in place, it served to give Rwanda an ideal that would firm the people's confidence in what lay ahead. It was thus that the end of the reign of Ruganzu I Bwimba also marked an important milestone in the evolution of Rwanda, as the budding process of *ku-aanda* was about to take root. It ushered in a new reality, namely the historical movement from being a clan-based principality in a confederation to a fully fledged monarchical state. This momentous leap would mainly be achieved by Bwimba's grandson, Prince Mukobanya.

While still under the reign of his father, Cyilima I Rugwe[24] (Bwimba's son), Prince Mukobanya would distinguish himself by attacking and conquering the confederate principalities and incorporating their territories within Rwanda. This would trigger an expansion process of *ku-aanda* that would last nearly five centuries.

King Kigeri I Mukobanya (±1378-1411): Launching the *Ku-aanda* Process

As already noted, by the reign of King Ruganzu I Bwimba the society had greatly matured leading to a strong military structure being put in place by the reign of his son Cyilima I Rugwe (1345-1378). It was, however, beginning with the reign of King Kigeri I Mukobanya that the legitimacy of the military institution can be explained as a mechanism of cultural development, in which the conduct of war became a legitimate social function supported by the binding national feeling of Rwandanness through an extensive institutional infrastructure. The military institution became an indispensable characteristic of the social order if people were to not only survive the predatory behaviour of strong neighbouring kingdoms such as Gisaka or Bunyoro-Kitara[25], but gain both in culture and prosperity.

During this period, Rwanda refined the social structures that were essential to the functioning of genuinely large and complex social orders and, in doing so, brought into existence a new and more versatile military institution. The period also saw the practice of war firmly rooted in the Rwandan society and experience and, perhaps more importantly, in the people's psychology. War, warriors and the military institution not only became normal, but the very core of life revolving around a structured system of alternating kings of peace and war in a socio-military complex permeating all levels of society.

It may be necessary to first explain this royal cycle of a structured system of alternating kings of peace and war, before appreciating the achievements of Kigeri I Mukobanya and the process he was about to initiate.

Through the royal cycle of alternating[26] kings, beginning with Cyilima I, the process of *ku-aanda* came to be articulated and channeled. The royal cycle revolved around a four-generation martial axis that defined the role and mission of each of the five kings in the cycle. The titular names of the kings in the cycle were Cyilima, Kigeri, Mibambwe, Yuhi, Mutara.[27] The royal cycle to the throne alternated in the following respective order:

> Mutara – Kigeri – Mibambwe – Yuhi;
> Cyilima – Kigeri – Mibambwe – Yuhi;
> Mutara – Kigeri – Mibambwe – Yuhi;
> Cyilima – Kigeri – Mibambwe – Yuhi; etc.

Each cycle could only begin with a King Cyilima or Mutara, both of whom were referred to as 'cattle or pastoral kings'. As pastoral kings they were tasked to accomplish the royal ritual of ensuring the care and well-being of the cattle and their increase in numbers as an indication of the kingdom's prosperity *(Inzira y'ishora)*. These were therefore peacetime reigns in which Rwanda had to concentrate on the domestic economy in order to gain in resources and the "energy" required to accomplish the tasks of the next two reigns, which were characterized by war and conquests.

To emphasize the importance of the royal cycle already in progression, kings Mutara and Cyilima also had to designate the matri-dynastic[28] clans from which the next three queen mothers, or the biological mothers of their successors, would be chosen. This was deemed necessary, as it would determine the character and therefore the quality of warriorship of the next Kigeri and Mibambwe, including those of Yuhi and Cyilima.

This designation of the matri-dynastic clans especially followed from the tradition established by King Mutara I Semugeshi (1543-1576), whose aim was to deter the monopolization of the institution of the queen mother by the family of Ndiga of the Abega clan. It is King Mutara I Semugeshi who is also credited with the articulation of the martial four-generation royal cycle[29].

After a King Mutara or Cyilima, therefore, the cycle would then continue with a king Kigeri followed by a king Mibambwe, both of whom were "warrior kings". It may be noted that the kings bearing the names "Ndahiro" or "Ruganzu" were also described as warrior kings. However, their bearers, King Ndahiro I Ruyange (1180-1213) and Ndahiro II Cyamatare (1477-1510), including King Ruganzu I Bwimba and Ruganzu II Ndoli (1510-1543), had died at the hands of the enemy and were therefore deemed an unwelcome omen on the institution of the monarchy. Due to this, King Mutara I Semugeshi in his articulation omitted them in the martial royal cycle leaving the names Kigeri and Mibambwe to represent the war and conquest stage in the cycle.

Theoretically, a King Kigeri would open hostilities and wage wars of conquests, with a King Mibambwe continuing the general war plan by consolidating and stabilizing the conquered territories. Thus, while a King Mutara and Cyilima were mainly intended for internal stability and prosperity, a King Kigeri and Mibambwe dealt with external relations, either militarily or diplomatically.[30]

The four generation royal cycle in the process of *ku-aanda* would finally close with a King Yuhi, who was described as the "king of fire" (Umuliro). He was, in essence, the stabilizing link between the pastoral kings and the warrior kings in the symbol of fire. In Rwanda's traditional folklore, fire is a symbol of Rwanda and its people as being perennial or enduring in the continuum of time. In Rwandan culture fire symbolises the energy that engenders transformation and change. For this reason there was always an undying fire in the royal court.

As a king, Yuhi's function also consisted of safeguarding the "fire" of the cattle (*Igicaniro*), for which he was also indirectly referred to as a pastoral king. *Igicaniro* in its essence was that fire lit at a new camp to gather cattle and dispel "nuisance flies", and therefore held the symbolism of bringing together and securing the unity of the people in the process of *ku-aanda*.

It is in this framework of the royal cycle that the role of Kigeri I Mukobanya may be conceived as a "warrior king" when he broke the confederation of petty chiefdoms marking the beginning of Rwanda's influence and power leading to prosperity, while still a prince. Mukobanya is extolled in the poem below.[31]

Ungana ya Nkuba Nkubiri	You are like that Thunder, the Whirlwind
Yakuburaga iz'ibihugu byose	That conquered all the territories
Abigira icya Mugabo umwe	Unifying them under one King
Nimwumve ikubitiro ry'ubukombe	Celebrating the first triumph of the Lead-Bull
Nimwumve umushyamo w'iyo Mfizi	Beware of the bellow of the Lead--Bull
(...)	(...)
Ngo irakubita ishyira mu cyico	How deadly the bull's lethal horns
Iz'amakeba igakomera impunzi	That revels in the rivals' flight

Under his father's reign, Mukobanya started the *ku-aanda* process by opening an eastern front at the head of two battalions, *Ababarabiri* (the-action-oriented-ones) and *Ibidafungura* (the-tough-ones), by first attacking the petty-kingdom of *Abongera*, whose domain straddled Nyabugogo River and included parts of Bwanacyambwe and the south of Buriza in Kigali Province.

This conquest of Bwanacyambwe and the capture of the kingdom's royal drum, Kamuhagama, is told by Kibarake in the poem *"Batewe n'iki uburake?"*[32] (What is it that upset them?).

Se asagirijwe agasigirira indekwe	Seeing his father in trouble, seized the bow
Ese we ko yiraririye iza Nkuba	And attacked Nkuba (last King of Abongera)
Nkomati ya Nyirankomane	The warrior son of the "Aged-Knock-Kneed" one (Cyilima I)
Atazijishuriwe akazizana	Who stumped the enemy (Nkuba) to submission
Iyo adahaguruka kwiyerekana	Hadn't he overrun and paraded
Kamuhagama	Kamuhagama

Bwiru bwa Muhanyi	Who would have dared
mwayironse he?	capture it?

In short order, the mountain range of Jari under the petty-king Mugina was next when Mukobanya captured the royal drum, *Bushizimbeho,* before turning to Busarasi in Bumbogo, Rulindo District, which also included the localities of Shyorongi-Kanyinya. With its petty King Sambwe (son of Cyabugimbu) ousted, Mukobanya installed his step-brother, Karimbi, chief of Busarasi, thus starting a trend of centralized administration and governance using relatives close to the throne. The poet Muguta mentions this conquest of Busarasi in the poem *Nigire inama nanoga.*[33]

Ni we wacuze incoro	It is he [Kigeri I] who bereaved
Y'Abanya Cyabugimbu na	The descendants of Cyabugimbu
Cyabashi	and Cyabashi
Iyo ncuro ayogoje mw'Igesura	In the ravages of war

Then Prince Mukobanya turned his sights west across River Nyabarongo and took Nduga Kingdom when he defeated King Murinda and his spirited army at Bwiyando near Kinyambi, east of the present-day Catholic Parish of Kamonyi in former Gitarama Province.

All told, Prince Mukobanya, while his father King Cyilima I Rugwe was warring to the north-west across River Nyabarongo, conquered the large kingdom of Nduga in which he installed close relatives and other trusted aristocrats to effectively administer and govern the now much extended kingdom of Rwanda. The king therefore directly administered his unified and centralised kingdom at his pleasure and could appoint or sack a chief depending on the appointee's loyalty to the court.

While this policy would last for the next two reigns, it was found only usefully applicable to the conquered kingdoms with a dynastic code similar to that of Rwanda – for instance, those having a dynastic drum as the symbol of their sovereignty, such as the kingdoms mentioned above.

In principalities where a dynastic code did not exist, such as in the northwest in former Ruhengeri and Gisenyi Provinces *(Inkiga)*, the local kings (called *Abahinza*[34] as opposed to *Abami*) were not replaced by administrative chiefs appointed by the Rwandan court. The Bahinza were only required to recognize the central administration by regularly paying homage through taxes *(amakoro)* to the Rwandan king and they would be allowed to continue being in charge of their principalities.[35]

This policy of selective 'indirect rule' started with the reign of Mukobanya's grandson, King Yuhi II Gahima (±1444-1477), when the process of *ku-aanda* reached the Inkiga region in the northwest. The region was significant as it included historic sites such as the residences of the father of the nation, King Gihanga at Buhanga.

On the whole, King Kigeri I Mukobanya's reign left the legacy of a strong and formidable kingdom that in the royal cycle would continue with consolidation of the enlarged territory with King Mibambwe I Sekarongoro Mutabazi (±1411-1444) before the closure of the cycle with King Yuhi II Gahima.

It was in the succeeding reign of King Ndahiro II Cyamatare that the turn of events would halt the process of *ku-aanda* following a crack in the strength of the monarchy and consequent desecration of the land in an occupation of part of Rwanda that would last eleven years.

King Ruganzu II Ndoli (±1510-1543): Restorer of the Monarchy and *Ku-aanda*

The process of *ku-aanda*, therefore, was not always smooth. As Rwanda continued to gain both in territory and prosperity, so would it encounter forces of destabilization, both from within and outside the kingdom. There began to occur internal rivalries between princes with ambitions to power. The situation was further complicated by neighbouring kingdoms harbouring intentions to occupy Rwanda to assert their hegemonic ambitions.

This was the case during the reign of King Ndahiro II Cyamatare (±1477-1510) when the kingdom of Bunyabungo in today's Eastern Democratic Republic of Congo, joining forces with the Kingdom of Bugara, saw the opportunity to overrun a Rwanda already destabilized by internal rivalries between princes hungry for power.[36]

Princes Juru and Bamara had forcefully occupied the eastern part of River Nyabarongo (in today's Kigali City) after rebelling against their brother, King Ndahiro II. Taking advantage of this internal crisis, Banyabungo led by Ntsibura I Nyebunga and Banyabugara under the leadership of Nzira son of Muramira jointly conspired to attack Rwanda and do away with it.

On getting to know of the imminent attack, King Ndahiro II also had a premonition of his own demise and knew that he would have to sacrifice himself if his heir was to inherit the throne. He decided to send his son, Prince Ndoli, accompanied by sympathetic royalists to exile in Karagwe (in present-day Tanzania), where the young prince's aunt, Nyabunyana, was queen to King Karemera Ndagara.

In the same bid to spare his progeny from the impending threat of the Banyabungo, King Ndahiro II also sent his son Mucocori – accompanied by his maternal uncle Bigirimana – to the northern volcanic ranges to live there. These two would be the fathers of Abagiri[mana] and Abacocori, today constituting the main lineages of the Abagogwe people of the northern region.

However, after a confrontation with the Banyabungo and being wounded, King Ndahiro II effected a tactical withdrawal. This would nevertheless rush him to his death after being cornered by the conspiring war party of King Nzira ya Muramira of Bugara. He was killed at Rugarama Hill (today referred to as *"Rubi rw'i Nyundo"*) as he retreated to his residence at Bayi in today's Nyabihu District in Western Province. Thus the saying, *Karore i Bayi*, the meaning of which eventually came to be used as a curse with the words, "may the worst befall you like it happened at Bayi." With the demise of the king at Bayi, three Rwandan army formations, namely *Inkindi, Ingata* and *Abahunga*, also perished, which made for a great tragedy.[37]

The death of King Ndahiro was, however, seen as a national sacrifice, making him a *umucengeri* of the mould of his great great great grandfather, Ruganzu I Bwimba. This is memorably recalled in Nyirarumaga's second poem, *Aho ishokeye inshotsi ya Gitarama*[38] (When he rushed to the river the thirsty bull of Gitarama) in which the poetess compares the king rushing to the battlefront to die with a thirsty bull rushing to quench its thirst.

Aho ishokeye inshotsi	When Ndahiro courageously faced his death
Ya Gitarama, ya Gihwera na Kigarama	At Gitarama and the horrible massacres of the royal party
(...)	*(...)*
Zuhiza Rugina	When the battle turned into bloodbath

The tragedy was especially worth noting as, in gross contravention of the then established etiquette of war, Ntsibura's party went on to kill King Ndahiro II's entire entourage, which included women and children, among them the Queen Mother, Nyirandahiro II Nyirangabo, and the queen, Nyabacuzi (mother of Ndoli). Killing women and children in war was considered taboo and extreme recklessness. This place of their death came to be called *"mu Miko y'Abakobwa"* (Women's Graveyard).

In their victory, the Abanyabungo were to occupy Rwanda for the next eleven years, symbolized by the capture of the royal emblematic drum, *Rwoga*. To Rwandans the drum was now not only lost, but desecrated at the hands of the occupiers.

In the end, it would take the death of King Ntsibura I Nyebunga in the eleventh year of occupation that, Kavuna, a special envoy from Rwanda, was sent to Karagwe to inform Prince Ndoli that it was "time to come home".

As was custom with such emissaries, Kavuna would not be allowed to return home alive for having overheard a royal testament and had to drown himself in River Kagera. This gave rise to the saying, *kuruha uwa Kavuna* – "sacrifying yourself for Rwanda unrewarded as Kavuna."

Accompanied by a strong escort detail led by Muyango[39], brother to King Karemera of Karagwe, Prince Ndoli crossed into Rwanda incognito and was crowned King Ruganzu II Ndoli in present-day Gatsibo District in Eastern Province. Upon enthronement the new king re-organised and recognized his father's royalists, the *Abaryankuna,* who had sent Kavuna with the message to come home. He then made them court advisors, priests and prophets, who would later come to be known as Abiru for their unwavering loyalty *(abatagoma).*

Also upon enthronement, King Ruganzu II Ndoli would set a national programme of future conquests, voiced in a keynote poem he composed with the aid of the poet Rwozi: *Riratukuye ishyembe icumita ibindi bihugu*[40] (It is always red the horn that it plunges into the womb of other nations) referring to the bloody course of action it would take to re-launch the process of *ku-aanda.*

Riratukuye ishyembe	It's always red the horn
Icumita ibindi bihugu	That plunges into the womb of other nations
(…)	*(…)*
Ngaha irarikurungiye iry'inkaba,	How sharp is the blood-soaked horn
Iryo yahoze yisha u Buguru	He used to submit Bugara
Iryisha i Gisaka	And fight Gisaka
Na njye nkarivuga ndi imvuzi	I, therefore, extol that
ya Mvukuye abahange	warrior's spear,
ya Mpangaje ya Muhita-vuba	In short-lived liberation battles
Uko isogota ngahimbarwa[41]	Forever restoring Rwanda's glory

The new king's priority was to re-capture the eastern part of Nyabarongo that his father's brothers – Juru and then Bamara[42] – had usurped. It was on accomplishing this that he set about restoring Rwandan sovereignty by installing the *Karinga* to replace the Rwoga, as the new royal emblematic drum. With the Rwandan dignity thus restored, he went on to form a powerful army, *Ibisumizi,* famous among Rwandans to this day, and whose eight battalions[43] under the command of the celebrated Muvunyi wa Karema would constitute a formidable force that would relaunch and reinvigorate the process of *ku-aanda.*

Muvunyi wa Karema finds his accolades and enduring recognition for his celebrated killing of King Katabirora ka Mirogosa of Bushi in today's Bukavu area in Congo. The killing was following a famous bet with King Ruganzu II in which the stakes were that, if the commander won by killing the Bushi king, then King Ruganzu would abdicate his throne and Muvunyi would become king. King Katabirora had challenged and insulted the authority of the Rwandan monarchy, to a point of sending emissaries to tell it to the face of the king.[44]

As it transpired, Muvunyi won the bet when he killed Katabirora, but declined to take the throne in deference of King Ruganzu II for the deep respect he had for the Rwandan monarchy. Besides, he was well aware of his lack of entitlement to the monarchy, royalty being a divine calling. As the poet Semidogoro puts it:

Umwami uyu ntawe umwigera	The King has no human equal
Ngo aha aturanye na we	Even some of his entourage
(…)	*(…)*
Ubwami ubu ntiburonkwa nk'icumu	For royalty is not bought like a spear
(…)	*(…)*
Umugabe abuzwa inkara	A King is ordained by oracles
Agaherezwa ingoma[45]	And assumes the throne

For the heroic feat Muvunyi was rewarded with a herd of cattle, *Indamutsa*, and fief still remembered as Remera ya Humure in Gatsibo District.

In a vengeful war for his family's death, Ruganzu II Ndoli with his able commander would go on to conquer Bugara and personally kill King Nzira ya Muramira, who had conspired with the Banyabungo to kill his father. Ndoli also went on to take the territory comprising Southern Bufumbira in present-day Uganda.

Other regions that Ruganzu II annexed included Huye District, specifically the localities of Ruhande ruled by Mpandahande, Bwanamukari under Chief Nyakarashi and Burwi of Nyaruzi son of Haramanga, the last king of the *abarenge* dynasty. Earlier on, inhabitants in the Nduga principality, in former Gitarama, had killed Mateke, the local tyranical usurper, and had surrendered to Ruganzu II's inexorable advance. This led Ruganzu II to take Bwishaza in Kibuye, Bugoyi and Byahi in Rubavu District, and Bwishya in North Kivu in the Congo. All these territories were conquered with the help of additional battalions he created, notably the *Abaruhije, Nyantango* and *Nyakare*.

Ruganzu II Ndoli finally met his death on his way from Kinyaga in Nyamasheke District, after receiving a fatal arrow in the eye from one Bitibibisi[46] in an ambush by inhabitants of Rusenyi in present-day Karongi District. He died in Nyantango at a place that henceforth came to be known as *ku Gaciro mu Matyazo ya Nyantango* (the place of the king's death).

His valiant army, *ibisumizi*, ashamed to survive the death of their Commander-In-chief, remains forever etched in the Rwandan psyche for committing a mass suicide by setting two camps to annihilate each other to the last man. To see to this, only commander Muvunyi and his *umugaragu* (special client and bodyguard), Kamara, would remain to ensure that all were dead. It was only then that, upon his request, Kamara finished off Muvunyi and buried the bodies of the dead comrades in aardvark's dens *(mu myobo y'inyaga)* before breaking the news to the court. This act is recalled in the caution, *"Nakireke si we Kamara …"* (you need not bother, as you are not the final man, Kamara).

Oral tradition extols King Ruganzu II Ndoli as one of the most celebrated of Rwandan conquerors for having recouped the dignity of the monarchy and the prowess of his people, as attested by the territories he was able to recapture and annex to Rwanda.

King Ruganzu II accomplishments are also attributed to his Regent Queen Mother, the celebrated poetess Nyiraruganzu II Nyirarumaga. The Regent Queen Mother is credited with the establishment of the Institution of Court Poets, *Intebe y'Abasizi.* However, Ruganzu II's greatness is better recalled by the poet Nyakayonga son of Musare during the reign of Mutara II Rwogera (19th Century) in the poem, *Ukwibyara gutera ababyeyi ineza*[47] (Self procreation makes joy for parents).

Uwo ni Cyungura Umwami wo ku Cyuma	He is the Conquering King of Cyuma (Nyundo)
Azanye Cyubahiro, yitwa Cyiha-bugabo	He brought Karinga the Proud-Achiever
Karuhura se uwo yarushwa ate?	That Redeemer, who can equal him?
Yahoreye se ashishikaye	The ardent avenger of his father (Ndahiro)
Ingabo ye ayigeza mu "Bugara"	Who conquered all the way to Bugara
Umuganda awigiza mu rumira	And established frontiers beyond the dense forest
Aho mutaragera	The pioneer of that far flung area
Uwo mugabo mwamugera nde?[48]	That man with whom would you compare?

Kigeri II Nyamuheshera (±1576-1609): The Great Conqueror

The process of *ku-aanda* attained its climax under Ruganzu II's grandson, King Kigeri II Nyamuheshera who would reach westward as far as Tonga in Masisi in today's Democratic Republic of Congo, only for his progress to be halted by the dense and expansive Congo Forest (*Iyo literwa inkingi* - "where pillars support the sky"). Rwandans believed that the Congo Forest marked the end of all inhabited world. While at his furthest point in Masisi, Mount Muhabura (which literally means "showing the way" or "beacon") was the landmark that would provide the bearings to lead his troops back home.

Moving northward past Bufumbira in present-day Uganda, the tireless king subjugated the regions surrounding Lake Edward, which Rwandans called Rwicanzige, and fixed Rwanda's furthest border at the escarpment of Kabasha *(ku rutare rwa Kabasha)* beyond which lay the kingdom of Bunyoro-Kitara, the birthplace of the revered cultist, Lyangombe,[49] which could thus not be "desecrated" with a military attack.

In the southwest, at the head of his army *Inkingi* (the Pillars), Kigeri II subdued Bukunzi and Busozo and crossed the Rusizi River to Bunyabungo where he conquered the Bishugi, including the entire region encompassing the northwestern ridge of Kivu (Buhunde and Buzi). Then following in the footsteps of his grandfather Ruganzu II Ndoli northwards, he annexed the Kamuronsi, the Gishali and the Tongo in present-day North-Kivu. On his way back across the Virunga volcanoes, he also annexed the Buberuka, and went on to attack the region of Kigezi in modern Uganda. It was from this expedition in the region of Bushengero that his army imported a new type of beans to Rwanda that continues to be cultivated to this day. Another expedition in the same region brought in the type of exotic goats called *Akamenesho* (the-better-breed) because of their larger size.

In all the conquered regions mentioned above, however, Kigeri II would leave their local chiefs in power but obliged them to pay him annual homage.

Kigeri II also regained Bwanacyambwe as a reward after helping Kimenyi III Rwahashya keep at bay Banyandorwa who, led by Gahaya I Rutindangeli, had attacked Gisaka and forced Kimenyi III to take refuge in Rwanda. This safe return of Bwanacyambwe is noted by the poet Bagorozi when he says, *Kimenyi wahawe urumuri arunda hasi*[50] (Kimenyi who had been given fire-support surrendered Bwanacyambwe).

Kigeri II, therefore, remains the greatest of Rwandan expansionists. His military exploits and heroism are attested by his being accorded the military award of *Umudende*, the first honour in a system of ascending numbers of seven to the highest honour of 21. A soldier who had killed seven enemy combatants would be awarded the *Umudende*, the one who had killed 14 would be awarded the *Impotore*. The highest honour was of the award Gucana-Uruti, granted to a general who had killed 21 enemies.

In the case of King Kigeri II Nyamuheshera, his award or decoration was in recognition of having killed or ousted seven foreign kings and annexed their kingdoms. Nyamuheshera's decoration remained hanging in his *Ikigabiro* (official residence) in Bumbogo near Gutamba in Kamonyi District until the 1960s.[51]

Kigeri II's *Umudende* award and his far-reaching conquests are recalled by the poet Kibarake in his poem *"Batewe n'iki uburake"*[52] (what is it that upset them?).

Mburanye Mirindi nyira-imyiri irindwi,	I plead Kigeri II, the decorated conqueror
Kurya na kuno ari myinshi	Of as many as seven kingdoms
Yanyaze iz'i Butavuga n'i Buhanuye	Who Raided Bunyabungo and Bushi
Anyaga i Bwuzure	And overrun Buz

Bwuzuriza-nshotsi bwa Shorera,	The Magnanimous Raider, son of Mutara II
N'iz'i Gishali arazisanza.	Who also raided Gishali
Iz'i Bunyoni yaziteranije	And conquered Bishugi and
n'iz'i Bwite	Bwito
Rusaza rwa Sagiro mu Busanza.	The Old-man of Sagiro in Busanza (Congo)
Ese wowe iyo adasubiza	The Great Sailor could only be halted by
iya Ngiga,	The Congo Forest
Ngondo ya Rukuge	Having conquered the farthest lands,
Yari yaciye kure Rureba[53]	That Visionary Conqueror took Rwanda to its greatest limits.

King Cyilima II Rujugira (1675-1705): The Great Military Strategist

The Rwanda military might reached its height during the reign of Cyilima II Rujugira. Though bearing the name of "pastoral kings", he proved to be one of the greatest military strategists[54] and defender of his kingdom in the unceasing process of *ku-aanda*. By devising the innovative strategy of *Ingerero* (military forts), which he posted along the frontiers of Rwanda, he was able to halt and counter-attack a coalition conspiracy of neighbouring kingdoms jointly moving to overrun and annex Rwanda.

Taking advantage of a declining Rwanda towards the end of the reign of Yuhi III Mazimpaka (1642-1675), due to the king's senility and rivalry of his children about the soon to be vacant throne, the three neighbouring kingdoms of Burundi, Gisaka and Ndorwa conspired an offensive to take Rwanda:[55]

Mu Bwami buheze	With the end of the reign of the senile king
Inzigo ziza iwe magaga,	Rivalries and conspiracies were rife in the kingdom

Kwa Baniha-tamu ba Mugera-ruzi	Hostilities came from [Burundi]
i Nyabugenda iyo	The [kingdom of Ntare son of Mwambutsa]

The bond between the two conspirators with Burundi originated from the network of matrimonial relationships that King Kimenyi IV Getura of Gisaka had managed to establish over time. His mother, Muhehure, was the princess of Bugesera, with one of his wives, Nyiragasumba, being the daughter of Ntare III, formerly King of Burundi. In the same extended family was also one of Kimenyi's daughters, who was married to Gahaya II Muzora of Ndorwa. Rwanda would later join the same extended family, through Cyilima II Rujugira marrying Rwesero, niece to Kimenyi IV. With these extended family relations, Kimenyi IV contrived to manipulate the politics of the sub-region. This is how he managed to bring together the other two kingdoms against Rwanda.

However, knowing the danger his kingdom faced, Cyilima II devised a three-fold defensive plan. He mounted, first, a military wall along the frontier of the main rival Burundi in order to be able to free his hand in attacking Gisaka and Ndorwa. This strategy of "military wall" or "military border forts" (*Ingerero*) would give rise to the intimidatory Rwandan saying, "*U Rwanda ruratera ntiruterwa*" (Rwanda is never attacked, but will always attack).

As a tactician the king knew that a pre-emptive attack has the advantage of not only shifting the damage of war into the enemy territory and therefore gaining on the initiative, but also provides the element of surprise forcing the enemy to fight a defensive war.

Second, he decided to form as many military formations as the society could economically bear. This effectively made him the Commander-in-chief of the largest army ever of all the kings of Rwanda, with more than twenty military formations,[56] each the size of today's infantry battalion.

As a third strategy, he resorted to the use of Abacengeli (offensive liberators) whose blood was believed to have divine blessings, enabling annexation of other kingdoms. This was a sacred tradition shared within the sub-region of Rwanda, Burundi, Gisaka and Bugesera. The *Abacengeli* "always had to precede the warriors, as told in the poem of the same title *Abatabazi bagira ubatemera* by Ndamira ya Muhabura during the reign of Cyilima II Rujugira.

Iyo intambara yagimbye	When war becomes inevitable
Amagambo ageze imagume	And diplomacy is no longer an option
Abagabe bashyamiranye kwakana ingoma	Kings readying for war
Bati: reba indongozi y'abatabara,	Resort to offensive liberators (Abacengeri)
Yagizwe urutsiro n'Imana	Anointed by God to redeem the country
Iyo ikagimbura ibintu	[The liberator] declares the war
Inka n'ingoma zikabona inzira	And the nation is mobilized
Abazima baziri mwo,	With the brave at the front,
Abazimu bo mu banzi akabarimarima	And the anointed liberator banishing the ghosts
Ababisha ntibacane ngo wake bagapfa.	of the enemy
Igihugu cyabo kikagerezwa buzima	The enemy territory is overrun
Haragimbye ingabo zihabwa imbonwa[57]	Thanks to the anointed liberator.

It was deemed that military might or strategy alone would not be sufficient to overcome a combined force of such as Burundi, Gisaka and Ndorwa. With Burundi being a powerful enemy, the spilling of royal blood was called for and King Cyilima II gave ascent for his son, Prince Gihana, also the commander of the military formation *Abalima,* to sacrifice himself and die a *Mucengeri* against Burundi. Gihana was, however, followed by another *Mucengeli,* Chief Rubona, the commander of *Abadahemuka* as the spilt blood of the prince had been "neutralized" by that of Rulinda rwa Gakamba, a notable from Burundi, who also performed a similar act of *Ubucengeri* self-sacrifice for his country to counter the Rwandans.

As narrated by Karera ka Bamenya in the poem, *Ruhanga rutsindiye igihugu*[58] ([Mutara III] the Redeemer of Rwanda), after exchanging a series of Abacengeli in which many lives were sacrificed, and most of whom were of royal birth, Mutaga III Sebitungwa himself decided to finally come in person and was killed at Nkanda by one Rutanda, the commander of Urwasabahizi, a Rwandan military formation originally from Bugesera. Hence the Burundian curse *"wa mugesera we"* (bad as the king's murderer) referring to the Bugesera killer, Rutanda. The frontier was then fixed at Nkanda forming the current border between Rwanda and Burundi, where the Province of Buyenzi hence became part of Rwanda.

Wazishakiwe na wa Mwami Cyuhira	You inherited the reign from that Pastoral King [Cyilima II]
Umunsi Cyusa atsinda Cyumya,	The day the Respected-man defeated Mutaga III (Sebitungwa)
Ku Cyambara-bagore	At Nkanda locality
Ntibaragaseka i Busumba-birenge	A royal loss Burundi would never recover
Umwana w'Umwami w'ino, Yahwanye n'Umwami w'i Butanguranwa Amutesha Rugabo[59]	The royal prince (Gihana) Our offensive liberator in Burundi Triumphed over their king.

After Burundi, it was the turn of Gisaka to be attacked by Cyilima II Rujugira. His son, Prince Sharangabo, the commander of *Abakemba*, supported by his younger brother Ndabarasa commanding the *Abaliza* and *Imvejuru* reached Shenga in Buganza after defeating Mudiligi, the army chief of Gisaka. They had captured Yoboka, the prince of Gisaka, forcing the army chief to withdraw eastward.

As for Ndorwa the military formations *Igicikiza, Imanga, Abatanguha* and later *Abarota* under the command of Kamali and Prince Ndabarasa, were to recapture the former Rwandan capital (near Gasabo) that had been captured after the death of Prince Gihana. This included the neighbouring areas of Rutunga. In the north, the Ndorwa army chief, Nyabarega, was also unable to resist the advance of Prince Ndabarasa, who was eager to secure the ranges of Rutare, the celebrated royal burial grounds for kings bearing the name Kigeri.[60]

Despite the limited gain in territory, it is the large size of his army and strategic foresight in countering a combined enemy that King Cyilima II Rujugira came to be known as the greatest defender of the nation.[61]

After Cyilima II's gains, the process of *ku-aanda* in the royal cycle of kings would continue unabated, with Mibambwe III Sentabyo capturing Bugesera and Mutara II Rwogera capturing Gisaka. The process of *ku-aanda* would end with the reign of King Kigeri IV Rwabugiri (1853-1895) and the coming of colonialism, which we shall discuss in a later chapter.

Notes

1   Joseph Nye, *Bound to Lead: The Changing Nature Of American Power,* New York, Basic Books, 1990.
2   A. Kagame (1972), op cit. p. 50.
3   Bernard Lugan, *Rwanda: le génocide, l'Église et la démocratie,* Éditions du Rocher, 2004, p.13. (A. Kagame (1972), Vansina (1962) and Delmas (1950) differ on the date of the beginning of Rwanda under Gihanga).
4   A. Kagame (1972), op. cit., p.39. The myth of Gihanga as having been a real person is given credence by places such as Buhanga in Northern and Southern Provinces, which are named after him, including holy shrines such as Mount Kabuye, Nyamirembe ya Humure, etc. Besides, some of his military formations (such as Gakondo and Abanyansanga), his royal drums (Cyimumugizi), and most importantly his hammer (Nyarushara), which symbolized Gihanga as the smith and

therefore the forger of a nation, could still be found at the royal court as recently as the 1930s (pp.39-47).

5   B. Muzungu (ed.), *Cahiers* No 21, Dec. 2002, p.8.

6   Idem.

7   A. Kagame (1972: 54) or Muzungu (2003:86).

8   Buganza, Bwanacyambwe, Buriza, Busarasi (later called Bumbogo) and Busigi.

9   E. Ntezimana, "Le Rwanda social, admnistratif et politique à la fin du dix-neuvième siècle", in Gudrun Honke (ed), *Au plus profond de l'Afrique : Le Rwanda et la Colonisation allemande* 1885-1919, pp.73-80.

10   A. Kagame, *Les Milices du Rwanda précolonial*, IRSAC, 1962, pp.15-36.

11   Ian Linden, *Church and Revolution in Rwanda*, Manchester University Press, Manchester, 1977, p. 12; J.P.Chrétien, *The Great Lakes of Afrika: Two Thousand years of History*, Zone Books, New York, 2003, p.158.

12   Table of Rwandan Kings, see Annex.

13   Lévi Strauss, *Anthropologie structurale*. Paris: Plon. See also his « The Structural Study of Myth » in *Structural Anthropology*, 1963 (First published in 1955).

14   P. Kanyamacumbi, *Société, culture et pouvoir politique en Afrique interlacustre. Hutu et Tutsi au Rwanda*, Edition SELECT, A.T.R.I.O, Kinshasa, 1995.

15   *Cahiers*, No. 29, of March 2005, pp. 88-104.

16   Ibid., p.91 (The ku-aanda process ends with the capture and integration of Gisaka under Mutara II Rwogera).

17   *Cahiers*, No. 27, of Sept. 2004, pp. 148-152.

18   Ibid., p. 151.

19   Vansina (1962); Lemarchand (1970: 19).

20   President John F. Kennedy during his inaugural speech on 20 January 1961.

21   *Cahiers*, No.27, Sept. 2004, pp. 43-52..

22   Ibid., pp. 45-.46.

23   U.S. President Harry Truman, 1945-53, insisted on presidential responsibility which he demonstrated by displaying a buck on his desk saying, "the buck stops here".

24   Hence Mukobanya being nicknamed by Rwandan poets *"Mugabo-mu-nka Nyirazo akizirimo"* [Translation: the co-regent of the aging king].

25 J.W. Nyakatura in his *Abakama (Kings) of Bunyoro-Kitara,*
    Kisubi, Marianum Press, 1999, pp. 73-74; Linden (1977: 13);
    Delmas (1950:183).
26 Ian Linden (1977), op. cit., p.15
27 A. Kagame (1972), op. cit., p.114
28 There were five matri-dynastic clans, namely, Abasinga,
    Abakono, Abega, Abaha, Abagesera who provided Queen-
    mothers while Kings were only from Abanyiginya clan. That
    is how traditional power sharing and broad-basing was ensured
    among the major clans of the country.
29 A. Kagame (1972), op. cit., p.115.
30 As an example, King Mutara I Semugeshi diplomatically
    concluded a non-aggression pact/agreement *(imimaro)* with
    Mutaga II Nyamubi of Burundi at Nyaruteja in a place
    henceforth called *mu twicara-bami twa Nyaruteja* [meaning "the
    Nyaruteja Peace Pact Hub"].
31 The poem is titled, *Ndabukire Imana yunamuye u Rwanda* by
    Sekarama, in *Cahiers,* No.26, March 2004, pp.82-97.
32 *Cahiers,* No. 24, Sept. 2003, pp.113-122.
33 *Cahiers,* No. 27, Sept.2004, p.47.
34 *Abahinza* were different from Abami in that the first, unlike
    Abami, did not usually have a dynastic drum symbolizing their
    sovereignty. Their administrative structure had also many
    different aspects (mainly based on Ubukonde) reflecting their
    local customs. For more details on Bahinza see de Lacger (1959:
    82-89).
35 De Lacger 1959: 108.
36 B. Muzungu, *(2003),* op.cit, p.132.
37 A. Kagame, *Les Milices du Rwanda pré-colonial* (1962: 52-53).
38 *Cahiers,* No 23, of May 2003, pp.22-26.
39 Muyango, son of Ruhinda, later became the ancestor of many
    Abahinda clans still found in Rwanda.
40 B. Muzungu, *Cahiers,* No. 23, ibid, pp.28-37.
41 Ibid., p.28.
42 Juru is the ancestor of Abenejuru, and Bamara (father of Byishi)
    of Abanyabyinshi. They later fled to Congo upon the return of
    Ndoli and make up the majority of the initial group of
    Congolese Banyamulenge.
43 *Ibisumizi, Ingangurarugo, Imisambi, Udusambi, Insambuzi,*
    Abadakonja, Abakonjabyuma and *Abaganda.*

44   Inanga ya Ruganzu na Katabirora, Radio Rwanda Archives

45   *Cahiers,* No. 27, Sept. 2004, p.149.

46   Hence the saying *"si umugabo ni Bitibibisi"* [this is a strong man like Bitibibisi (the one who could kill a powerful king)].

47   *Cahiers,* No. 29, March 2005, pp.88-104.

48   Ibid., p.95.

49   Lyangombe was believed to be the holiest spiritual leader whose birthplace (Kitara) could not be attacked as it amounted to sacrilege.

50   *Cahiers,* No 24, of Sept. 2003, p.59.

51   A. Kagame (1972), op. cit., p.122.

52   *Cahiers,* No. 24, of Sept. 2003, pp.113-122.

53   *Cahiers,* No. 24, of Sept 2003, ibid, p.119.

54   Walter Rodney (1972:127) wrote that "Rujugira ...put permanent military camps at strategic places".

55   As told in the poem, *Riratukuye ishyembe icumita ibindi bihugu* by Ruganzu II Ndoli, completed by the poet Bagorozi under Cyilima II (*Cahiers* No 24, of Sept. 2003, pp.81-82).

56   *Abakemba, Indilira, Imvejuru, Abadahemuka, Urwasabahizi, Abadaha, Abarima, Intarindwa, Inzirwa, Ababito, Abatanguha, Ibisiga, Igicikiza, Imanga, Abarota, Abashubije,Abashumba, Abanyoro,* etc.

57   *Cahiers,* No. 28 of Dec 2004, pp. 24-29.

58   *Cahiers,* No. 29, March 2005, pp.246-256.

59   Ibid., p.253.

60   B. Muzungu (2003), op. cit., p.189.

61   Ibid., p.193.

2

The Rwandan Monarchy
(Ubwami)

Pre-colonial Rwanda can be described as a "theocracy", in which all power derived from God *(Imana)*, who was the Creator *(Rurema)* and Provident *(Rugira)*, and who bestowed upon the king divine authority to guide and shepherd His people. The king was believed to have been anointed by God while still in the womb, and thus was born with "the seed of kingship in his hand"[1] *(Umwami avukana imbuto)*.

Finding its highest expression in the monarchy, religion guided social cohesion and permeated every aspect of life, including the military. As perceived, therefore, Rwanda was God-given. It was privileged, for God was resident in Rwanda. He may spend the day elsewhere, but at night he always came back to Rwanda *(Imana yilirwa ahandi igataha i Rwanda)*.

It was drawing from this perception that Rwanda in the minds of the people was invincible and inviolable, for God was always with them acting through the king. Rwanda could not be attacked or occupied, and was eternal. The Kinyarwanda saying is that *Agakambye ugatega u Rwanda:* whatever will be, "for better or for worse", the people of Rwanda are resilient and will always overcome.

God worked through anointed individuals, such as *Abiru,* who appointed the king as the vicar of God, alongside a Queen Mother who was also divine and exercised almost the

31

same powers as the king. Both the king and queen mother were bequeathed emblematic drums as a symbol of Rwandan sovereignty under God. For instance, the *Kalinga* royal drum was for the king and the male population and the *Cyimumugizi* for the queen mother and the female lot. Upon enthronement the king ceased to be a man, and therefore ceased to be a member of his clan or any of the three social categories of Hutu, Tutsi or Twa. The poet Semidogoro explains:

Umwami si umututsi, ntabe	The king is neither a mututsi nor
n'umunyiginya	of the Nyiginya clan
Ni umusumba asumba abantu	He is above every human
Agasumba n'abisumbuye[b]	Even those of the highest status

This was because the king was entrusted with the divine mission of reigning over the people and Rwanda on behalf of God. The people's confidence drew from the knowledge that God was *Niyigena* (it-is-God's-will), *Ntirushwamaboko* (Almighty) or *Itangishaka* (Unconditional Provider). It is from this, therefore, being the representative of God, the king was divine and not an ordinary man, as spoken in the above poem, "*Umwami si umuntu*" (the King is not an ordinary man). In the poem Semidogoro is reminding Rwandans during the short-lived reign of King Mibambwe III Sentabyo (1741-1746) of his divine prerogative.

Henga mbwire u Mwami aho	Let me reveal to the king where
Imana yubatse	God dwells
(...)	*(.....)*
Imana nyibona mu ijabiro umu	For I see His Divine Presence in this royal home.
Nsanga ari we Mana twambaza	And methinks the king represents the God we worship

| *Indi Mana ni we uyizi* | And only him knows the Almighty |
| *Tubona Ngendo twebwe*[3] | But we only see you the walking and physical one |

God governed through the king, who therefore could not engage the people in any national enterprise, whether waging war or managing any national misfortune, without consulting God for His divine will. The king would consult diviners *(abapfumu b'i Bwami)* or seers *(abahanuzi)* to seek God's approval *(kuraguza)* or "green light" *(Imana zeze)* to undertake such an enterprise. The institution of the monarchy therefore always sought divine guidance, despite the particular missions of the kings in the afore-mentioned four-generation royal cycle in the process of *ku-aanda*.

Always guiding the monarchy and the nation was a set of laid-down procedures known as Ubwiru (traditional Monarchical Code or "Constitution"). Couched in 17 "Articles"[4] and administered by *Abiru* (guardians of *Ubwiru*), the monarchical code was an all- encompassing set of "laws", sacred rituals and procedures on how to manage the nation, including enthronement of the king *(Inzira y'Ukwimika)*, conduct in the event of his death, or during a contest of the king's legitimacy – Inzira ya Gicurasi, y'Ikirogoto and y'Urugomo, respectively.

In the enthronement of the king, for instance, *Inzira y'Ukwimika* would take place under the guidance of the Abiru. The Abiru would follow the laid down procedure of enthronement to crown the King's successor whose mother had to come from the pre-established matri-dynastic clans chosen by Mutara or Cyilima kings. The Abiru would indicate the clan of the mother to the next Kigeri and Mibambwe, and the family of Abega clan which became a tradition since the reign of Cyilima II, and hence Abega having the monopoly of mothering Yuhi and Cyilima kings.

According to the "fundamental principle"[5] of succession to the throne, supreme power was entrusted, not directly to the heir prince, but to his mother. In other words, royalty was granted to matri-dynastic clans, *Ibibanda*, in the person of the daughter that the oracles would designate as Queen mother. If the designated Queen mother already had an only son, the latter was automatically the future king to reign with his mother. In case she had several sons, divine oracles had to choose one among them. In principle, therefore, all the sons of the designated queen mother were eligible for the royal office. That is why the "un-chosen" princes were often frustrated, to the extent of some resorting to revolt against their brother-king as was the case under Kings Ndahiro II Cyamatare and Mibambwe III Sentabyo.

After the death of the reigning king, therefore, the Queen mother (who in most cases was no longer alive) would have to step down, *kunywa* (voluntary suicide), for the next queen mother and her son to take over.

The *Ubwiru* included, among other things, procedures on disaster management, such as *Inzira ya Rukungugu* in case of drought, *Inzira y'i Kivu* in case of floods or *Inzira ya Muhekenyi* in case a cattle epidemic. It also included economy-related procedures like *Inzira y'inzuki* for a good harvest in bee products and *Inzira y'ishora* for prosperity, mainly in cattle. Other procedures were military related, such as *Inzira y'inteko* (war procedure), *y'Inkiko yabyaye umugaru* when dealing with a troubled frontier, and *Inzira y'Urugomo* when dealing with a rebellion.

In the day-to-day life, the monarchy was the culmination of socio-economic and political administration that followed the natural organisation of the traditional society. There was the family *(urugo)* at the lowest level, followed by the lineage *(inzu)* and the clan *(ubwoko)* up to the national level *(igihugu)*. Flowing from this the king was at the top of the hierarchy as the head of all families and the people, under whom the people found their unity *(Rubanda rw'Umwami)*.

The King was also known as *Sebantu* (the father of all the people and clans). As the "father", he was the ultimate proprietor of all lands and cattle in the hands of the larger family of the nation *(Umuryango wa Bene-Kanyarwanda)*. And, given his divine attributes, the King was also the guarantor of personal wealth, health and justice for all. Common greetings in Kinyarwanda emphasized this guarantee from the King in saying *Gira Umwami* (Greetings in the name of the King).

Administratively, and for the sake of levying royalties *(amakoro)*, the king politically governed by appointing governors *(Abatware b'Umwami)* who would in their turn appoint three pivotal territorial chiefs in every region in the nation. These were the Préfets of the Soil and those of Pastures and their sub-Préfets, who under them had Hill chiefs. The hill chiefs used messengers to communicate all administrative instructions to family leaders. Along with these Préfets were also different levels of Army Commanders for military matters, who also liaised with family leaders at the lowest level and had the king as their Commander-in-chief.

In the event of a dispute, the family leaders settled all simple cases within the family, or would represent the family in case of a family-to-family dispute in the Gacaca, the traditional councils and tribunals made up of elders of the village and leaders of the two families in conflict.

Rooted in society, the Gacaca derived its impetus and legitimacy from *ubumwe bw'Abanyarwanda* (Rwandan unity), and complemented the same unity by being the cement that strengthened social relations in the name of justice.

The administration of justice in Rwanda also followed the natural social structure that began with the nucleus family, followed by the lineage, the clan and eventually the nation under Mwami, who was the guarantor of justice for all. As noted, the family heads settled all simple cases within the family, and would represent the family in case of a dispute with another family in the Gacaca.

In essence, every Rwandan knew all the channels of arbitration to resort to in case of any litigation, starting from his own family head up to the king. This would include the political administrators, such as the Préfets of the Soil or Pastures (*Abatware b'Ubutaka and b'Umukenke*) depending on the case, whether it was about land or cattle and pastures.

There also would be the military préfet who would settle socio-military cases and traditionally would be of a higher authority than the other Préfets in case of an appeal.[6] As we shall see, the military institution was the core administrative and socio-political organizing institution with the king as the Commander-in-Chief.

This centrality of the military can be illustrated in that, since everyone in the society had to belong to a military formation, one's commander would play the role of legal advisor in any instance of legal administration up to the King's Tribunal without having to pay any "legal fees". The king was always the final arbitrator in case of any sustained dispute through the established channels.

The saying was that "The king does not kill; it is his entourage who are the conspirators" (*Ntihica Umwami, hica rubanda*). This emphasized that he was above personal, petty issues and trivialities in the society and that he could not conspire against his own people. He was the caretaker of justice among his people in all matters and was easily accessible to all through army commanders. The king would regularly travel all around the country to avail himself to the people.

The Rwandan king said to have most epitomized the royal judicial responsibility is King Mibambwe II Sekarongoro Gisanura (1609-1642), nicknamed *Rugabishabirenge* [the Generous King], for his love of the poor and victims of injustice.[7] His sense of justice is recalled in the saying *urubanza rwaciriwe i Mutakara* (justice has been served as at Mutakara), signifying fair-play in a given ruling. Mutakara, near today's Ruhango township, was Gisanura's royal capital from which he ruled and dispensed justice, hence the above saying.

Given the foregoing, justice would only be possible because of *ubumwe* (unity), first within the family and on to the nation as a unified whole under the king. As for the monarch, the king's excesses were checked by the *Abiru* and *Abasizi* who were the keepers of tradition as prescribed in the monarchical code. They would advise the king accordingly in case of incapacitation or abuse of power. For instance, as spelt out in the *Ubwiru*, its guardians, the Abiru, could invoke *kumunywesha* (royal suicide) in case the monarch or the queen mother abused power and "overstayed" the monarchy. For instance, the king was not allowed to have grey hairs while still in office. This meant that he was becoming "too old" to rule. As once put by King Mutara II Rwogera in the 19th Century,

"Sinamerera imvi munzu umu	I can't grow grey hairs in the palace
Ngo nkurwe ku iteka no gutunga	Till I am forced to resign
Ibya Gahindiro mfite"[8]	For having refused to abdicate power

As for the role of poets as advisers, the example is in the above quoted poem by Musare, *"None ko wamaze ubuhingwa"*[9] (Now that the conquest is over, why not return home) inviting King Kigeri III not to overstay in Ndorwa. The poets' advice to the King was always an informed one as they drew it from past experience, being guardians of Rwanda's oral history. A historical event or an action which had incurred negative consequences to the nation had to be recalled and avoided in the future. Similarly, positive deeds had to be extolled and encouraged.

Negative examples had to be discouraged; for instance, a warrior king such as Kigeri was not to cross River Kibilira as its water had been "tainted" with Ndahiro II's blood in his retreat after being wounded by Ntsibura's warriors. Similarly, some king's names like Ruganzu and Ndahiro were removed from the royal cycle titles as their bearers had been found death at the hands of the enemy.

No reigning king was also allowed to have a bald head, as it would be used to suggest that either he was too old to rule effectively or had been too long in power to abuse it. The example was always given of King Yuhi III Mazimpaka, who was unable to rule due to senility. On *Abiru's* insistence he was forced to appoint a regent king, Karemera Rwaka, to rule in his stead. Karemera did not rule for long, as "bad omen" befell him, when he went blind and his mother, Rukoni, suffered mental illness.[10]

The same applies to the queen mother, who was never allowed to marry again, have another child or survive the death of her reigning son. This was a strong custom that could not be contravened in any way, as there could never be two queen mothers. The most recent example is that of Queen Mother Nyiramavugo Nyiramongi to Mutara II Rwogera who died in 1853. Upon the death of her son, she was compelled to abdicate *(kunywa)* in order to uphold the tradition of not having two queen mothers.

Perhaps worthy of note, queen mothers were interred in the same localities as their husbands – and not with their sons who were formerly monarchs.[11] Queen mother Nyiramavugo I Nyirakabogo, for instance, the Queen mother of King Mutara II Semugeshi, was buried at Butangampundu (in today's Rulindo District) where her husband Ruganzu II Ndoli had been interred. Kings and queen mothers dying a violent death (i.e., sudden disease, suicide or death in the hands of the enemy) had to be buried at Butangampundu as well. Thus, King Ruganzu II was buried at Butangampundu instead of Ruhanga (Tare) where other Ruganzu kings were initially buried.

Kings with the royal names Cyilima or Mutara would first be mummified, then interred at Rutare in today's Gatsibo District in Eastern Province. Rutare was also the royal cemetery of the kings bearing the name Kigeri. Traditonally, a Cyilima would be laid to rest by a Mutara or vice versa, making mummification necessary to preserve the dead king for as long as it would take to enthrone a Mutara, which would be after three reigns approximating one hundred years.

For example, the Cyilima II (1675 – 1708) should have been buried by the following Mutara III Rwogera, who unfortunately died unexpectedly in 1853 without fulfilling this royal obligation. The same applied to Mutara III Rudahigwa (1931 – 1959) who became too Christian to perform such a traditional obligation and also died a sudden death. It is for these reasons that the remains of Cyilima II are still there, and are currently preserved at the Rwanda National Museum in Huye.

Other kings were also mummified, for at least four months, to avoid decomposition before being laid to rest during period it took to anoint and enthrone the new king.[12]

As for kings with the title Mibambwe and Yuhi, they were respectively buried at Remera y'Abaforongo in Rulindo District and Kayenzi Tumba in Kamonyi District. The choice of Remera y'Abaforongo for Mibambwes' royal burial site was decided by Mibambwe I (Sekarongoro Mutabazi) who had his preferred residence on a hill (Ngabitsinze) that had been rewarded to the descendants of his brother, Forongo, a *mucengeli* who sacrificed his life for him during the second attack of the Banyoro.

Royal tombs, residences and other historical sites were of great religious importance as they were used to carry out traditional rituals, many of which were presided over by the King himself or High Priests *(Abiru b'Abanyamihango)*. Many of those localities were almost sacred, such as Gihanga's residences, and were important because they symbolized Rwanda's power and sovereignty. Such places were not only culturally meaningful to Rwandans, but also could be abused to denigrate Rwandans' sense of dignity, as was the case during the colonial period when King Yuhi IV Musinga opposed the putting up of churches near such sacred sites, or the use of the trunk of the sacred *Ibigabiro* (royal) tree in the construction of the churches.

The most sacred sites remained Gihanga's residences, most of which were named after him, such as Buhanga. His most venerated residence is found in Umurera (Nkotsi) in today's Musanze District in Northern Province, as this is where he was enthroned king, while his burial place is on Muganza Hill in Kamonyi District. These became shrines at which many royal rituals were conducted, either to give offerings or implore Gihanga's assistance as the first Rwandan patriarch.

Notes

1   Ian Linden (1977), op.cit., p.12.
2   *"Umwami si umuntu"* (the King is not an ordinary man) was composed by the poet Semidogoro ya Gasegege and presented to King Mibambwe III Sentabyo (1741-1746). See *Cahiers* No 25 of Dec. 2003, pp.39-45.
3   Ibid., p.42.
4   There were 17 ways of doing things, called *Inzira*. See B. Muzungu, 2003, op. cit., p.368 or A. Kagame, *Inganji Kalinga*, Kabgayi, 1943.
5   A. Kagame (1975), op. cit., pp.76-77.
6   A. Kagame, *Le Code des institutions politiques de Rwanda pré-colonial*, IRCB, Vol.xxvi, fasc.I, Bruxelles, 1952., p.7; Kagame stresses that the army was the basic social institution that guaranteed private property rights in return for military obligations.
7   A. Kagame. (1972) op. cit., pp.122-23.
8   *Cahiers*, No. 17, March 2000, p.52.
9   *Cahiers*, No. 30, June 2005, pp.38-47.
10 A. Kagame (1972), op. cit., pp. 130-131.
11 Ibid, p.107.
12 Ibid, p.115.

3

The Traditional Rwandan Military: *Ingabo z'u Rwanda*

The Rwandan military *(Ingabo)* started in the family as a small protection unit that played more of a socio-economic role, with the main concern being the preservation of the means of subsistence. As earlier observed, King Gihanga's military formations, for instance, were meant for the security of his family and his economic assets.

From a small force for family and clan protection, therefore, the *Ingabo z'u Rwanda* grew into a fully articulated national army with specialized military units not dissimilar to the modern army by the time of the of reign of King Cyilima II Rujugira.[1]

The family *(urugo)* formed the basic social unit in the organisation of the country in almost all respects, and more so the military.

Above the nuclear family was the extended family *(Inzu)* or lineage *(Umuryango)*, headed by a patriarchal chief *(Umutware w'Umuryango)*. The lineage head settled all socio-administrative problems of the family he represented, including being the army representative in his lineage.

After the lineage, however, there was a departure from this family-based structure of having a military clan head. This arose due to the need to develop a more practical army structure in the hierarchy of command and effectiveness. This explains why the clan was not emphasised in the military structure.

Due to the clan's amorphous nature and the broad distribution of its members state-wide, it would be difficult to rally them under one command. It was for this practical reason that after the lineage head came regional army chiefs *(Abatware b'Umuheto)* bringing together several lineage armies in their locality.

The *Umutware w'Umuheto* traditionally appointed the successor of a lineage head. If the former lineage head only possessed cattle exclusively gotten through the cattle-based clientage *(ubuhake)*, then it was up to his pastoral chief to appoint the successor.

An example of a lineage force can best be illustrated by the military force Abarashi of Gahunga at the foot of Mount Muhabura in the Northern Province under the command of Rukara rwa Bishingwe during the reign of Kigeri IV Rwabugiri (1853-1895).

The famous Abarashi started as a family protection unit made up of descendants of Nyakarashi from the Abacyaba clan who evolved to become an effective fighting force under army chiefs Bishingwe and his son Rukara as successive lineage leaders.

The army unit comprised four generations of successive family "platoons", namely, *Abemeranzigwe, Abakemba, Urukandagira* and *Uruyenzi.* All were commanded by their respective lineage leaders beginning with Ndagano, Rukara's great grandfather who lived during the reign of King Yuhi IV Gahindiro (1746-?).

The platoons were manned by family members, with *Uruyenzi* being in the family of Rukara himself, *Urukandagira* that of his father Bishingwe, *Abakemba* under his grand-father, Sekidandi, and *Abemeranzigwe* under Rukara's great grandfather, Ndagano.

The famous *Abarashi* therefore started as a family protection unit made up of the descendants of Nyakarashi who, due to their exploits, would be incorporated into the national army

Ingangurarugo under King Kigeri IV Rwabugiri. They also illustrate the hereditary nature of the traditional Rwandan army.

The significance of the *Abarashi* is that they did not fall under a regional army chief, but directly under the king, who was at the same time the supreme patriarchal chief of all the families in the country and therefore the Commander-in-Chief of the national army.

The hierarchical structure of the society, from the nuclear family through to the extended family, the lineage, the clan up to the national level coincided with the modern army structure from the section level, the platoon, the company, battalion up to the national army.

The Section Commander, therefore, coincides with the head of the nuclear family, the Platoon Commander with the extended family head, the Company Commander with lineage chief and the Battalion Commander with the clan head (*umutware w'ubwoko*) who, in this case due to the above-mentioned practical reasons, was replaced by the Regional Army Commander.

In this hierarchical structure, each nuclear family had its contribution to the military institution, thereby forming the basic unit of the army's organization. By this virtue almost every able-bodied Rwandan male, whatever his social category, including the King, had to belong to the army.[2] This included the women and children in the material or moral support they had to offer their men. In this manner the military was rooted in society in a symbiotic relationship that enabled socio-political and administrative organization.

To draw a simple analogy to this symbiosis, the Rwandan state can be likened to the simplest of single-cell organisms. As such, a single cell organism comprises of three major components, namely the nucleus, the plasma and the membrane. Taken this way, the nucleus is the society's leadership, the plasma the people or citizenry and the membrane the military. The people or the plasma through its leadership produces its own protective shield *(Ingabo)*, which in turn protects the fragile plasma or society. Therefore, there exists an inherent symbiotic relationship between the people, their leadership and the *Ingabo*.

Though three categories of administrative organization of the state were applied, the military took precedence as the core social and administrative institution. Thus the Prefects of the Soil and those of Pastures found themselves under the army chiefs, all due to the fact that every citizen was *Ingabo* (defender of Rwanda).

The second reason for the military to take precedence was that, due to there being no pastoralists in every part of the country, and therefore no Prefects of the Pastures, as in the north-western regions which were mainly organized around the land, only the military covered the entire country. The triple chieftaincy system of administration was mainly functional in central, south and eastern Rwanda.

It was therefore due to its universal inclusion of every member of the society and its having the widest reach statewide that the military institution had to emerge as the core socio-political structure of the nation that helped in the centralization of administration and in ascertaining social and national cohesion. Its credibility was such that the army chiefs were accorded the significant role of being arbiters to whom every one resorted in case of disputes with one's superior, who would either be the land or cattle-chief.

Given the foregoing, therefore, it cannot be gainsaid that with its influence on the people the military institution would emerge in its role as the enduring institution of socialization, so that while it drew from the society, it gave back to it through socialization in a complimentary manner evoking the symbiotic relationship afore-mentioned.

Also given the institution's broad reach, the army was drawn from geographically diverse areas and assigned for a number of years of common service outside their home region. This made the military institution a melting pot of diverse Rwandans from different backgrounds. In the process it gave identity to the members going by the military formations to which each individual belonged. Hence, *Abataganzwa, Abashakamba* and *Uruyange* or *Abakemba* would describe each member of each formation. This would be passed on to one's descendants as an enduring identity. Thus the socio-categorization of Rwandans, whether Twa, Tutsi or Hutu, were irrelevant as socialization took place in the army where each individual drew his identity from the military formation one belonged to.

As we shall see, this socialization took place in the traditional military schools called the *Amatorero* where everyone's discipline and good conduct, their sense of bravery and patriotism, their honesty and integrity, moral behaviour and even their mannerisms were moulded to make not only a good soldier, but an *impfura y'u Rwanda* (gentleman of Rwanda).

The military influence on the society can be seen not only in the people's names, but in their environment and prized property such as cattle. So there are people's names such as Rwatangabo ('The-one-who-pierces-the-shield), Rusingizandekwe (the-One-who-praises-arrows), Nyiriminega (The-Owner-of-Arrows), etc. The names often reflected a father's military ambitions for his children.

In the same context, streams such as *Amazi atukura* (the stream of red-waters), and names of localities such as *Ruhashya* (the successful defender), *Rusatira* (close attacker), mu *Irasaniro* (battlefield), *mu Iviro* (place of bloodbath), speak of military battles or war manoeuvres that took place there mainly between Banyarwanda and Barundi.

Additionally, many traditional provinces, including Nyaruguru, Ndara, Mvejuru, Bashumba-Nyakare, Nyantango and Impara were named after the military formations that were deployed there.

Even in "cattle-lore" (*Amazina y'Inka*) the herds had been "militarized". In traditional folklore, herds of cattle are imagined in war with others and the most triumphant are praised in the same vein as men. It however may be mentioned that herds of cattle symbolized traditional military formations to which they were often attached.

Examples of such are the *Abashakamba* and their respective cattle formations were the *Umuhozi,* the military formation *Uruyange's* cattle equivalent was *Ingeyo* and the military formation Intaganzwa's was *Uruyenzi* and the military formation *Abakemba, Imisugi.*[3]

The traditional military formations or "social armies"[4], which as we have seen can be likened to regiments or battalions in today's modern army articulated and gave form to the traditional army, often indicating each reign's military strength. The very first military formations are traced to the social armies of King Gihanga Ngomijana (1091-1124), which included the *Abanyansanga, Abahiza* and *Gakondo,* etc.[5]

The highest number of military formations in its history was around 20 under the reign of King Cyilima II Rujugira that saw the traditional Rwandan army amass its greatest strength, making him one of the greatest defenders of Rwanda.

Other than working to achieve such exploits and providing national security and sovereignty, some of the armies' duties included fulfilling social and economic obligations. This went back to the very beginning, where the army was basically more family or socially significant than towards the end of the pre-colonial Rwandan state. As observed, all of King Gihanga's military formations and for many generations of kings hence had more socio-economic than military functions.[6]

This changed with the reign of King Cyilima I Rugwe and his military formations of the *Ababarabiri* and the *Abariza,* who initiated a more martial tradition. With his co-regent son, Prince Mukobanya, breaking the confederation rules with his neighbours and attacking them to incorporate their clan kingdoms into his, the martial nature of the military formations in this dawning era of conquests in the process of *ku-aanda* was established lasting more that five hundred years to the reign of King Kigeri IV Rwabugiri (1853-1895).

Socialization and Military Training

By the time of King Kigeri I Mukobanya in the late 14th Century, a tradition had already been established of creating and training a social-army or military formation. The formation of a new social-army would take place upon the enthronement of each new king, or depending on the king deeming it necessary to address a pressing need. This would also happen after assessing his kingdom's security threat.

Usually, after a new king was enthroned, his direct subordinates would bring him their sons not as yet attached to any military formations in the preceding reign.[7] The first intake of these young men would then form the first company of about 150 to 200 recruits and be given a name. This company would form the nucleus of the elite military formation comprising the new king's agemates, with its name *(umutwe w'umurangangoma)* being given to the national army under the new king's reign. For instance, the *Ibisumizi* were formed upon the enthronement of Ruganzu II Ndoli, the *Abakemba* under Cyilima II Rujugira, the *Abashakamba* under King Yuhi IV Gahindiro and the *Ingangurarugo* under Kigeri IV Rwabugiri.[8]

These would basically constitute the king's personal guard (today's presidential guard) and would be entrusted to the Head of the King's Palace *(Umutware w'urugo rw'Umwami)* for training and development.

In addition to this first company and under the same reign, four or five military corps would later be formed in the same manner and given a different name. These would actually replace aging corps of preceding reigns, who would eventually retire as their generation died out.

A man would usually remain in his military formation throughout his lifespan unless the king decided to deploy him elsewhere. Also, a soldier would usually belong to the army subunit of his father since, as already noted, the military institution functioned along hereditary lines.

As observed, however, the military being rooted in the society demanded that every Rwandan male belongs to a military regiment *(Itorero)*. The *Itorero* formed the basic military formation within the *Umutwe w' Ingabo* or battalion. In the *Itorero*[9], strong bonds were formed between the recruits, where one learnt military tactics and about past exploits, including those of their fathers and grandfathers, and how one should emulate them and perfect their military ability.

Training usually took 5 to 6 years in traditional military schools *(amatorero)* which, as the name suggests drew from the Itorero. From the amatorero graduated the elite of the land from whom important chiefs were chosen. During the day in the schools, the recruits studied war dances *(Imihamilizo)*, archery *(Kurasa)*, shield tactics *(Ingabo)*, fencing, i.e., sword tactics *(Kurwanisha inkota)*, and the use of different types of spears *(gutera icumu)*. These included practising marksmanship *(kumasha)*, throwing javelins *(gutebanwa)*, jumping *(gusimbuka)*, singing *(Indilimbo z'ingabo)*, and *Kwivuga* (proclaiming one's courage and heroism through self-praising poems).[10]

During the evenings, usually in the convivial African tradition of get-togethers around the fire, recruits were instructed in Rwandan cultural mores, civics and artistic values such as eloquence *(kuvuga neza)* and poetry, courage *(Ubutwali)*, honesty *(ubupfura)* and patriotism *(gukunda igihugu)*. All these drew from and were passed on through the rich oral tradition in folklore and art that included songs, poems, myths, epics and legends such as of *abacengeri* (voluntary martyrs or offensive liberators). Rules of conduct which were not learned in the family would be acquired or incarnated in the military, thus the saying *"Utarumbiye mu ngobyi arumbira mu ngabo"* (it is in the family or in the military that one acquires - or loses, proper conduct).

The result of this was the deep entrenchment of the military institution in Rwandan socio-cultural life, leaving a marked impact in the individual in the socialization process. This may be reflected in the popular traditional dance *Umuhamilizo* and personal poems *ibyivugo* in which the difference between the military and the non-military aspect of the individual could not be distinguished. For example, the Intore dance was initially a war dance which has been proudly taken over by the larger society.

In sum, the belonging of the male youth in the *Itorero* was a national duty, but most importantly an initiation into responsible adulthood. This was so imperative that failure to belong to *Itorero* would result, for instance, in one missing a spouse in the perception that such a person was not man enough, a notion that persists to this day in betrothal ceremonies. In traditional Rwanda in a betrothal ceremony a man had to identify himself with the military formation to which he belonged, to gauge his character and suitability for the bride.

While *amatorero* formed the main induction channels into the national army, foreign troops could also be inducted into the Rwandan national forces. These included former invaders who preferred to stay like in the case of *Indara*, created by Yuhi III Mazimpaka, who were mainly composed of Banyoro invaders who had failed to return home. They would also be soldiers whose territory was conquered by Rwanda or refugees in Rwanda seeking asylum. This is the case of *Nyakare* who came from Burundi under King Ruganzu II Ndoli, or the *Ibihura-mutwe*[11] also from Burundi who were integrated into *Inzirabwoba* by Prince Nkoronko under King Mutara II Rwogera; or *Urwasabahizi* and *Abarota* from Gisaka, who came under Cyilima II Rujugira.

Local armies, especially those along Rwandan borders, could also become part of the national army because of the bravery they may have demonstrated in protecting their area.

This is again the case of *Abarashi* who were integrated into *Ingangurarugo* by King Kigeri IV Rwabugiri for their skill and bravery. These also included the *Abangogo*, initially inhabitants of Kingogo in Ngororero District that Mibambwe II Gisanura declared his "army" and integrated into the national forces.

The king could also settle in a new area and decide to create a local army or incorporate an existing one into the royal troops. The best example is that of *Abadaha* and *Abatanyagwa* created by Cyilima II Rujugira for his daughter, Mitunga. They were initially composed of inhabitants of Budaha in Ngororero District before being integrated in the national army.

The king could also allow his son or one of his favourite chiefs to create a local army for security reasons in the region. One example is that of *Inzirwa*, created under Cyilima II again by one of his military chiefs, Ruyumbu, to guard the Rwandan border with Mubali at Gakuta as well as the border with Burundi, at Busozo.

In the end, the prowess and socio-political organization of the Rwanda military force was such that it was impenetrable, even by the Arab slavers. The slave trade never affected Rwanda. The Arabs captured slaves from the vastness of the Congo and other surrounding areas. Indeed, if there had ever existed any divisions or conflicts between the Hutus and Tutsis during this period, it would have been a veritable recipe for slave trade.[12]

When the explorer Henry Morton Stanley reached Karagwe in 1878, he met one Ahmed Ibrahim, an Arab, who found a way to explain away his frustrations, saying the Banyarwanda were "a great people, but covetous, malignant, treacherous, and utterly untrustworthy...They have never allowed an Arab to trade in their country, which proves them a bad lot."[13]

Cattle Armies and the Socio-economic Role of the Military

In principle, the traditional army comprised two sections under the same command. The first comprised the combatants *(Ingabo)* and the second of special cattle-herders *(Abashumba or Inkomamashyi)*. This combination obtained as many military corporations had a corresponding "cattle formation" made up of cows from combatants' families. Hence the situation was such that, parallel to the fighting troops, there existed corresponding *armées-bovines* (cattle armies)[14], mainly to cater for the formation's subsistence needs.

Some of the "duties" of the *armées-bovines* included production of milk and breeding of milking cows *(inkuke)* and bulls for beef *(indwanyi* or *ibiniha* in case of an infertile cow) for the royal court. The cattle were also raised for many other reasons in accordance with the Dynastic Code *(Ubwiru)* or for religious reasons, such as providing young sacrificial bulls for divination (Amamana) or raising royal bulls *(Rusanga)*.

The *armées-bovines* were often bequeathed to the military formation after its creation by the king, or as part of the spoils of war *(Intorano)*. *Indorero*, for instance, were pillaged by King Ruganzu II Ndoli after defeating Nzira son of Muramira, the king of Bugara. The cattle were given to his army, *Ibisumizi*, for having beaten Nzira's personal army, *Abakongoro*.

However such cattle-armies as *Umuhozi* and *Inkondera* respectively attached to *Abashakamba* and *Inyaruguru* social-armies mainly came from the soldiers' families rather than from war booty. However, some fighting armies had no known corresponding cattle-armies, with some cattle-armies also having no corresponding fighting armies.

While cattle played a central role in the society and the army, the traditional Rwandan military played a crucial socio-economic role in all its endeavours. It is credited to King Gihanga as being the initiator of one of the earliest socio-economic initiatives when he charged his military formation, *Gakondo*, to prepare the First Fruits Ceremony *(Umuganura)* by providing required crops, mainly sorghum *(amasaka)*, millet *(uburo)* and vegetable *(isogi)*. *Umuganura* would be as a "agricultural show" where the best crop and fruits of each year's harvest would be exhibited to give thanks to *Imana*. This formed the basis for the spread of early crops *(imbuto nkuru)* that are used in Rwandan traditional ceremonies such as *Guterekera* and *Kubandwa* (traditional prayer ceremonies). After the court, the same ceremony would be performed throughout the country on lineage basis, which led to dissemination of those crops nationwide.

In addition to popularising these early food crops and livestock products, new varieties of crops and animals were introduced later in Rwanda by the army returning from military expeditions abroad. Examples are given such as in the 16th century, when the army of Kigeri II Nyamuheshera, *Inkingi,* brought in a type of beans from Bushengero in present-day southern Uganda, which proved better than the local *igiharo (sennonis)*. From the same region of Kigezi, *Inkingi* also brought a herd of goats that the king termed *Akamenesho* as they were a better breed and larger than the local variety.

In the 19th century, introduction of a new variety of the sweet potato by the army of Kigeri IV Rwabugiri "revolutionalised the traditional food production system"[15]. The new potato introduced by *Ingangurarugo* from its expedition in Gikore in Bufumbira in June 1879 yielded more than one tuber and more times in a year than the local variety, *gafuma*. People still recall that Rwabugiri himself ordered each of his soldiers to tie one sweet potato-plant to his bow when coming back home, and that to multiply them, he created a nursery in his royal residence at Giseke.

Under the same reign, around the year 1874, the military formation *Uruyange* returned from the expedition of Butembo in today's Democratic Republic of Congo with a new food crop,

Amashaza (cow peas). Rwabugiri again spread them throughout the country after experimenting with them at his royal residence at Rubengera in present-day Karongi District in Western Province. It is highly possible that the former name of Bwishaza, in the same province, is associated with this introduction of the peas in the region. The name may therefore mean the "region of peas".

It actually may be surmised that the Rwandan pre-colonial military's battles were in most cases economically driven. Either to raid cattle as in the expedition of Mirama under King Kigeri IV Rwabugiri,or to bring back their own raided ones as in the expedition of Buhunde-Butembo, or to get petty-kings to recognize the authority of the King of Rwanda by paying homage in the form of taxes *(amakoro)* to the royal court (e.g. Expedition of Bumpaka). We look at the reign of King Rwabugiri in the next chapter.

Notes

1 Walter Rodney, *How Europe Underdeveloped Africa,* 1972, EAEP, Nairobi, pp.126-127.
2 A. Kagame (1952), op. cit., pp.17-79.
3 Table on Rwandan kings and their armies in Appendix.
4 A. Kagame, *Les Milices du Rwanda pre-colonial,* Butare, 1962, p.8.
5 Appendix.
6 Ian Linden (1977: 13).
7 A. Kagame (1962), op. cit., p.8.
8 Appendix.
9 Ian Linden (1977), op. cit., p.13.
10 A. Kagame, 1952, op. cit.
11 This "integrated force" still survives in the RDF. For instance, Lt Emmanuel Shyaka of the RDF 201 Brigade traces his ancestors to the *Ibihuramutwe,* Burundian Force that was integrated by Nkoronko. His lineage from Abagesera clan, beginning with him: Shyaka, Sebuhuku, Kangabo, Murangira and Nkoronko.
12 Ian Linden (1977), op. cit., p.21.

13   Henry Morton Stanley (1878), op. cit., p.455.

14   A. Kagame, *L'histoire des armées-bovines dans l'ancien Rwanda,* IRSAC, 1960.

15   B. Muzungu (2003) op. cit., pp.267-268..

4

King Kigeri IV Rwabugiri (1853-1895):

The End of *Ku-aanda* and the Advent of Colonialism

Upon being enthroned and taking reign of the now fairly prosperous kingdom of Rwanda in 1853, King Kigeri IV Rwabugiri would end up being one of the longest reigning and distinguish himself among the greatest of the warrior kings. With a total of more than fourteen military expeditions[1] at the head of his celebrated army, *Ingangurarugo*, he was not a king to trifle with, as his nickname or "sword-name" was "*Inkotanyi-cyane* (the tireless combatant or indefatigable warrior)".

King Rwabugiri aspired to quell ongoing rebellions in the neighbouring kingdoms that traditionally paid homage to Rwanda. This made him stand out as the most accomplished king in his quest for centralization of authority, and was always willing to take on his neighbours at the slightest provocation. His legend was that he could not tolerate the sound of the morning drum (*Ingoma z'indamutsa*) from a neighbouring kingdom, which he interpreted as an impudent insult to his royal might and prowess. It is said that upon hearing the drum, he would attack the neighbouring king the very next day.

In the poem *Ntambe Ineza*[2] (Let me celebrate), Sekarama, who witnessed most of the battles waged by King Rwabugiri likens him to Ruganzu II Ndoli:

Kavura-shavu Nyirishema ryinshi,	The-Consoler The-Very-Proud king
Kigeri uri Umugabe watwitse ibirwa	Kigeri you are a king who ravaged Kivu islands
Ugatera igishyika ibyaro	And threatened all petty-kingdoms
Urihoza mu ruganda	You always refurbish your spear
Rugambirira-tabaro	You the-Premeditator-of-wars
Rwa Mutabazi wa Cyamatare	Just like Ruganzu II son of Cyamatare
Zirahangwa no gucanirwa	As soon as people are given a king
Akazibyukurukamo[3]	He immediately attack them

King Kigeri IV Rwabugiri strove to centralize and, true to his proud, uncompromising and distrustful character, as described by those who knew him, personally supervise and consolidate the kingdom. So focused was he to enable the perfect environment for this personal supervision and consolidation, that his was the continual destabilization of local leaders and ruling families in the regions he ploughed through. Many of the aristocratic or ruling familes perished during his numerous expeditions[4] or were deported to other areas. An example of this was during the expedition of Butembo in Kivu in 1874, where he killed the commander of *Uruyange* battalion, Giharamagara cya Rwakagara. In 1873 he had allegedly avenged his mother's death by killing his uncle Nkoronko, who was the commander of *Inzirabwoba* and Prince Rwamhembwe rwa Nkusi the commander of *Abashakamba.*

This rout of ruling families was not only a strategy aimed at close personal control of his kingdom, but a reform measure in the established form of decentralized administration and revert to the centralization akin to that of Kigeri I Mukobanya. It was thus that to ensure personal control, Rwabugiri created and multiplied his royal residences *(amarembo)* in most regions in the kingdom. The royal residences became major administrative centres of the provinces *("Ibiti"* or *"Intara")* with "boundaries" that could however change at the pleasure of the king. At these residences he installed his wives (sometimes two in one area) and appointed a body of handpicked administrators, the majority of whom owed everything – their honour and wealth – to Rwabugiri and were therefore most loyal to him.

At the same time, the distrusting monarch also put in place an omnipresent network of spies to oversee his residencies, administrators and their assistants. Any motive or pretext to commit mischief reported to him was sufficient to dismiss or even execute the transgressor. Rwabugiri would appear at any time. Oral accounts attest to his improvised military expeditions and visits to the provinces being as frequent as they were tireless and legendary[5].

The relocation of the entire ruling families, their installation in the newly occupied regions to replace local hereditary chieftains, including exiles generally forced to flee at the advance of Rwabugiri, abound in many oral accounts. These seem to affirm that, all things considered, the beneficiaries of Rwabugiri's administration were individuals initially unknown to the communities they ruled and were often people of "low descent", whether Hutu, Tutsi, Twa, or merely "lowly" residents of the newly conquered territories[6].

The monarch would elevate them from their modest stations in life and bestow upon them heavy responsibilities, such as in the case of Bisangwa and his brother Sehene. The brothers were descended from one Rugombituri (Migambi), a young destitute, who was adopted by Mutara II Rwogera's royal court and became a noble, thus the saying *amagara aramirwa ntamerwa* (you become noble when well fed). Bisangwa was made chief of Bugoyi in present-day Rubavu District and given command of the area's army battalion, *Inkaranka*. Sehene was made a notable of Mayaga in today's Nyanza District, responsible for the royal cattle herds and therefore a highly regarded noble in the royal residences of Kamonyi, Rwamaraba and Gitovu.

Another example of a person who gained favour with the king, long before the two brothers, was Nzigiye ya Rwishyura who rose through the ranks to become a *de facto* "Prime Minister" during Rwabugiri's reign.

It is on the basis of examples such as this that oral accounts attest to the end of the reign of Kigeri IV Rwabugiri, as the disenfranchised aristocracy bore murderous animosities towards him that included assassination plots, and fueled the political instability that ensued. Indeed, the removal of ruling families' source of power and privilege ensured the political instability that would characterize the last decade of the 19th Century and early 20th Century – a situation in which colonialism would take root, compromising Rwanda's might and signaling the end of the process of *ku-aanda*.

The first official colonialist in Rwanda, the German Lieutenant, Gustav Adolf von Goetzen, met Rwabugiri at Kageyo in Ngororero on 30 May 1894. It is said that upon entering the court, von Goetzen had slapped the king's chief of protocol, Nkwaya, who had barred the German's way for trying to by-pass protocol and go directly to the king. And to make his point, von Gotzen showed the might of the German's by letting go two awe-inspiring cannon blasts.[7]

However, sizing up the white man with his small contingent of 127 askaris, Rwabugiri decided he could not accept the brashness and superiority displayed by the German. Despite caution from his trusted ally, King Rumanyika of Karagwe, that the *mzungu* was not an enemy to trifle with, "with his long stick that loudly smoked from one end"[8], Rwabugiri ordered his army commander, Bisangwa, to lay a night ambush to his visitors on their way home.

Bisangwa, who had grown to become a respected, battle hardened and tactical warrior at the head of the national army,

Ingangurarugo, must have employed his vast experience, but his military operation was no match to the bullets and sound of the German firearms. The *mzungu* had made his point, and from then on Rwanda with its festering political instability would never be the same.

The Political Crises

It is generally acknowledged that the political crises of the period 1890-1900 can be attributed to King Rwabugiri's desire to settle the question of his succession according to his wishes[9], regardless of the "constitutional" provisions *(Ubwiru).* Having overstayed in power, there emerged several court intrigues of upstarts seeking favours without questioning the king's overstay. By the same token, Rwabugiri distanced himself from his peers and close advisors, such as his brothers-in-law led by Kabare ka Rwakagara, who would have dared question him to his face about his personalized rule. This is probably one of the main reasons the king decided to designate a successor. Such a designation of a successor was not bad in itself, except that as a Kigeri, he was not allowed to designate a regent. According to *Ubwiru,* only Cyilima and Mutara could.

This happened when, in 1889, Rwabugiri by-passed the laid down procedure in the Monarchical Code, *Ubwiru,* and decided to forcefully appoint his son, Rutalindwa, regent king. While this was an unheard of Kigeri appointment, he went further and designated his favourite wife, Kanjogera, Queen Mother. The problem that would unfold to greatly weaken the monarchy was that Kanjogera was not only step-mother to Rutalindwa, but was also not from the Abokono, the designated matriarchal clan for the next reign. Additionally, Kanjogera had her own son, who she felt more deserving of the throne than the motherless young regent king. This conflict of interest would create the recipe for the troubles that lay ahead after the death of King Rwabugiri.

Accounts of the king's leadership from his descendants and the families who interacted with him in the regions he conquered stress his administrative reforms and autocracy. Rwabugiri's exploits lasted almost half a century and left a leadership vacuum when he died unexpectedly in September 1895. However, the fact that hereditary privileges were removed from traditional ruling families can be seen as a positive step in the evolving dynamism of the society. At the same time, the promotion of outsiders from other parts of the kingdom to leadership could have resulted in more consensus and cohesion in the communities they ruled. This may be so, as the new rulers with no local alliances had no other interest than to please the king - like in the case of Nzigiye ya Rwishyura who went on to become Rwabugiri's closest confidant.

Thus the ruling power and administration had become very personal and unpredictable. Rwabugiri had managed to change the traditional way of administration and mis-advisedly subverted official statutes of the monarchy making his rule devoid of checks and balances. The traditional nobility was marginalized and in their place Rwabugiri appointed those who owed him personal loyalty. The most worried were the Abega clan, who had provided three consecutive queen mothers[10] before Rwabugiri, and had therefore established a strong nobility of the Abakagara sub-clan to which Kanjogera belonged. While the royal residences or chief towns resembled the beginnings of modern administration, there was much rivalry, infighting and intrigues among the courtiers, making these centres of power greatly unstable.

Meanwhile, politically marginalized, the great families were, amid much open competition, waiting in the wings for the opportunity to regain their lost power long before the sudden death of Rwabugiri.

The Battle of Shangi and the Palace coup of Rucunshu[11]

The death of King Rwabugiri was therefore not unwelcome. As it would turn out, the king, as always, still harboured ambitions to consolidate western Rwanda (now eastern Congo), mainly through loyalties and other homages. However, there emerged local attempts of revolt from this region against the king, which would eventually pave the way for complicity towards Rwabugiri's death with accomplices very close to his court.

Oral accounts still mention many poisoning attempts or other forms of attempted assassinations of Rwabugiri during his last expeditions against Bushubi in today's Tanzania and Rusozi in Bushi in Congo and Ankole in Uganda. In the end, versions of the accounts allege that his death on Ibinja Island in Lake Kivu, during his last expedition in 1895, was the result of poisoning by his Bashi housemaids and servants who were monitored by highly placed "Banyarwanda" with the complicity of his favourite wife, Kanjogera[12].

After Rwabugiri's death, his co-regent son Rutarindwa became King Mibambwe IV (1895-1896). However, as the young king struggled to consolidate his power, the long disempowered family groups jostled with each other in order to regain their former privileges. These struggles took the form of mainly the royalists (pro-Rutalindwa) against the Abega clan (pro-Queen Mother Kanjogera). The command of the military formations was similarly split along these two factions.

On the King's side, there were three powerful battalions led by royalist commanders, who had been appointed by Rutalindwa's father, Rwabugiri, and who vowed total loyalty and obedience to the late king. The first battalion was the previous reign's Royal Guard, *Ingangurarugo*, commanded by Bisangwa bya Rugombituri. The second was *Inyaruguru* in the Southern Command headed by Prince Muhigirwa, who was regarded as the main supporter of his brother King Rutalindwa. Some of Rutalindwa's brothers such as Baryinyonza preferred siding with the Queen Mother's camp for their personal security. The third force was the *Abarasa* commanded by Mugugu wa Shumbusho in the Eastern Command, Gisaka, where he used to liaise with traders from Bujinja (in today's western Tanzania) to bring clothes and trinkets and other items from the East African coast.

In the opposing camp there were two less powerful battalions, the *Uruyange* under the brother of the Queen Mother, Kabare ka Rwakagara, and the *Abashakamba* under Rutishereka rwa Sentama. This camp was not only weak in terms of military strength, compared to the royalists, but also was at the time made up of less experienced troops. This was the main reason why Queen Mother Kanjogera and her two powerful brothers, Kabare and Ruhinankiko, wanted to change the command of the first camp at all costs if they were to conspire against Mibambwe IV.

Mugugu was the first to be gotten rid of because he was a royalist and had an old axe to grind with the Queen Mother. Some years previously, the Queen Mother had wanted to take over the royal residence of Sakara in Gisaka, which at the time was under the command of Mugugu. Chief Mugugu opposed the idea, as he did not want the then Queen Kanjogera to tamper with his dealing with the Bujinja traders for King Rwabugiri. On those grounds Mugugu was eliminated and his battalion given to Rwayitare, the son of Rutishereka.

Come July 1896, despite these rivalries, another blow to Rwanda's stability would strike. A military contingent from the Congo Free State under the command of Lieutenants Long and Deffense,[13] the Belgian African army *Force Publique,* strayed into Rwanda and established themselves at Shangi by installing military stations at Nyamasheke and Musaho (Karongi District) on the shores of Lake Kivu.

This prompted conspirators to urge the young King Mibambwe IV to dispatch the army, which was led by the elite companies from *Ingangurarugo* and *Inyaruguru* battalions, to dislodge the Belgian force. Prince Nshozamihigo was made the expedition commander, who charged Chief Bisangwa and Prince Muhigirwa to form the vanguard force with their respective elite companies, *Ibisumizi* and *Ijuru*. The two powerful commanders were sworn royalists to the young king, thus the reason they were chosen to lead the attack against the white invaders in spite of a long standing caution by the late King Rwabugiri never to affront the Europeans. Force Commander Bisangwa formed the advance party with his *Ibisumizi* and attacked first. Though at first it had an upper hand in the surprise dawn attack, the Rwanda army would later be tragically overrun and annihilated.

What would hence become known as the battle of Shangi took the lives of Bisangwa and many other commanders. In their victory, the *Force Publique* soldiers would memorably rampage through Cyangugu. The Rwandan historian, Emmanuel Ntezimana, notes that "the violence, pillage and torching of homes by the FP with the connivance of Congolese local populations (i.e. Bashi, Bafulero of South Kivu and the Barundi) are still recounted in Cyangugu."[14]

With a humbled army, Rwanda had broken its backbone, and the national spirit had been weakened at Shangi. Yet the royal court rivalries and intrigues continued unabated. In the end, it would lead to a face-off of two opposing camps. On the one side were the followers of Mibambwe IV Rutarindwa and, on the other, those of the Queen Mother Nyiramibambwe Kanjogera who wanted to reign with her own son, Musinga, as king.

Prince Muhigirwa, who had preferred a withdrawal instead of undertaking a suicidal confrontation at Shangi, was now desperate after the death of his two comrades, Bisangwa and Mugugu. He therefore opted for defection rather than clinging to his brother's weakened camp. Besides, King Mibambwe IV was believed to have lost his mind, as he would not listen to any advice from his supporters. From this time on "Rucunshu" was inevitable. The only obstacle remaining was Commander Sehene, who had taken over the command of *Ingangurarugo* after the death of his brother Bisangwa. It is alleged that Kabare quietly organized the murder of Sehene.[15] It took a while to discover who the conspirators were.

Meanwhile, the intrigues and tension between the two heads of the nation became so heightened that it is said by the end of 1896, "everyone" was walking with a weapon on high alert at the royal residence of Rucunshu. The queen mother and the king could only communicate through messengers, an indication of a serious break-down of the unity of the monarchy.

In the heightened tension it would only be a matter of time before the now infamous palace coup of Rucunshu, which, ironically, would be triggered by what might have been a minor, if innocuous, incident: It happened that a swarm of irritated bees attacked the courtyard of pro-Rutalindwa Batwa warriors, from the *Urwililiza* Company. Other than get stung by the killer African bees, the warriors sought to take refuge in the nearest compound, which happened to be that of the Queen Mother. Since they were armed and shouting as they fled from the bees, the guards on the Queen Mother's compound perceived this as an attack. It was in this confusion that the fateful coup would ensue.

Initially, the pro-Rutarindwa warriors had an advantage, but the Kanjogera sympathizers finally gained the upper hand, for Kabare had the precaution of leaving behind his men who would misinform and deceive the intervening troops to attack the royalists' camp. In defeat and with no way out, King Mibambwe IV Rutarindwa was forced to commit suicide together with his wife Kanyonga, their three sons, his brother Karara and their sympathisers. The royal court was torched, after gaining hold of the royal drum, *Kalinga,* and Kanjogera's son, Musinga, was declared king by the Queen Mother's influential brother, Kabare.

The battle would only last half a day, and most of the army regiments would only learn about the royal suicide before arriving at Rucunshu. Meanwhile, the Queen Mother and the young Musinga moved from Rucunshu to instal themselves at Rwamiko in Marangara in central Rwanda. Their victory was not definite, however, as the royalists to the former king still harboured ambitions to the throne.

The struggle between the ex-royalists and the coup makers would persist for the next two decades.[16] Meanwhile, having served for only one year, King Mibambwe IV Rutalindwa reign never had an impact in Rwanda's history and was therefore rarely mentioned in the official list of Rwandan monarchs. Also, according to *Ubwiru*, the death of king at the hands of a rival prince makes the winner automatically Imana's chosen king, who in this case was Musinga and his maternal uncles.

However, the delicate situation towards the end of the 19th century would have its ramifications in the entire kingdom. It had a great repercussion on the hierarchy and organization of the army. The instability was proportional to the long and personal reign of King Rwabugiri who died without being able to complete his reforms or stabilize his consolidated regions. Meanwhile, Queen Mother Kanjogera, helped by her brothers, continued with her court intrigues and purging under King Yuhi V Musinga until the latter, as he matured, decided to oppose the consuming intrigues and become his own man.

This new wave of purges was now pitting the supporters of the two brothers of the Queen Mother, Kabare and Ruhinankiko, who vied for political influence and hegemony at the Court. The time for several army commanders who had escaped death at Shangi and Rucunshu had come. The major ones to die were Prince Muhigirwa and his brother Baryinyonza first, later followed by Commanders Rutishereka, Mutwewingabo of Abateke family, Kampayana, Sebuharara and his cousin Cyaka, among others. The same intrigues affected their respective forces, which were sometimes obliged to confront each other in defence of their beloved commanders.

But with the squabbles and a humiliated and divided army, Rwanda had reached its lowest ebb. Therefore when on 22 March 1897 the German Captain, Ramsay, handed Mpamarugamba (standing for King Musinga) the German flag and the letter containing the "Protection Accord" that proclaimed Rwanda a German "protectorate", the royal court jumped at the offer. Mpamarugamba was a trusted courtier who often represented the king to unknown Europeans, and also because Musinga was still too young to negotiate national matters. Ramsay, on the other hand, had that previous year (May 1896) set up a military post to oversee the District of Ujiji in the vast German East Africa, which included Buha (today's Kigoma, Tanzania), Burundi and Rwanda.

Musinga's court, however, knew or cared little of this background. What mattered was that, on the balance, being allies with the Germans meant that the Court would benefit from the protection of the white men, neutralizing the many enemies that were created in the Rucunshu coup, not to mention the ever threatening Belgians still in their military garrisons in Shangi. Though the Belgians had been shown the letter of German protection by the now more confident Rwandans, they would not budge and clung to Shangi as an outpost of the Congo Free State.

As it would turn out, however, a large contingent of rampaging Congolese armed rebels numbering 5,000 came sweeping through the area forcing the Belgian *Force Publique* to abandon their stations at Musaho (Kibuye) and Nyamasheke at Shangi which, overwhelmed by the rebel numbers, they could not defend. The rebels took over the stations and abandoned them on their own volition in April 1898 and moved on.[17] As this was happening, it became a sign for Rwandans that the Germans were a worthy ally, mistakenly believing that it was the German letter of protection shown to the Belgians that had driven them away. Besides, the German offer of protection was the more agreeable policy of indirect rule, which left the king and his court to rule as they pleased.

In May of that year, Captain Bethe took over from Ramsay, and in November of 1898 set up a German military outpost at Shangi. In that same year, the Germans had founded the Military District of Bujumbura that oversaw Rwanda and Burundi. A skirmish, however, arose when Belgian Officers, Hecq and Hennebert, attempted to re-capture Shangi and surrounding territories. This led to the Hecq-Bethe Peace Treaty of 23 November 1899 affirming the Germans' right to Rwanda and allowed Bethe to authorize two military posts for the Congo Free State in Cyangugu and Nyakagunda that started operation in April 1900.[18]

That same year, in the month of February, the White Fathers led by Bishop Hirth made their way into Rwanda on a recommendation by Bethe to Musinga's Court to allow them begin evangelizing. It was a recommendation the Court could not refuse, which saw the missionaries first settle at Save near Butare town.

The year 1901 turned out to be an eventful one in which Prince Rukura of the Abagesera Dynasty of the Gisaka Kingdom was making claims to the Gisaka throne, with some complicity among the Abarasa Battalion that was based there. The Abarasa were not only originally from Gisaka where they had served under its last chief, Ntamwete wa Kimenyi IV Getura (last king of Gisaka), but also were resentful of the elimination of their former commander Mugugu wa Shumbusho, and his replacement with Rwayitare of the *Abashakamba*.

On becoming aware of this complicity, King Musinga sent the *Abashakamba* Battalion under Chief Sebuharara to quell the revolt, but found that the *Abarasa* had fled to Burundi for fear of engaging the more powerful *Abashakamba*. However, with the support of the Germans, Rukura was captured in Bushubi and jailed in Bukoba, both in present-day Tanzania.

Coming from Bujumbura to assess the turmoil in Gisaka, Lt. von Grawert (Bwana Digidigi) and his troops found that Rukura had already been captured and took him to Bujumbura for imprisonment. Prince Rukura was eventually released after denouncing his dynastic claims to Gisaka.

By then the court had become quite dependent on and appreciative of the German's military might, despite the inevitability that it no longer mattered that the Ingabo had become an irrelevant force.

Meanwhile, by 1909, as the court remained busy with internal wrangles, new challenges were arising in the north of the country where a rebellion was beginning to brew. One Basebya, a Twa deserter from the *Abashakamba,* who also did not recognise Musinga's authority, was terrorizing Buberuka and the neighbouring zones of Kibali and Bukonya (in Northern Rwanda). With his terrorising gang, *Ibijabura,* and accompanied by starved villagers, Basebya attacked Musinga's royalists during the night and set fire to their homes after pillaging them. Kabare sent a punitive expedition against Basebya mainly comprising of the Company *Indengabaganizi,* and under the command of Ruhararamanzi rwa Shumbusho, the chief of Buberuka. The confrontation saw the escape of *Ibijabura* and their leader Basebya to Kigezi in Uganda.

Shortly after, there arose a "pretender" to the throne, a certain Ndungutse, whose real name was Birasisenge and hailed from Bugwangali (Ngarama) in Umutara region. Rumour had it that one of the wives of Kigeri IV Rwabugiri, Muserekande had two sons: one Biregeya with Kigeri IV, and the other Ndungutse with Mibambwe IV Rutalindwa, who as such was the true heir to the throne. When he showed up in Buberuka he was acclaimed by sympathisers of Basebya, including Rukara rwa Bishingwe, the commander of *Abarashi.*

By this time, the famed warrior, Rukara, was a fugitive for having killed the White Father, R.P Loupias (Rugigana). The White Father had been sent by the Court of King Musinga to deliver a verdict of the king following an altercation in the North where Rukara had been in conflict with Sebuyange over their respective spheres of influence in Gahunga and Kabaya.[19]

A joint expedition made up of German troops under Lt. Gudovius (Bwana Lazma) and the Company *Iziruguru* under the command of Rwubusisi rwa Cyigenza, was sent by the court to quell the northern rebellion. After manoeuvres that took several days, Ndungutse was shot down by Gudovius on 13 April 1912, while Basebya was captured by Chief Rwubusisi and sentenced to death at Kajwi in Nyarutovu on 15 May 1912. As for Rukara, he was arrested and executed in his area of Murera while his son Manuka, the real murderer of the White Father, was imprisoned.[20]

The arrangement of complementing one another in times of need would serve both sides well. On the one hand, the Germans helped King Musinga to do away with rebels, and, on his part, the king helped the Germans fight the Belgians in 1916 by conscripting his men *(Indugaruga)* to fight alongside the German troops all the way from Gisenyi to Tabora in Tanzania, as we shall see in the next chapter.

Notes

1   Appendix.
2   *Cahiers,* No.26, March 2004, p.57-73.
3   Ibid., p.71.
4   Ian Linden (1977), op.cit., pp. 19-20.
5   E.Ntezimana, op.cit., pp.76-77.
6   Ian Linden, (1977),op.cit, pp. 19-20.
7   « Au plus profond de l'Afrique: Européens et Rwandais font connaissance » by Gudrun Honke (ed), *Au plus profond de l'Afrique : Le Rwanda et la Colonisation allemande* 1885-1919, p.86. A. Kagame (1962), op. cit., pp.15-36.
8   A. Kagame (1975), op. cit., p.92.
9   Ian Linden (1977), op.cit., p.23.
10   Nyiramibambwe III Nyiratamba, Nyirayuhi IV Nyiratunga and Nyiramavugo II Nyiramongi.

11   Lemarchand, op.cit. pp.57-58 ; Yuhi Musinga: *Un Reigne Mouvementé,* unpublished MS ; Pagès, *Un Royaume hamite au centre de l'Afrique,* ERCB, Brussels, 1933, Vol.1, pp.195-232.

12   A. Kagame, 1975, op. cit., p.103.

13   Ibid, p.113.

14   E. Ntezimana, « Le Rwanda Social, Administratif et Politique à la fin du Dix-neuvième Siècle » in Gudrun Honke (ed), *Au Plus Profond de L'Afrique: le Rwanda et la colonisation allemande, 1885-1919 (Wuppertal: P.Hammer),* 1990, p.73.

15   A. Kagame (1975) op. cit., p 119.

16   Lemarchand, op. cit., p.57) observes that 'Rucunshu marks the beginning of a long civil war between the Bega and the Banyiginya clans, in a way reminiscent of the protracted struggle between the House of York and the House of Lancaster in 15th Century England'.

17   A. Kagame (1975), op.cit, p.143.

18   Ibid.

19   Ibid, p. 162.

20   Prof. Roger Louis, *Ruanda-Urundi 1884-1919,* Clarendon Press, Oxford, 1963, pp.156-157; A. Kagame (1975), op.cit., p. 163.

5

The Demise of the Traditional Rwandan Military

The beginning of the demise of the traditional military can firmly be traced to the slave trade in the Great Lakes Region, and particularly to the Belgians' colonization of the neighbouring Congo under King Leopold II,[1] long before the German colonization of Rwanda. However, while communities surrounding Rwanda were being ravaged and scoured for slaves and labour for Leopold's Congo, Rwanda remained largely unscathed for its military prowess and strength of leadership.

Things changed in 1894 with von Goetzen's meeting at Kageyo with Rwabugiri, and more so with the defeat of the ambushing[2] elite troops, *Ingangurarugo*. It is however the battle of Shangi that sealed Rwanda's military fate with the death of the top commanders at the front, foremost among whom was Bisangwa. And with the patronage of the Germans with their more modern military equipment to prop up the monarchy against its many enemies and rebellions, the *Ingabo* finally caved in and proved impotent in the dispensation.

In this progression of events, however, the watershed of *Ingabo's* glorious past and what the future would hold for Rwanda was marked by the end of the First World War with the defeat of Germans. As spoils of war, Belgium claimed Rwanda as a trophy for colonial exploitation and, not least, as a grudge for Rwandans' active support of the Germans during the War.

While the Germans had been relaxed in their rule by letting the monarchy reign as it pleased, the Belgians held a more violent attitude in their tighter control[3] of Rwanda. This found its roots in Belgium's commercial exploitation of the natives in the Congo through the notoriously brutal military organization, *Force Publique*.[4] This approach to colonial rule that the Belgians transplanted in Rwanda from the Congo brought with it all the violent historical baggage of the *Force Publique*, which it may serve well to recall.

The *Force Publique*

The *Force Publique* finds its genesis in the cruel violence of the slave trade that also accompanied the European explorers in the region, with the most notable being Henry Morton Stanley.[5] Stanley first made his name with his successful search, between 1871 and 72, for the famous Dr. David Livingstone who had gone missing. With the impending Scramble for Africa, Livingstone in the 19th Century Western imagination embodied the European ambitions for the continent to exploit its resources, evangelize the natives and learn as much as possible of the "Dark Continent".

However, when Stanley embarked on the search of the famed explorer, he started with a heavily armed retinue of 190 men,[6] making it hitherto the largest African exploring expedition. Except for Stanley and two British sailors, all of the members of this expedition were Africans experienced on the slave routes and the brutal raids that this entailed. These were drawn from various regions of the continent along the slave routes such as the Kamba in today's Kenya, the Sukuma in Tanzania, the Nubians from Sudan, Hausa and Senegalese from West Africa, etc.

The explorer came to believe in these African mercenaries for his future expeditions. And, for more supply of them, including paid porters and slaves, eventually came to rely on the "most powerful of Zanzibar-based slave traders by the name of Hamed bin Mohamed el Muljebi, popularly known as Tippu Tip. His nickname was said to have come from the sound of the slaves-traders principal instrument, the musket,"[7] a weapon which most in Stanley's retinue could ably use.

In the end, having made his name, explorer Stanley caught the eye of the King Leopold II who sent him on a five-year exploration tour (1879 – 1884) to stakeout Congo for the Belgian king, who harboured strong ambitions to personally own and commercially exploit the vast region. Stanley accepted the challenge and utilized the African mercenaries to great effect in accomplishing the king's wishes.

As the first commercial companies under contract from the king started arriving to exploit the forests of the Congo for rubber, a culture of violent brutality to ensure forced labour using the mercenaries on the local population had already been established by Stanley in his bid to build a road upstream to open up Congo for exploitation.

In 1888, King Leopold II formally organized Stanley's African mercenaries into what was to become the *Force Publique,* a multi-purpose military organization. Not only was the *Force Publique* an army for Leopold's Congo, which now belonged to the king as a piece of real estate, but a counter-guerrilla strike force, an army of occupation, and a corporate labour police force, all in one. From a few hundred, this army grew to more than nineteen thousand officers and men by 1900, and became the most powerful military force in central Africa.[8]

The *Force Publique* was divided mainly into small garrisons of several dozen African soldiers under one or two white officers. Records show that the initial handful of military posts grew to 183 by 1900, and to 313 by 1908.[9] The posts were organized around the growing economic system that was militarized for maximum commercial exploitation of the Congo and its people. Thus, with *Force Publique* garrisons found in the most commercially strategic places across the land, they often supplied their firepower to the companies under contract. In addition, each company had its own militia force and when hostages had to be taken or a rebellious village subdued, this militia and *Force Publique* soldiers often joined hands in the incursions.

In order to ensure production quotas were achieved in rubber plantations, for instance, wives would be held hostage to force husbands to deliver in order to secure their release. Also, for failure to adequately produce, the *chicotte (ikiboko)*, a whip made of raw, sun-dried hippopotamus hide that could inflict deep cuts on the body, was used in savage beatings that left gaping wounds of which even children were not spared. The *chicotte* would also be used on chiefs in public humiliation for their villages' failure to deliver their quotas.[10]

Rebellious villages were wiped out and, with this happening too often the amount of ammunition expended grew so much without adequate supply that a system had to be devised to account for the bullets. It was decreed that for every bullet used to kill an African the right hand of the dead body had to be severed and submitted to account for the bullet.[11] With this policy, the brutality moved a step further when the soldiers started severing hands of the living to account for bullets they never spent on the victims, but which they might have used for game hunting or sold to rebels and slave traders.

The brutality practised, as has been described above, became the life of generation after generation of the *Force Publique* soldiers that their sheer cruelty is to this day still painfully imprinted in the social memory of many communities in the Congo, not to mention the Shangi communities in Cyangugu.[12] The cruelty remains the most enduring and defining characteristic of the *Force Publique*. We shall see much of this brutality being replicated again in Rwanda in a later chapter.

It still remains to be said that it was not just the villagers who suffered the colonially-instigated brutality, but the *Force Publique* soldiers themselves at the hands of their white officers. The soldiers were poorly fed, with worse wages and were not spared of being flogged with the *chicotte* for the slightest offence. It is attested that many tried to desert, with their frustrations breaking into mutinies.

One particularly notable mutiny broke out in 1897 in northeastern Congo among six thousand soldiers and porters, who had been forced to march for months through forests and swamps in Leopold's bid to extend further inland, and could take it no more. The ensuing fight lasted three years, causing much loss on the *Force Publique* on many occasions. It was this group of rebels that chased away the *Force Publique* from Musaho and Nyamasheke near Shangi, as we saw in the previous chapter. The rebels, however, did not stop there and the fight was still going on "in 1900 when two thousand of the Congolese rebels chose to stay in the German territory where they finally gave up their arms for the right to settle."[13]

The First World War

The *Force Publique* won the day, nevertheless, and remained the military force to reckon with in the region when the First World War broke out in 1914. The Germans did not see it that way, however, under the over-confident leadership of von Bismack in Europe and a vast territory in Africa, including Rwanda, from which to draw the foot soldiers. So when the war broke out the Germans opened hostilities against the Congo Free State by occupying Ijwi Island on Lake Kivu.[14]

Not least by virtue of its proximity to the island and the Congo mainland, Rwanda could not escape the war. Therefore the Court of Yuhi V Musinga had to receive a request to avail soldiers for the big war. This was inevitable as the Germans had helped the Court keep at bay its many enemies and had helped quell a number of rebellions, the most recent being the one in the north under Basebya, Rukara and Ndungutse.

It was thus that the Court availed a semblance of the emasculated *Ingabo* with the military force, *Indugaruga*, whose contingent composed of members of the Royal Guard taken from

Indengabaganizi and *Iziruguru* companies. Members of these two companies had received military lessons and some education at the Nyanza School of Chiefs'sons, opened by the Germans in 1907 not just to benefit the elite, but also lay the foundation of African support in the budding colonial administration in Rwanda.

The *Indugaruga* had learnt well their military lessons and, when they were sent to the Northern front in Gisenyi at Bugoyi, distinguished themselves in military tactics. The heartened Germans recruited more local combatants and posted them at Gatsibo in Byumba where they often would be visited by the supportive local Chiefs Rwubusisi and Nturo who offered their moral support.[15]

The northern front in Gisenyi remained in position for the two years that the Belgians allied themselves with the French in the conquest of Cameroon (1914-1915), as they prepared an offensive against German East Africa. With everything finally ready, an expanded *Force Publique* army of 15,000 Congolese soldiers and 800 Belgians, with 30,000 East Africans, 30 000 Afrikaners and an additional British reinforcement, the offensive was launched under the Belgian Commander, General Tombeur, on 18 April, 1916.[16]

Hostilities between the German and Belgian troops on the Rwandan territory around the year 1916 seriously devastated the country, starting from the north-west.[17] *The Diary of Nyundo*, a Catholic newspaper at the time, noted that this Catholic Mission was completely looted. The paper noted that in the plains of Rwerere, the Belgian soldiers captured many goats and women that they abused as a much coveted booty. They also destroyed banana plantations in banana-rich Bugoyi, requisitioned food products and porters and all this in an unprecedented vandalism.[18]

In the southern front, as the offensive warmed up, Col Olsen, Commander of the Belgian Southern Brigade, captured Nkombo Island on Lake Kivu and occupied Cyangugu, then advanced towards Kigali. On the northern front in Gisenyi, Col. Molitor tactically stationed part of his Northern Brigade there, and proceeded behind the volcanoes in Bufumbira in Uganda in order to be able to quickly assault Gatsibo before advancing towards Kigali. He reached Lake Muhazi on 30 April 1916 from where he joined with British troops in the final push that would take Kigali on May 6.[19]

Meanwhile, the commander of the German front, Capt Wintgens (Bwana Tembasi) had avoided being surrounded by tactically abandoning the Gisenyi position to save himself and his outnumbered contingent, which was then under the shelling of Congolese troops that Col. Molitor had left behind. This tactical withdrawal was bewildering and irritating to the Rwandan combatants, who could little understand the reasons for the persistent abandoning of positions and, echoing the *Ingabo* fighting spirit, took it as extreme cowardice for not engaging the enemy.

Nevertheless, the German Capt. Wintgens took flight in the face of the advancing Belgians and, in a surprising gesture of concern for Germany's subjects, left King Musinga with a Belgian flag as a safety measure. The Belgian flag, Capt. Wintgens explained, was to be raised when the Belgian force arrived at Nyanza to avoid the king's Capital being razed to the ground in bombardment. This was sound advice, and when the attacking Belgians reached Nyanza, another flag was circulated by one Nyakazana, son of Mushyo who hastened and presented it to the Belgian Commander at Nyanza as a mark of submission and request for cease fire.[20]

The doomed *Ingabo*, in the name of Rwandese German soldiers, *Indugaruga,* did not comprehend the significance of this continual retreat or pullout and, upon arriving at Nyanza, tried to persuade the King that they could defend the capital against the Belgians. The concerned king had to order them not to act, claiming that he did not wish the war between the Europeans to be between him and the Belgians. Then he ordered them to give back their weapons to the Germans after reaching the eastern border at Rusumo.

As it would turn out, however, the Rwandan troops did not actually wait to reach the border. They gathered their weapons and abandoned them and headed back at Buhimba, not far from Nyanza by now occupied by the Belgian troops under Commander Muller. Some *indugaruga* die-hards, however, continued with the Germans to Tabora, which fell on 20 September 1916 at the hands of the Belgian, French and British forces.[21]

Up to this time, Rwanda had been a part of German East Africa under the 1884 Berlin Conference agreement. Now, after the end of the First World War in 1918 and in the aftermath of a vanquished Germany, there arose the League of Nations, the precursor to the United Nations, under the stewardship of the American President, Woodrow Wilson. The main aim of the League was that never should such a brutal and costly war ever happen again, and took upon itself the task of regulating international affairs as a mechanism to ensure this.

Of course, the League failed in its ideal with the breaking out of the Second World War, ironically again against the Germans under Hitler's Aryan delusions. But under the League of Nations mandate, Rwanda and Burundi, as a single territory Ruanda-Urundi, were ceded to Belgium in 1924.[22] Together with Congo, they were administered as Congo-Belge with the Governor General based in Leopoldville and a vice-governor for Ruanda-Urundi, each of the two being under the overall administration of a *Résident.*

By then the *Force Publique* had been firmly established; for beginning in 1916 it took over as a provisional military administration and as an occupational force even as the First World War raged on. The force took root as a multi-purpose[23] national army so that, just like in Leopold's Congo, the *Force Publique* in Rwanda became a counter strike force, an army of occupation[24], and police force.

The provisional military administration, however, being an occupying force in wartime, came to an end on 31 December 1918 with Major Declercq, the Belgian military Resident, handing over to the civil Resident, M.van den Eende, whose main task was to fight the famine caused by the war campaign especially in Bugoyi where the scorched earth tactics had been used by the outnumbered German force. With this civilian rule, the country was divided into four regions, namely, Kisenyi, Ruhengeri, Nyanza and Shangugu, each with a military post and a *Résident de Territoire.*[25]

Though the *Force Publique* would be greatly reduced, it would continue with the mission to maintain order and public safety, as both a military and territorial police force. By December 1925, the force comprised three Belgian officers and four Non-commissioned officers; 580 Congolese corporals and privates, of whom approximately 250 were deployed in Rwanda and the rest in Burundi.[26] Rwandans or Burundians were never recruited to form any part of the *Force Publique.* Such recruitment was not needed, and though the force may have appeared small, it was diligent and effective in its reputed brutality serving the Belgian colonial administration.

It is to these colonial administrators and their cohorts, the Roman Catholic Church, we shall now turn to in what would befall the country in the denigrating, but ironic use of the Rwandan pre-colonial socio-military structure and institutions to bring a proud people to their knees, literally, and divide a nation.

Notes

1   Adam Hochschild, *King Leopold's Ghost: A Story of Greed, Terror and Heroism in Colonial Africa,* Pan Books, London, 2002.
2   Due to the friendly welcome extended by Rwabugiri, von Goetzen does not dwell much on this ambush which Rwabugiri convinced him was provoked by nearby peasants rather than his troops. In fact, as Lemarchand (1970:48) observes, the friendly welcome

'came as a disappointment to von Goetzen, who apparently felt robbed of a splendid opportunity to display his martial qualities; at the time a lieutenant in the Second Royal Regiment of Ulans, von Goetzen's comments were indeed worthy of his calling: "Feeling strong and being moderately equipped with weapons, we certainly would have liked to cope once with a more serious enemy."

3   Lemarchand (1970), op.cit., pp.77-79.

4   Adam Hochschild, op. cit., pp.124-133.

5   Ibid.

6   Ibid.

7   Ibid.

8   Ibid.

9   Ibid.

10   The whip would also be used to great effect in Rwanda to enforce labour.

11   Adam Hochschild quotes an American missionary, Ellisworth Faris, who recorded a conversation he had had with a state officer by the name of Simon Roi in his diary in 1899: "Each time the corporal goes out to get rubber, cartridges are given to him. He must bring back all not used; and for every one used he must bring back a right hand!...As to the extent to which this is carried on, [Roi] informed me that in six months they, the state, on the Momboyo River had used 6000 cartridges, which means that 6000 people are killed or mutilated. It means more than 6000, for the people have told me repeatedly that the soldiers kill children with the butt of their guns" (p.226).

12   The Rwandan historian, late Emmanuel Ntezimana, originating from the same province of Cyangugu attests that "...violence, looting and setting fires to local houses perpetrated by Congolese soldiers and guides from Bushi are still narrated by oral traditions"(see Gudrun Honke, op. cit., p.79).

13   Adam Hochschild, op. cit., p.128.

14   Chrysologue Nduwayezu, « La *Force Publique* au Rwanda depuis 1916 à 1960 » (Mémoire in ESM, Kigali, July 1987), p. 11.

15   A. Kagame (1975), op. cit. p.171.

16   Ibid., p.172

17   Ian Linden, (1977), op. cit., p.127

18   Jean Rumiya, *Le Rwanda sous le Régime du Mandat belge* (1916-1931), Paris, 1992 ["On June 21, 1916, the Belgian askaris came to

seek porters near the Mission. They took many goats and all they found in the huts", pp.60-61.

19   A. Kagame (1975), op. cit. p. 172.

20   Idem.

21   L. De Lacger, *Le Rwanda ancien et moderne*, 2è ed, Kabgayi, 1961, p.459.

22   Alison Liebhafsky Des Forges, , *Defeat Is The Only Bad News: Rwanda Under Musiinga*, 1896-1931, Yale University, Ph.D., 1972, p.236.

23   'As in the days of the German protectorate', Lemarchand (1970: 65) says, 'the [colonial] military was entrusted with a wide range of administrative functions; and, like their German counterparts, the Belgian Residents were forced into a variety of roles, acting as trouble-shooters, judges, counselors and law-enforcing agents, and relying for assistance on a mere handful of European deputies, "whose sphere of action depended on the Resident and varied according to political circumstances".'

24   According to Lemarchand (1970: 63), the establishment of military rule through Ruanda-Burundi in 1916 was not only a normal conclusion to Belgium's victories in East Africa but a necessary condition for the realization of its ultimate political objectives. 'One of the goals of our military effort in Africa', said the Belgium Minister of Colonies, Jules Renkin, in 1916, 'is to assure the possession of German territory for use as a pawn in negotiations. If, when the peace negotiation open, changes in possession of African territories are envisaged, the retention of this pawn would be favourable to Belgian interests from every point of view.'

25   J.P. Harroy, *Rwanda: Souvenirs d'un compagnon de la marche du Rwanda vers la démocratie et l'indépendance*, Hayez, Bruxelles, 1984, pp.75-80.

26   L. Lacger, *Ruanda*, 2è édition, Kabgayi, 1959, p.487.

Traditional spears, symbols of monarchical power

Warriors armed with bows, arrows and a shield in pre-colonial era

The agaseke, traditional basket, symbolizes the resilience of the Rwandan nation and its values. It is enshrined in the Court of Arms

Iriba rya Gihanga, a well on top of Mount Kabuye from which the mystical water used for blessing the enthronement of new kings was drawn. Left to right: Gérard Nyirimanzi, Prof. Josias Semujanga and Claude Bizimana

King Kigeri IV Rwabugiri, the tireless conqueror of the 19th century whose 'sword name' was 'Inkotanyi-cyane', a name that would later be adopted by the Rwanda Patriotic Front (RPF)

A commander, left, with his soldiers in pre-colonial era

Back row L-R: Rwidegembya, Kanuma, Kabare, Mwami Yuhi V Musinga, Nkwaya, Mushigati, Cyitatire and Nyagatana

Colonel Molitor (centre), the Commander-in-Chief of the Belgian North Brigade in Congo, enters Kigali on 8 May, 1916

Mwami Musinga (centre) with his wives and Queen Mother Kanjogera (2nd left). Standing, with the colonial hat, is the Belgian Resident Major Declercq

Traditional military commanders, François Rwabutogo (left) and Paul Nturo (right), led the Inshongore group that conspired with the Roman Catholic Church and the colonial administration to dethrone Mwami Musinga

Mgr Léon Classe, Apostolic Vicar of Rwanda, 1922-1945

Mwami Charles Rudahigwa (1931-1959) and his wife, Rosalie Gicanda

Mgr Andre Perraudin, extreme left, President Grégoire Kayibanda, extreme right, who was formerly the Bishop's personal secretary

6

The Joint Conspiracy between the Catholic Church and the Colonial Administration

It is difficult to tell apart the missionary project from the colonial project, as the Church in Africa supported colonization and the colonizer, and vice versa. The Church was within colonization, much as the colonizer co-habited with the Church. In Rwanda, this co-habitation became the Belgo-Roman Catholic Church conspiracy that would, first, divide a people, and then play one side against the other. Colonel Logiest himself, the last colonial Resident of Rwanda concedes:

> For many years, the Tutelle [Belgium] and Catholic missions...
> worked hand in hand in such a way that Rwandan people could
> not distinguish between the two and considered them to be one
> power. A power that supported and developed the ascent of
> the Tutsi caste.[1]

For this to happen, it had to take a colonially orchestrated breakdown of the cultural core that held the Rwandan society together.

As we shall see in this chapter, there needed to be a complete change of Rwandans' cultural self-perception that would see core institutions, including the *Ingabo,* the *amatorero* (traditional military schools) and the monarchy serve the colonialists. To undergird it all, the Church and the colonial administration would introduce a racist ideology that would inform the divisions, hatred and brutality that would characterize Rwandan life henceforth under the *Force Publique,* as will be detailed in the next chapter.

It all began with the first missionaries in Rwanda, who came in the wake of the first German colonizer, von Goetzen, five years after he had claimed German ownership of Rwanda to King Rwabugiri in 1894. The modest caravan of these missionary White Fathers, who included Mgr. Hirth, Fathers Brard and Paul Balthelemy, and Frere Anselme, wound its way in December 1899 to Bujumbura and Shangi military stations in search of the German officers in charge of Rwanda. The aim of their journey was to ask for the assistance of Lieutenants von Grawert of Bujumbura Military District and Bethe of Rwanda Military Detachment in Shangi to influence the Court of King Yuhi IV Musinga to establish the Catholic Church in Rwanda.[2]

Accompanied by the local army chief Rwabirinda rwa Rwogera of Impara in former Cyangugu, two askaris and an interpreter provided by Bethe, the caravan reached the Nyanza Royal Court on 2 February 1900. Prince Mhamarugamba, standing for the king, in consultation with Ruhinankiko, the *de facto* "prime minister", cordially received the missionaries and invited them to pick a site of their own choosing anywhere in the South. The White Fathers picked the fertile Save area and occupied it on 8 February 1900. Save is close to Astrida (Butare), which was the capital of Ruanda-Urundi during the colonial rule. Hence its choice by the first missionaries, which marks the beginning of their joint conspiracy against Rwandans.

Here they hoped to firmly plant the Roman Catholic Church and spread it throughout Rwanda, as they had just suffered a defeat in Uganda where the Protestants had been the first missionaries. The Catholic Church had not only found the Protestants, but Islam already entrenched and neither was willing to give the Catholic missionaries a foothold in Uganda.

In Rwanda, however, the Catholics were the first to arrive, and were determined to hold on to their prize of a virgin land waiting to be Christianised. Their strategy was simple: target the leaders of the people, as Bishop Leon Classe would later advocate, to stay a step ahead of the Protestants.

In his letter to his Superior General dated 28 April 1911 Bishop Classe would advise, arguing a case for the Roman Catholic Church from its base in the Kivu Apostolic Vicariate of the Congo:

> To my humble view, the vital and important work in Rwanda before all the others is that of the Tutsi or Chiefs. The struggle between us (the Catholics) and the Protestants will be won by those who will gain the hearts of chiefs first. Without chiefs, we will not have the people on our side in a serious manner. .... The king is the spirit of the country. Whatever the circumstances, we must win the hearts of the chiefs. Chiefs will always look at Nyanza.[3]

The missionaries, however, found German colonial machinery that was just embarking on the policy of favouring the Tutsi aristocracy as "born leaders", in their general policy of indirect rule. The Germans had seen their opportunity in the *Ingabo z'u Rwanda* and its mechanisms of self-perpetuation, such as the *amatorero*, which could be exploited in the service of the colonialists. As a crucial strategy, this would not only enlist the traditional military through its own structure of command and training, but the colonialists would also effectively control and mould the already proven Rwanda military prowess through the traditional educational structure.

Indeed, *uburere* (education) is where Rwanda had found its strength and prowess, as the socio-military society had demonstrated throughout the pre-colonial period. Socialization in pre-colonial Rwanda took place in the traditional military schools, *amatorero*, where everyone's discipline and good conduct, bravery and patriotism, honesty and integrity, moral behaviour and even their mannerisms were moulded to make not only a good soldier, but an *impfura y'u Rwanda.*

In this knowledge the potential became apparent to the colonialists for the exploitation of the socio-military education structure, targeting mainly the aristocracy, and opened the School of Chief's Sons at Nyanza in 1907. Setting up the school in Nyanza was not a coincidence, as it was not only the Rwanda's capital holding the seat of the monarch, but was where the elite of the nation was trained in the traditional *itorero ry'i bwami* (Elite school).[4]

The aim of the School of Chiefs' Sons was initially to train assistants *(abasesita)* to the white administrators to read, write and speak Swahili, the official language of German East Africa for which also they would be interpreters. However, taking over the traditional role of the *amatorero,* the school started training Rwandans in modern warfare as the First World War drew closer. Military training included the use of guns as an important part of the school's programme.[5] Indeed, the *Indugaruga,* the Rwandan army formation that King Musinga availed to fight alongside the Germans during the First World War were among the first graduates of the school at the beginning of the war in 1914.

However, come 1916 as the world war progressed, it was the Belgians who would claim victory over German East Africa, thereby marking the beginning of a new era of colonial occupation in Rwanda. While the Germans had been content to let the king rule on their behalf with both mutually aiding each other in times of need, if one recalls the *Indugaruga* fighting alongside the Germans or, vice versa, the German help in the suppression of the Basebya and Ndungutse rebellions in 1912, the Belgians would prove to be different.[6]

Insecure as the new colonizers and lacking a clearly formulated policy they saw King Musinga as a hindrance and a bit too presumptive of the Belgians in his monarchy. Therefore while the Germans would usurp the *amatorero* and thus the *Ingabo*, the Belgians would denigrate and humiliate its Commander-in-Chief, not only to assert their power, but to demonstrate the end of Rwandan sovereignty.

As Captain Stevens, heading the Belgian occupation in Nyanza would write to the new *Commissaire Royal*, "Musinga has been simply laughing up his sleeve at us and scorning the orders we give him. He intends to play the leading part in the politics of his country and to relegate the European authorities to the background."[7] Following this, on 25 March 1917, King Musinga was bundled off to jail at gunpoint, only to be released not long after, when Rwanda proved ungovernable without its monarch.

Though the Belgians could thus demonstrate their power, they would not gain control over Rwanda until the Orts-Milner Convention of 30 May 1919, whose formalities relating to Rwanda's status as a mandate territory under the League of Nations would however not be completed until 1924.[8]

The Catholic Church was by then quite entrenched and in deep cahoots with the Belgian administration. Though the missionaries were French, they had sworn to help administrate the Congo Free State after the Belgian Government bought it from King Leopold, and with the experience did so for Rwanda, in order to earn their place in the Belgian dispensation. Moreover, there were the francophone sympathies between the Walloon administrators and the missionary White fathers headed first by Mgrs Hirth and later Classe, both of whom were said to have descended from the northeastern region of France in Alsace-Lorraine. Along with their inability to manage a foothold in Uganda with the more entrenched Protestants, these were the factors that influenced the Catholic Church's behaviour in Rwanda in their close collaboration with the administration.

The missionaries were able to demonstrate their worth in the collaboration and, in the vision of first targeting the leaders in their efforts to give the Church a more commanding presence and credibility in the eyes of the people, had by the early

1920s already acquired a prize convertee in the name of Chief Rwabutogo rwa Kabare, the highly regarded commander of the military formation *Uruyange*. Rwabutogo had been a graduate of the Nyanza School of Chiefs' Sons, and due to his zealous Catholicism had been appointed secretary to Louis Leenaerts, the Nyanza Administrator and schoolmaster, who was better known to Rwandans as 'Bwanakweri', nicknamed so for supposedly always being right and could not be contradicted. His opinions had always to be agreed to with *"ndiyo Bwana"* (yes Sir).

However, his newly acquired religious fervour, which Rwabutogo was now eager to impart to the young *Intore,* could not be proselytized in the secular school having been long forbidden by the Court. Rwabutogo found a solution by turning his house into a clandestine evening class to offer catechism lessons to the young *intore* of the capital. When it finally came to the attention of the king about what Rwabutogo was up to, it led to King Musinga being provoked to the extereme where it is said that he started making "martyrs" at the capital to serve as examples. Following this, the young catechists under Rwabutogo's tutelage were cautioned by Mgr Classe not to reveal themselves as Catholic converts unless they were in a large group, as it would make the angered king pause before exacting his wrath.[9]

To counter the increasing influence of the Catholics at the capital, King Musinga decided to overtly favour the Seventh Day Adventists, who had established themselves at Gitwe not too long before. The King invited its founder, Pastor Meunier (Munnyeri), to openly preach at the capital on regular basis. This, however, would only aggravate matters. For instance, one Thursday afternoon, as Pastor Meunier was preaching to the crowd, which included a good number of young Catholic converts from the official School at Nyanza, the young men decided to heckle the pastor by noisily proclaiming themselves staunch Catholics. They then organised a demonstration at the Court and mocked the King for his being against the Catholics.[10]

Among the demonstrators were catechists under instruction by Chief Rwabutogo and Thaddé Gishoma, a former Seminarian also hired by Classe and the Nyanza Administrator as instructor at the School, to sabotage the Court. The young men were part of the four companies composing the *Incogozabahizi* under training at the Court. It was a sad day for Rwanda that the young demonstrators, who would soon replace their fathers in leadership roles, would break taboo by defying[11] the Rwandan king's authority and publicly embrace "Christ the King". Other young men under training in regional *amatorero* followed in these steps after learning of the 1925 events in Nyanza and became Christian converts. Bishop Classe had at last achieved his aim of winning over the hearts of the future leaders.

In these future leaders the Belgians had planned to obtain firm command over the kingdom by placing the young men in positions of power. Leenaerts had explained the plan to Musinga, who could do nothing and foresaw the demise of his monarchy and the end of Rwanda as he knew it. These young leaders were his *intore* as the king and had been trained to attend to him and defend him. It is reported that on the day the young leaders were assigned their posts, "the formation of *intore* marched together for the last time to the royal enclosure to dance and declaim their praises to the Mwami. As they sang him a song of adieu, Musinga wept openly."[12] Although several hundred *intore* were left at Court, they were greatly disorganised by this dispersal of their leaders as well as by the struggles between supporters and opponents of the Court, as we shall see with the case of *inshongore* below. Gradually the company disintegrated, with most of its members drifting away from the Court and no new *intore* were ever called to serve Musinga.

Though defeated, the traditionalist king could never give away his heritage; so he later had to be forcefully replaced by his more "modernist" son, Prince Rudahigwa, who had also attended the same School of Nyanza in the regiment *Imirimba,* a less known company of the *Incogozabahizi.* After the youthful subversion of Nyanza, the Belgian administration opened similar schools of chiefs' sons at Gatsibo, Ruhengeri, Rukira and Cyangugu.

The schools would later be replaced by the Groupe Scolaire d'Astrida, opened in 1929, with the Catholic Church assuming overall administration of the entire educational system. This led to the Government schools gradually being phased out in the 1930s[13] and being taken over by the Catholic Church. This demonstrated the shared goals and therefore the harmony between the Church and the colonial administration. Graduates from this school called themselves *Indatwa,* in continuing with the traditional naming of *amatorero* graduates as they passed out to become *Intore* warriors.

The name *Indatwa* referred to the purest breed of the royal herds, *Inyambo,* of which the graduates likened themselves in the perception that they were the better of their predecessors. The graduates used the name to stress their educated sophistication as the new colonial Rwandan elite *(evolués).* Indeed, the essential characteristic of education from the time it was taken over by the Church was that it served only the Tutsi for the short-term needs of the Belgian administration, yet another example of the Belgo-Roman Catholic Church conspiracy.

Religion and the Demise of the Traditional Rwandan Military

It is a strange coincidence that Rwandan traditional religion bore some striking resemblance to the Roman Catholic faith.[14] For example, the Catholics worshiped God through His Son, Christ the King, while Rwandans worshiped *Imana* represented by the king and father of the nation, *Sebantu.* The important reference in the example is the king being the God-chosen intercessor between Him and His people. Perhaps more striking, however, is the sign of the cross Catholics make on their head and chest of the "Father, the Son and the Holy Spirit", which resembles a similar sign by Rwandans in their traditional religion. The Rwandan "cross sign" would accompany the following words in a *kubandwa* rite:

Mu gahanga uri indahangarwa	The forehead makes you invincible
Mu gituza kigutuze mu Rwanda	As the chest settles you in Rwanda
Intugu ziguture abanzi[15]	And the shoulders ward off your enemies

This coincidental sign of the cross confirmed to the missionaries that the Tutsi were lapsed Ethiopian orthodox Christians who they supposed "migrated" to Rwanda and conquered the "original" Bantu inhabitants.

However, before we come to that, religious worship in pre-colonial Rwanda had two aspects. The first was the worship of *Imana*, the creator of the universe *(Rurema)* through direct or blood ancestors *(abakurambere)*, and the second through adopted ancestors *(imandwa)*[16], who would be prayed to intercede in difficult times under the cult of Lyangombe. The worship of direct ancestors was called *guterekera* (to offer gifts).

The worship of the adopted ancestors was called *kubandwa*, which in the traditional ritual was in honor of *imandwa* (friends or disciples of Lyangombe) who interceded to solve life's difficulties, whether it was a wish for wealth, children, good health, etc. Some scholars[17] have even postulated a similarity observing that worship of ancestors is no different from the worship of saints in the Catholic Church.

The ritual of *kubandwa*, likening it to sacrament, has two stages, *kwatura* and *gusubizaho*, that has been compared to the "baptism" and "confirmation" of the Christians. These are the two stages required to initiate one into the sacred companionship of *imandwa* (best disciples of *Imana*).[18]

With such similarities it is arguable that the more sophisticated of Rwandans during these early days of Catholicism may have began to fancy the Christian religion as something of a modernization of their traditional way of worship. Such sophisticates included commanders Nturo ya Nyilimigabo and Kayondo ka Mbanzabigwi of the military formations *Imbabaza-abahizi* and *Impama-kwica*, respectively. Also included in this group was Chief Rwabutogo, Commander of the formation *Uruyange*.

There can be no better illustration of the demise of the military than with this example of Christian infiltration through the highly respected commanders. By converting to Christianity the commanders became "princes of the Church" and abdicated their military obligations to the Rwandan people. Among others, the commanders would form the group that came to be known as *Inshongore* (the Proud, Vain Ones)[19] that would conspire with the Roman Catholic Church and the colonial administration in dethroning King Yuhi VI Musinga as a pagan monarch, and replace him with his son King Mutara III Rudahigwa, a protégé of the church and former member of the formation, *Incogozabahizi*.

The *Inshongore* were not without opposition, however, which was actively demonstrated by a formation of *intore* studying at the Nyanza School that, though it admired the European way, felt compelled to defend the Mwami. These young men became known as the *"Ibyaanga-batwaare"* (the haters of the *Abatware*), referring to the army chiefs who formed the *Inshongore*. The intore were said to even physically rough up the Abatware and verbally attack them. Neither did they spare their classmates who supported the *Inshongore*.

"As the conflicts between *intore* who supported the Court and those who opposed it multiplied, the high morale and strict standards of conduct which had characterised earlier military formations crumbled. The *intore* drank too much, brawled constantly among themselves and with others, and even raped the young women of the vicinity."[20] This previously unheard of behaviour from those supposed to be *impfura z'u Rwanda* led to the displeasure of the king who ordered the *intore* punished, before the Belgians ordered the company disbanded, more so to safeguard the *Inshongore*.

It is said that a poet of the Court gave *Inshongore* the name, taking it from a pack of Nturo's hunting dogs. The Court and its followers, explains des Forges, "found the image of yapping dogs chasing after their master most appropriate for those who sought the favour of the Europeans." The poet Munyanganzo was to lament:[21]

Ikizi nzaba mpari	Surely I will be there
Impaga y'abanzi ishize	With the alien's threat long gone
(…)	*(…)*
Abayoboke batsinze abayobe[22]	When the patriots triumph over the bootlickers

This was a worthy lament, as it will be recalled that with the Rwandan king being the Vicar of God, the religious institution in traditional Rwanda was of great importance in ensuring social cohesion in every aspect of life, including the military. The poet therefore was invoking the doomed truth that Rwanda was God-given, and therefore God- privileged, as *Imana* was a resident in Rwanda. But now, not only the commanders of the *Ingabo z'u Rwanda,* including the Commander-in-Chief himself, were subjugated under Jesus, the king of the Christians, but were also firm allies of the very enemy of Rwanda, the colonialists. The poet's lament, therefore, was of a Rwanda that would hopefully bounce back in its usual resiliency.

This was powerful symbolism of a vanquished people that would find its climax with the overthrow and banishment of the traditionalist King Musinga to Kamembe on November 12 1931, and the enthronement of the Christian King Mutara III Rudahigwa four days later. Overseeing it all, by-passing the sacred tradition that required a king to be enthroned by Abiru, was Msgr. Classe and the new Governor Voisin. In the wake of the enthronement of the new king by 1933 there followed a snowball effect of conversions to Catholicism by Rwandans that, defying belief in its massive proportions, the Belgians could only describe it as the Rwandan *tornade* (tornado).[23]

In 1943 the new king was baptized with the names Charles Léon Pierre, drawn from his colonial godfathers Charles le Bon, Count of Frandle, Msgr. Léon Classe and Pierre Ryckmans, Governor General of Belgian Africa. This was followed in 1946 by the consecration of Rwanda to Christ the King, with which the country effectively became a Christian kingdom. Rudahigwa put it this way in his speech, as he surrendered Rwandan sovereignty symbolized by the royal drum, *Kalinga,* to Christ the King:

> Lord Jesus, it is You who have made our country. You have given it a long line of kings to govern it in Your stead even at a time when they did not yet know You.24

By this time, the traditional Rwandan greeting, *"Gira Umwami"* (greetings in the name of the king) had been corrupted and replaced with *"Yezu akuzwe"* (Praise Jesus). This Christian greeting persists to this day, even among Muslims and Christians alike, signifying the extent of Christian influence and obliteration of the Rwandan culture.

Even the institution of *Ubusizi* was not spared in the Christian cultural onslaught. Teachers and descendants of families of the dynastic poets began to produce rich and fascinating Catholic poetry of the Rwandan mould. In the 1940s Bruno Nkuriyingoma[25], a descendant of a large family of court poets from Kiruri[26] in Nyaruguru, composed his *Izuka rya Yezu* (The Resurection of Jesus) in the classical form of dynastic poems traditionally in the praise of the *Abami.*

In similar fashion, Frederiko Kaberuka, a catechist from Nyange Mission, composed the praise poem *Igisingizo cya Papa*

Piyo XII on the enthronement of Pope Pius XII in 1939, while it is reported that events like building of a church, the presentation of a Papal (Gregorian) medal to the king, were all occasions for the creation of new verses in the epic vein. The *Isoko y'Amajyambere*, "The source of progress", is a cycle of thirty songs speaking of the Court's glorious history, followed by a sequence relating the missionaries' works until Rudahigwa's baptism in 1943.[27]

In the end, this was how the colonial writer de Lacger triumphantly described the disappearance of the symbols of the "pagan" past at the Court of the Christian king, Rudahigwa, in the wake of Rwanda's consecration to Christiandom:

> Of course, (…) everything that made condemned paganism prosper, talismans, ishyira shrine, iron bludgeon, fetish, isubyo gourds, dog-faced baboon, disappeared as if by magic. All this apparatus must have gone to Kamembe (Musinga's place of exile); it did not return from there. Kalinga, the drum however remained… the diviners' peat, herbs, sacrificers, workers of spells, seers, all these had scattered like a flight of nocturnal birds; those who remained, Abiru (members of the council of the crown), Abakongoro, Abagabe, were henceforth obliged to limit themselves to their nonreligious duties.
>
> The fire of Gihanga (legendary ancestor of the dynasty and of all Rwandans) died in its amphora; the huts of the great monarchs and of national liberators, Ruganzu, Rwabugiri, Gihana, were not rebuilt. Heroic rhapsodists and chroniclers, regular hangers-on and chroniclers, from now on frustrated from palatine manna forgot their way to the ibwami (royal court) or lost their inspiration. Yearly parental homage, pacifying expiation, communication with spirits, secret initiation into the cult of Lyangombe, sacred orgies, all these were swept away like dead leaves… All this past was repudiated as incompatible with the new order.[28]

The Making of the Rwandan "Races"

Even as Rwanda was being converted into a Christian kingdom, an elaborate enterprise to use the Tutsi as "best for command" in local administration was already in place, and had received official sanction from the Belgian Government.

In a 1920 directive, the Minister of the Colonies, L. Frank, had explicitly stated that the administration "must be composed uniquely of the Batutsi, in accord with the Mwami" and the distinctive Tutsi aristocracy.

However, it was the words of Governor General Ryckmans that best described this perception of the uniqueness of the Batutsi:

> The Batutsi were destined to reign over their people. Their fine presence alone already insured them considerable prestige over the inferior races surrounding them; their qualities, and even their defects, enhanced them even further. Proud, distant, in total control of themselves, rarely blinded by anger, avoiding any familiarity, insensitive to pity, and with a conscience never touched by scruples: no surprise that the good Hutu, less cunning and simpler, let themselves be enslaved without ever attempting to rebel.[29]

The words may have been spoken by a Belgian, but it was the Germans, not only as the first colonizers, but its intellectuals, who would provide the ideological basis of the superiority of the Tutsi. German ethnographers and linguists were the first to embark on the systematic study of African cultures, well ahead of their European counterparts.

It was the thesis of the 19th Century German philosopher Hegel, for instance, that Africa was the home of the "non-historical peoples" who had taken no part in the spiritual development of the world. In his view, humanity first started in Asia with the earliest inhabitants of Africa, the San, as his historian contemporaries would contend, coming from Asia. They saw the process of human occupation in Africa as a set of sequences in which the Pygmies and the San, low-statured peoples originating from Asia and possessing virtually no material techniques; then there came the fuzzy-haired Negro peoples coming from South-East Asia, with their rudimentary agriculture, their round and square huts, a few wooden implements, and bows and arrows as weapons.[30]

These were thought to have been followed by proto-Hamites from northern Asia, who used the hoe to cultivate cereals (sorghum), and also reared small-horned cattle. The intermarriage of these peoples with the Negroes was supposed to have given birth to the Bantu peoples. After this came the invasions of the light-skinned Hamites, who arrived through the Suez isthmus; they were said to have been the ancestors of the Fulani, Maasai, Oromo, Somali and Khoikhoi peoples, and to have disseminated further decisive culture elements such as the long-horned cattle, spears and leatherwork.[31] In this category the Tutsi were supposed to firmly belong.

Therefore, when the first colonialists came to the region and met the Banyoro, Batoro, Banyankole, Barundi, Banyarwanda, Baha, Bashi and Bahaya, they found the racial distinctions as they had been spelt out when they saw the Twa hunter-gathers, the agriculturalist Hutu Bantu, and the pastoralist Hima and Tutsi. They found what they wanted to see.[32]

These racial perceptions amounted to mere speculations and had no scientific basis. In the light of the most recent advances in human genetics, no biologist nowadays any longer admits the existence of races within the human species. Indeed, the United Nations Education Science and Cultural Organisation (UNESCO) made the declaration that "Race is not so much a biological phenomenon as a social myth."[33]

As the Genographic Project[34] has shown, every man and every woman on this planet can be traced to one particular man and woman in Africa through their Y- and X-chromosomes respectively. This, in effect, nullifies any racial argument.

Though the above arguments contradict the racial constructs, including the immigration theory, as espoused by the colonial administration and the Roman Catholic Church in Rwanda, on this basis as we see below the Tutsi came to be favoured as "best for command" and were destined to benefit from colonial education in preparation for taking over administrative posts, especially beginning in the 1930s. Between 1946 and 1954, for instance, 389 Tutsi and only sixteen Hutu enrolled in Astrida from Ruanda-Urundi.[35]

In this vein there necessarily had to be an absolute classification of every individual as Tutsi or Hutu, which ironically came with the official census of 1933-4 that arbitrarily identified Tutsi as separate from Hutu on the basis of the ten-cow rule. Whoever owned ten or more cows was classified as Tutsi.[36]

This may be contrasted with the fact that, in pre-colonial Rwanda, the difference between the Hutu and the Tutsi was vocational and social rather than racial or ethnic. The term "Hutu" meant 'agriculturist' or 'poor' or 'servant', while 'Tutsi' referred to 'cattle-keepers' who, *ipso facto*, had to be rich and therefore could be patrons. The Tutsi had a superior social status due to their economic affluence in terms of cattle at that particular time.

The poet Rukomo rwa Bujyugu, under King Mibambwe III Sentabyo (by 1741-1746), observes in *"Imana yabonye inka"*.[37]

Iteka zitera abantu ubwoko	They're [cows] always the measure of status and identity
(....)	(...)
Uwazitunze akaba umututsi	He who owns them becomes a Tutsi
Zironkwa n'umuhutu	When a Hutu gets them
Akaba yabaye umwega mu Rwanda	Becomes another from his peers
N'uwamunenaga akamutura umugeni"[38]	Even those who treated him as outcast offer him a bride

What the colonialists did, therefore, in the "10 cow rule" to suit their overall "divide and rule" strategy, was to transfer to the ethnic or racial register what used to be the socio-economic categories of Rwandans. This way, they re-engineered Rwandans and ascribed them a new identity.[39]

The 1926 Mortehan Reforms

The Mortehan Reforms were directly informed by the racial ideology and actively sought to favour the Tutsi over the Hutu through education and administration.

As Bishop Classe expressed it,

"If we want to position ourselves at the practical point of view and seek the country's interest, we have in the Mututsi youth an incomparable element of progress, which no one who knows Rwanda can underestimate."[40]

In this opinion the schools, all of them controlled by the Church, were thus instructed by the Bishop in a blatant policy of marginalization of the Bahutu:

Education for the Bahutu is necessary to train catechists, schoolmasters and tutors, and in order to instruct and train youth in general...Schooling for the Batutsi, here, must take precedence over schooling for the Bahutu. The Father in charge of schools must set his heart on the development of this schooling.[41]

In their marginalization and exclusion, the Mortehan Reforms had a political as well as economic agenda, mainly in terms of administrative efficiency, marshalling labour and collecting taxes. The Belgians wanted the system not just to conform to their ideal of bureaucratic organization but also to carry out their orders promptly by installing the newly educated Batutsi from the Nyanza School.

To begin with, there was the pre-colonial triple chieftaincy system[42] of traditional administration, made up of the chiefs of the soil, pasture and army chief, which had served the Rwandans well. This system was a useful means for the transmission of and execution of the orders of the monarchy, and not least the collection of taxes *(ikoro)*. It mirrored the aspirations of Rwandans, and had evolved to ensure social justice and cohesion, with the army chief being the supreme head in each locality.

While the traditional system of administration may have been useful[43] for Rwandans, it was too intricate for the Belgians and served no purpose in their colonial agenda. And thus it was that in 1926, Resident Mortehan undertook a series of administrative reforms that brought about fundamental changes in the Rwandan society.

With the urging of Bishop Classe, he decreed that the triple chieftaincy be suppressed, and replaced the existing 20 districts *(ibiti)* with *territoires*. The *territories* were divided into *chefferies* (chiefdoms), which in their turn were divided into *sous-chefferies* (sub-chiefdoms). By the end of the reign of Mutara III Rudahigwa there were 565 *sous-chefferies* in ten territoires nationwide and 45 *chefferies*.[44]

While land chiefs were traditionally Hutu, pasture chiefs Tutsi and army chiefs drawn from either of the two socio-economic groups, after the Mortehan reforms all Hutu and Twa chiefs were progressively removed in favour of the "more able" Tutsi, now invested with European education and therefore better able to serve the colonial masters.

Kagame provides a list[45] of forty Twa *Ibikingi* chiefs who were sacked in the reform process, and who included the notable *Sous-chef* Gisilibobo of Rukoma (Kagina). Others included Nyanjunga of Buberuka, Biganda bya Rwampungu of the Abasyete lineage of Bushiru in the north.[46] Many more Hutu chiefs and *sous-chefs*, mainly from the Inkiga regions, were sacked under similar circumstances, and all of them were replaced with Tutsi.[47]

In the Belgian process of "tutsifying" the Rwandan administration that informed the Mortehan reforms, the task of appointing Tutsi *chefs* and *sous-chefs* to replace the Hutu and

Twa was aided by Father Leon Delmas who, in his *Généalogies de la Noblesse (les Batutsi) du Rwanda,* would in the 1940s provide the "pedigrees" of all Tutsi notables to make sure that the "race" of new appointees was strictly of Tutsi descent. In the book he charted selected Tutsi family lineages going back many generations. A confident Father Delmas wrote:

> I am sure that I will reach all the clans and even the main families of Rwanda. Later, it will be easy to attach to those family trees those who will remain immutable, the names of the new ones, and those of their children, for example.[48]

Worthy of note is that abolishing the traditional triple chieftaincy also sealed the fate of the social role of the *Ingabo z'u Rwanda,* which formally placed the army chief as overall administrator, who as we have already seen, superceded the land and pasture chiefs. The administrative change was, however, not greatly felt by Rwandans, as many of the army chiefs were retained as chiefs of *territoires* and continued as they traditionally did with their loyal subjects.[49]

Nevertheless, the army chiefs could not mobilise or offer military training to their subjects, as was traditionally the case. The socio-military schools, *amatorero,* formally under the direct stewardship of the army chiefs had long been replaced by the Belgian schools beginning with the *Incogozabahizi.*

The Belgian military schools would come later, as the legacy of the new army-cum-police force, *Force Publique,* took its brutal hold on Rwanda.

Notes

1   G. Logiest (1988: 95).
2   A. Kagame (1975), op.cit., p.147.
3   G. Mbonimana."L'Instauration d'un royaume chrétien au Rwanda, 1900-1931", (PhD. thesis, Université catholique de Louvain, 1981), p.347.

4   A. Kagame (1975), op. cit., p.171.

5   Ibid.

6   G. Logiest (1988:89) admits that "indirect rule was only existing in words".

7   Ian Linden (1977), p.127.

8   Des Forges, op.cit., p.236.

9   A. Kagame (1975:178): They gathered at the court and kneeled down to pray and sing Catholic hymns. When King Musinga wanted to chase them saying he is 'fed up with their noise', they now started invoking out loud the Holy Spirit saying 'He threatens us? What can he now do against us since the Europeans are there to protect us?'

10   Des Forges, op. cit., p.283.

11   Lemarchand (1970:70) concurs that 'the new generations of chiefs had fully sensed the significance of the social forces that lay behind the spread of Christianity. They felt that the preservation of their traditional claims ultimately depended upon their endorsement of the new creed '.

12   Des Forges, op.cit., pp.289-290.

13   Ian Linden, op.cit.,p. 163.

14   B. Muzungu, Ph D Thesis, « Le Dieu de nos pères », 3 vol., Bujumbura, 1974, pp.75-81.

15   Interview with José Kagabo, a Rwandan historian teaching in France, May 2006.

16   Ian Linden, "The *Mandwa* spirits of the *Lyangombe* cult were thought to be of a higher order than lineage spirits, against whose malevolent designs they were said to provide protection from. They related the initiate to a spiritual world more extensive than that of the *inzu* and hill settlement, just as the *ngabo* united the peasant to lineages scattered throughout the Rwandan State. A sacrificial warrior hero, *Lyangombe,* headed the spirit order." – pp.13-15.

17   B. Muzungu Ph.D Thesis, op.cit.

18   T. Murasandonyi, "Le mythe de Lyangombe" in *Cahiers* No.5, May 1997, pp.45-65.

19   Des Forges, op cit. p.252 (She observes that "The Court sometimes called [Inshongore] "Abahababyi," "the accusers," because they carried tales to the administrator, or "Abangayuhi," "the haters of Yuhi," a reference to Musinga's reign name. But most often they were known as "Inshongore," "The Proud, Vain Ones." A poet of

the Court gave them this name, taking it from a pack of Nturo's hunting dogs. The Court and its followers found the image of yapping dogs chasing after their master most appropriate for those who sought the favour of the Europeans. The Inshongore were a diverse group united only by their fear of the court and their hope of using the administrator to protect them from it. A few sincerely admired the European culture; of these few, several were interested in Christianity and would soon convert to it. But the leaders Kayondo and Nturo, and most of the others, wanted only to use European power while continuing to ignore European culture.")

20 Des Forges, op. cit., p.285.
21 Ibid., p.252.
22 *Cahiers* No 24 of Sept 2003, p.185
23 T. Gatwa,, "*The Churches and Ethnic Ideology in the Rwandan Crises 1900-1994*", (Ph.D. thesis:, University of Edinburgh, 1998), p.128
24 Ian Linden, op. cit., p.200.
25 He was a well-known school teacher in the parish of Kibeho. He is also the author of "*Icyivugo cya Ruzagayura*" [A poem on Ruzagayura (famine in 1945)] that he composed in 1945. See Cahiers No 24, p.239.
26 *Cahiers,* No 24: " Poètes de Kiruri au Nyaruguru", Sept. 2003.
27 Ibid.
28 L. Lacger, *Le Ruanda* [Kabgayi: Vicariat apostolique du Ruanda, 1939], pp.549-50.
29 Josias Semujanga, *Origins of Rwandan Genocide,* Humanity Books, 2003, p.145 or Lugan (1997: 26).
30 Ki-Zerbo, J. (Ed), *General History of Africa Part I,* UNESCO, 1981, pp. 104-105.
31 Idem.
32 J. Semujanga (2003), op.cit., p.140; see also Gourevitch, *We Wish to Inform You,* p.55.
33 J.Ki-Zerbo, op. cit., pp.100-103.
34 A project led by the National Geographic to trace the genetic "Adam" and "Eve" by identifying mutations over the millennia in the Y- and X-chromosomes.
35 Ian Linden, op. cit., p. 197.
36 Mahmood Mamdani, *When Victims Become Killers: Colonialism, Nativism, and the Genocide in Rwanda,* Fountain Publishers, Kampala, 2001, p.98.

37   *Cahiers* No 22, March 2003, p.21-24.

38   Ibid, p. 22.

39   Alain Destexhe, *Rwanda and Genocide in the Twentieth Century*, Pluto Press, London, 1995, p39 (According to Destexhe, the differences in terms of physical attributes and mannerisms became "scientifically" indisputable. J. Sasserath, a Belgian doctor, in 1948 described the Tutsi and Hutu thus: "The Hamites are 1.90 metres tall. They are slim. They have straight noses, high foreheads, thin lips. The Hamites seem distant, reserved, polite and refined." Referring to the Hutu, "the rest of the population,' he said, 'is Bantu...possessing all the characteristics of the Negro: flat noses, thick lips, low foreheads, brachycephalic skulls. They are like children, shy and lazy and usually dirty.' The Twa were far inferior than the Hutu and the Tutsi, and 'keep themselves apart and are treated with contempt by the rest of the population."

40   Bishop Classe's letter to Resident Mortehan on 21 September 1927.

41   G. Mbonimana, (1981), op. cit., p. 352.

42   Lemarchand, Rwanda and Burundi, 1970, p.72; or Sandrart, *Rapport sur le Territoire de Kigali*, 1929, p.4; or Maquet, The Premise of Inequality in Ruanda, 1961, pp.96-128.

43   Lemarchand (1970:.72) notes that "[f]or Kagame, it was the elimination of the army chiefs from traditional power structure, and the resultant abeyance of the military code, which led to all the abuses associated with the buhake".

44   A. Kagame (1975), op.cit., p.187.

45   A. Kagame, *Le Code des institutions politiques du Rwanda précolonial* (Bruxelles, 1952, pp.118).

46   Interview with Mzee Ladislas Musuhuke, a former Sous-chef of Bukamba from 1925 to 1959.

47   As gathered from interviews with former colonial chief, Mzee Ladislas Musuhuke, pre-Mortehan Reform Hutu chiefs and sub-chiefs included descendants of Nyamakwa in Bushiru replaced by Chief Nyangezi, Nyakazana in Buhoma, Rukaburacumu in Rwankeri, Nyanjunga in Buberuka, descendants of Ndagano in Bukunzi-Busozo replaced by Rwagataraka, Batsinda in Bunyambiliri (Suti) replaced by Ntagozera ya Birasa, Bivete in Bukamba, Ngayabarezi in Buturo, Sekidende cya Segisabo, Rwandinzi and Ndizihiwe in Mulera, descendants of Rukara in Gahunga, those of Musana in Bumbogo and Minyaruko in Busigi.

Logiest (1988: 89) himself observes "that reform was unfavorable for the Hutu. In ancient rule, they [the Hutu] had several chiefs. They could therefore seek protection from one [chief] against the exactions of another and benefit from the rivalries between the Tutsi. In the new rule, this possibility was no more and they were subjected, without a counterbalance, to the arbitrariness of one chief or sub-chief, whose authority was more than ever reinforced by the Belgian administration". According to Lugan (2004:42/3) "with the reform undertaken by Governor Voisin, the three functions were put in the hands of one chief, and chiefs and sub-chiefs will be heretofore nearly all Tutsi". Indeed, in 1959 out of 45 chiefs only 2 were Hutu, while there were 549 Tutsi sub-chefs out of 559.

48 Father Leon Delmas, *Généalogies de la Noblesse (les Batutsi) du Rwanda*, Apostolic Vicaritae of Rwanda, p.2.

49 A. Kagame (1952:7) affirms, "[t]he army was the basic social organisation which ensured to each individual the enjoyment of his property, in return for certain obligations; it gave him the ready assistance of a public defender[avocat] in the person of the army chief, who was obligated to defend him before every tribunal, including the *mwami's*".

7

Living the Legacy of the *Force Publique*

With the alien *Force Publique* already established as both the military and policing institution in Rwanda, it was also underpinned by a racial ideology and a *"Tutsified"* administrative leadership that set the conditions for the brutality the FP would be famed for. It however would all be tied with the economic agenda of the Belgians in their new colony with the *Force Publique* playing their familiar violent role.

The effective brutality of the *Force Publique* cannot be gainsaid. Starting with their rampage in Cyangugu during the battle of Shangi when they looted, plundered and burned leaving a lasting memory with Banyarwanda of the area, they would still play a hand in the enduring humiliation of King Yuhi VI Musinga in the Belgian victory of World War One.

As has been reported, the Court barely had time to weigh alternatives in dealing with the victors before the Belgian advance guard arrived on 19 May 1916. The *Force Publique* stormed the royal palace and ordered two traditional protocol officers, Segore[1] and Rwamiheto, to immediately take them to Musinga. Unable to understand the command, which was given in Swahili, the two had tried to explain Court protocols in Kinyarwanda. But taking this as a sign of resistance, the Belgians shot both men dead. Frightened and humiliated by the killing of his men in his own royal compound, Musinga hurried to pay court to the Belgians, accepting their flag and promising to have no further contacts with the Germans.[2]

But this was only the beginning, as the king would in February 1917 be jailed on trumped-up charges that he had ordered his southwestern commander Rwagataraka rwa Rwidegembya to aid the Germans against the Belgian advance from Bukavu. This arrest and jailing of the king denigrated the very essence of the Rwandan sovereignty. It was noted that by jailing Musinga, the Belgians showed clearly that they had assumed ultimate power in Rwanda, something that no other foreigner had dared before. Implied in their treatment of Yuhi V was their right to remove him from the throne if they so chose.

Rwandans believed that the Belgians had acted to humiliate and destroy the dignity of the monarch and the nation of Rwanda, so as to prove that they had become the real rulers.[3] In their colonial mentality drawn from their experience in the Congo, the Belgians equated the Rwandan monarch with the Congolese tribal chiefs or sultans whose authority they could give or take at will. This provoked Rwandan anger and rebellion to the point of wanting to declare war on the Belgian authority, which grudgingly had to release King Musinga. According to the Banyarwanda, Rwanda was no more without its king *(Urwanda ntirura nze)* and could never be without its king. It was at this time the colonialists started thinking of grooming a more amenable successor, who turned out to be the King's son, Prince Rudahigwa.[4]

However, at the bottom of it all, as already noted, was the advancement of the colonial economic agenda that had began with the Belgian victory in 1916 over the Germans during the First World War.

From the very outset after winning the war, the Belgians, like the Germans, collected taxes and imposed forced labour, or *akazi* and *shiku*. They originally demanded one or two francs from each lineage of ten men, but by 1921 they were beginning to demand this amount *(umusoro)* from each adult man.[5] The

Belgians applied akazi and shiku by forcibly recruiting men to build the system of roads that would enable future economic development, and had men also transport material for their new administrative centres and the Roman Catholic churches.

Labour was now being demanded for terracing of hills and reclamation of swamps, in addition to planting compulsory food crops, such as manioc, in the wake of the famine that came to be known as *Rumanura* that ravaged Rwanda between 1915 and 1918. The famine had resulted from the desertion of the fields as a result of requisition of porters and the displacement of thousands of people in the Belgian onslaught into Rwanda against the Germans during the First World War. This was exacerbated by the devastation of fields and the destruction of crops as a tactic in the wake of the German withdrawal against the pursuing Belgians and their allies.

The *Diary of Save Mission* reports on the brutality of the Belgian onslaught through the *Force Publique* by describing "the parade of women for debauched soldiers who could only loot and steal". It adds that people remember the image of herds of cattle slaughtered and part of its meat taken away leaving the rest to rot. This was meant to punish King Musinga and the Tutsi, wrongly considered as the only owners of cattle.[6] By the same token, there was the destruction of crops and wide displacement of Rwandans in the ensuing famine, *Rumanura*.

In order to enforce the colonial economic policy of forced labour, it may serve to recall the *Force Publique's* brutality in Belgian Congo during the reign of King Leopold II. It may be recalled how, for instance, in order to ensure production quotas were achieved in rubber plantations, wives would be held hostage to force husbands to deliver on their allocations to secure their spouses' release. Also for failure to adequately produce, the *chicotte,* which the Banyarwanda came to call *ikiboko*—a whip made of raw, sun-dried hippopotamus hide— was indiscriminately used. The *ikiboko* could inflict deep cuts on the body, and would also be used on chiefs in public humiliation for their villages' failure to deliver their quotas.

This would also apply in Rwanda, with the "necessity" of flogging being institutionalized in the Law No.3/15 of 21 March, 1917. Thus it was that, as has been variously noted, many Rwandans saw Belgian rule as the beginning of the "time of the whip".[7] The Hutu, being the majority working the land, bore its brunt, with the Tutsi notables suffering from it occasionally. The humiliation did not spare the chiefs either, including the new ones in the *Tutsified* administration, as they too could face the whip for failure to deliver the required quotas in *akazi* and *shiku*. In the thirties, Harroy observes that "territorial administrators were appraised according to the number of kilometres of new roads they had inaugurated each year"[8]. Forced labour was required not just for roads, but also for erosion control, church building, anti-famine and cash crops, etc.

For instance, forced growing of cash crops such as *Arabica* coffee plants were distributed throughout the country in a wide range of soil types and climates, and when they did not grow or germinate, not only was the peasant's incompetence blamed, but also the chiefs' who oversaw them. Likewise, the imposed and compulsory food crops like manioc were often not disease-resistant and therefore did poorly, but of which peasants refusing to go through the motions of planting them were subjected to severe penalties by the *ingénieurs agronomes* (Agricultural Extension Officers). These penalties included beatings and fines of fifty to a hundred francs for failure to follow farming instructions[9], issued during the decree imposing compulsory planting of food crops by Governor Alfred Marzoratti in Law No 52 of 7 November 1924.

In order to ensure better production, just like in Leopold's Congo, quotas were set for the Tutsi chiefs. If the quotas were not met, the Tutsi chiefs were scolded by their white colonial administrators and had their cattle confiscated. They were beaten and jailed by the *Force Publique*, who also went on rampage in indiscriminate destruction of homes and crops of the peasants' the chiefs oversaw. Faced with such sanctions, the Tutsi chiefs in turn placed heavy demands on their subordinates. They sometimes forced their people to pay the tax two or three times over, or to sacrifice their labour more frequently than they were supposed to if such measures were necessary to meet quotas. Due to this, as has been noted, the peasants would be heard complaining, *"Amafaranga aratwiica"* (the francs [for taxes] are killing us).[10]

And thus, by virtue of the brutal effect of the *Force Publique*, it went on for a long time in a vicious cycle — the Tutsi chiefs avoiding the wrath of the Belgians through the *Force Publique*, and in their turn the peasants bearing with oppression lest they have it both from the Tutsi chiefs and the *Force Publique*.

There is an example of the Belgian administrator, who became known as *"Cumi n'abiri"* [sic], (Twelve blows).[11] It is told how this administrator did not take greetings from the average native kindly. Instances are given of his being annoyed when the Banyarwanda passers-by intruded on his thoughts with a greeting on the road, when he supposedly would respond with a wave of the hand saying, *"cumi n'abiri"*, as an order to the ever present *Force Publique* officers to give the "offending" Munyarwanda twelve strokes of the cane for having addressed him. In the same vein, other administrators were nicknamed *Kurimpuzu* (take-off-your-clothes), *Ruhenesha* (the one who makes you-show-your-naked buttocks), etc — so named according to their preferred methods of inflicting pain on the bared skin with the *ikiboko*.[12]

From their brutal experiences, the Banyarwanda had long associated anything bad or violent with the Belgians through the saying *"Kanaka ntagira nabi arusha ababiligi"* (you cannot beat the Belgians at malice or violence). The cumulative effect of all the brutality was that matters got so desperate for the population that many Rwandans started migrating across the border to Uganda and Tanzania to avoid the whip and hard labour, but also to look for greener pastures as early in the 1930s. These would form the large Rwandan diaspora providing the labour in the sugar, tea and sisal estates in East Africa.

It may be noted that the violence to advance the colonial agenda that would see migration of Rwandans was with the consent of the Roman Catholic Church. Despite this complicity, however, dissenting missionary voices would emerge drawing attention to the violence and the exodus with the advent of Father Laurent Deprimoz. Following his consecration in 1943 as Bishop Classe's co-adjudicator and then administrator of the vicariate, Father Deprimoz would be the first to allow the missionaries to give vent to their feelings about the colonial oppression of Rwandans.

Reverend Father A. Pagès, for instance, wrote a letter of protest to the Gisenyi Resident about the brutal corporal punishment meted out by the *Force Publique* to those who, in desperation to grow their own more productive traditional food crops, pulled up their potato crop before it was ready.[13] Then, a short while later, the rival Protestant Alliance sent their list of complaints to Leopoldville, the seat of overall authority in the Belgian colonies. Meanwhile, a Catholic chief of the Abanyambo in Mubali in the north-east pleaded with the Fathers to intercede on his behalf because his subjects were fleeing en masse into Karagwe to escape the whip and forced labour.[14]

These protests went unheeded however, as it was as much a colonial project as it was for the Roman Catholic Church to let things move as they did despite the brutality of the *Force Publique.* It may be recalled that when the Belgian Government had declined to buy Leopold's Congo in 1908, it was the White Fathers who persuaded the Belgian Senate to accept the deal and pledged to assist in governance and administration given their long experience in colonial Africa.[15] Since their institution in the 19th Century by King Leopold, the *Force Publique* had proved their reliability through to the middle of the 20th Century where they, with their brutality still intact, would take on a more political role in Rwanda.

This role is inherent in the nature of a military force that it is not merely an enforcer of economic agendas as the *FP* so illustrates, but, as we shall also see, a tool of power in the ever-changing political circumstances — circumstances of which by the mid-fifties the tide was beginning to change against the Tutsi.

By this time, led by King Rudahigwa, Rwandan elite had begun to agitate for independence threatening to upset the status quo for the Belgian administrators. This would lead to a turning of tables that saw the colonialists begin to favour the Hutu as opposed to the Tutsi chiefs. The irony was that while the sons of Tutsi chiefs had been the chosen ones to advance the colonial project as chiefs and padres, receiving the best education, as opposed to the Hutu and *"petit* Tutsi" who they were supposed to reign over, political expediency demanded that beginning in the mid-1950s the colonial administration and the Roman Catholic Church turned around and espoused the cause of the "oppressed" Hutu, by the "Tutsi".[16]

Another factor that led to the shift in power alliances in favour of the Hutu is suggested by Lugan:

> Since 1955, the Tutsi establishment began to collapse. The three partners associated to power in Rwanda at the time were... the mwami, the Belgian vice-governor and the apostolic vicar residing at Kabgayi. But in 1955, important changes occurred. In April, J.-P Harroy was appointed vice-governor of Ruanda Urundi by the king of Belgium, and he had chosen the Hutu camp against that of the Tutsi. Again in 1955, Msgr Deprimoz, the Apostolic Vicar in Rwanda, abandoned his duties due to sickness and was replaced by Msgr Perraudin, a Swiss missionary who had also espoused the Hutu revolution.[17]

Nevertheless, it is no coincidence that it was the elite and educated Tutsi who first agitated for Rwandan independence from the Belgian colonialists, in resonance with the prevailing "winds of change" across Africa with the widespread demand for independence at the urging of United Nations to free colonial territories. Yet, as if surprised by the independence movement that it had not perhaps foreseen, the Belgian administration would unload all its political errors onto the Tutsi for the demand of the country's independence and henceforth supported the Hutu against the Tutsi in order to continue their colonial enterprise.[18] It was thus that at the dawn of independence, the Tutsi were considered the "true" colonizers, while the Belgians espoused the Hutu cause leading to the chaos that would erupt in 1959 and see the killing and exile of tens of thousands of Tutsi.

However, the change of the Belgian heart towards the Tutsi during this period also coincided with the intensifying global politics over the strategic importance of Africa, as the Cold War reached its height pitting the West against the spread of Soviet Communism. At stake in the Great Lakes Region was its stability and the strategic importance of the mineral-rich Congo, which was causing concern with its agitation for independence. The movement led by Congo's charismatic pro-communist, Patrice Lumumba, was feared as likely to influence the Tutsi elite in their clamour for freedom, which raised Belgian and French alarm that Rwanda also risked going the communist way. The geostrategic importance of the Congo, which unequivocally bound the Belgian colony to France for being Francophone, could not in any way be risked away, leading to France's offer of military training to the *Force Publique* in the 1950s to keep communism at bay in the region.[19]

One of the Belgian officers to benefit from this training was Major Louis Marlière who would be "of great help"[20] to the infamous Colonel BEM Logiest Guy when he first came to Rwanda to quell the 1959 violence and maintain public order.

Employing a recently formulated French military doctrine[21] as a Lieutenant-Colonel in August 1957, Logiest and Major Marlière had distinguished themselves in what had been dubbed "operation tornadoes" by putting down an armed uprising in the Katanga region in the Congo.[22] The French military doctrine emphasized generalized violence in an agitated population to rout out insurgents among them. It applied brutal modes of coercion and extermination that flashed out elements of instability such as the Katanga rebels. This doctrine was applied effectively by Logiest with the Hutu-*nised* post-independence military in sustained counter-insurgency measures against the *Inyenzi* in the early to mid-1960s as we later shall see.

In the meantime, it may be recalled that Ruanda-Urundi together with the Congo were administered as Congo-Belge with the Governor General based in Léopoldville (Kinshasa). A contingent of *Force Publique* was deployed in Rwanda and another in Burundi. The Brigade headquarters of the *Force Publique* was based in Stanleyville (Kisangani) and had three battalions. One battalion was in charge of Province Orientale (Haut Zaire), the other for Kivu Province and the third for Ruanda-Urundi.

When the violence obtaining from the 1959 Hutu Revolution broke out, the *Force Publique* Battalion deployed in Rwanda could not have been adequate in containing the widespread chaos that erupted, and therefore needed urgent reinforcements. It was because of this need that Colonel Logiest, heading the Kisangani-based *3è Groupement* first came to Rwanda to "restore order" in a brutal week that lasted between 5 and 12 November 1959. The 11th Battalion stationed at Rumangabo and the 6th Battalion camped at Watsa, both of which formed the *3è Groupement,* were deployed to intervene in Rwanda in the 1959 turmoil, as the two had earlier successfully quelled a local riot in Stanleyville (Kisangani).[23]

The cruel irony was that instead of intervening to stop the chaos that had quickly degenerated into open massacres of the Tutsi, the Belgian Congolese forces stood by and watched as it took place, with houses being torched and the Tutsi being hounded into exile in their tens of thousands. On 10 November, for instance, one Platoon from the 11th Battalion had to actively intervene in the territory of Nyanza to prevent the Tutsi from defending themselves against their violent perpetrators. This was the "very last massive reaction of the Tutsi" as Logiest[24] would boastfully observe of the 10 November event." [T]heir chiefs realised that they can do absolutely nothing against such a highly disciplined superior force."

It may, therefore, appear that the extreme violence against the Tutsi was officially sanctioned. Logiest concedes that "against the gathering of the Tutsi, [FP's] fire weapons were used more than once. The Hutu, on the contrary, appeared much more docile. Some groups of Hutu could even march with the Belgian flag in front."[25]

In the end, with the 1959 Hutu Revolution marking their final assignment, the *Force Publique* would also leave a mark in its unfortunate legacy before it would be localized and become a Ruanda-Urundi force the following year. Specifically, for a society that had so much respect for its women and had no word for rape, it would be the legacy of the Belgian force to provide one.

It is reported that "hundreds of troops sometimes escaped the control of their officers and robbed and raped at will. They behaved so badly that the Belgians had to prohibit them from leaving their post without a European officer."[26] Yet this did not help. The sexual violence, especially, still continued at gun point, and has since been epitomised in the Kinyarwanda word for rape, *gufalinga,* the term deriving in the letters – F A L – referring to the Belgian automatic gun – *Fusil Automatique Léger* – that the *Force Publique* were eager to use and fondly referred to as FAL.

This is the kind of legacy that the *Force Publique* would pass on to its successor, the Garde Territoriale du Ruanda-Urundi in June 1960, the month Congo gained independence, and which saw most of the *Force Publique* returning home.

In these changing circumstances as the 1960s dawned, Logiest had in the meantime been appointed the Belgian Special Resident in Rwanda, while retaining the overall military command of the new *Garde Territoriale* in Rwanda. This new appointment is worthy of note, as it not only laid the foundation for the French doctrine as we shall later see, but also essentially militarized the colonial administration, in effect sanctioning military force as the leading political strategy in the Belgian hold on Rwanda that would continue long after independence.[27]

Meanwhile, the *Force Publique* mission in Rwanda had been taken over by the *4ᵉ Battalion Commando* of Maj Bruneau, and formed part of the *Garde Territoriale du Ruanda-Urundi* under the command of Colonel BEM Delperdange[28], Logiest's former classmate in Belgian military academy. The new force was to oversee the local elections taking place in Rwanda to vote for local councils and mayors in 1960, before the next level of the first national elections to take place in 1961.

Both these elections were a testament of the times, in that they were marred by extreme violence against the Tutsi, with Logiest at the helm in his militarized administrative office taking sides in favour of the Hutu in a convenient political expediency.

By January 1960, Logiest had already declared which side he was on:

> What is our goal?" he had asked, "It is to accelerate the politicization of Ruanda. ...[W]e must undertake an action in favour of the Hutu, who live in a state of ignorance and under oppressive influences. By virtue of the situation we are obliged to take sides. We cannot stay neutral and sit.[29]

As journalist Richard Cox of the London *Sunday Times* would note on the violence that Logiest's taking sides would derive,

> "between August and mid-September (prior to the 1961 legislature elections)...in the Astrida region alone there were over 150 deaths, 3000 huts were burnt and 22,000 refugees came to Astrida. The violence spread to Nyanza... to Kigali and finally, in a wave of terror on the eve of the elections, to the north-east region of Kibungo. Despite the vast troop reinforcements, despite armed police, despite every modern

method of control, the administrators and officers on the spot were 'unable' to bring the trouble to a halt until a few days—a convenient few days—before the elections."[30]

On the military front, after the new Congo Prime Minister, Patrice Lumumba, had directed that the *Force Publique* should have its own African commanders, many Belgian Commissioned and Non-commissioned Officers were now available to mould the just formed *Garde Teritoriale du Ruanda-Urundi* as they wished.

It was upon Logiest, both as Special Resident and Commander, to create a force of his fancy, of which, maintaining his unremitting bias he created a "Hutu force". This is how he put it: "I deemed it necessary to rapidly put in place a local force composed of 14% Tutsi and 86% Hutus, but in practical terms of nearly 100% Hutu."[31]

To ensure the force remained Hutu, an ingenious method of recruitment was applied. In the recruitment and enlistment of men to the *Garde Teritoriale du Ruanda*, a system called *Pignet* was introduced. It was used to sift the "able" from the "unfit" according to their body sizes. For instance, for one to qualify he or she had to score at least 5 or less points of *pignet*.[32]

Pignet worked on a formula that took the measurement of the height of the recruit in centimetres, less the sum of breadth of the chest in centimetres, plus the weight in kilogrammes. This system of recruitment favoured the short and stocky "Hutu" constructs to the exclusion of the taller and slender "Tutsi" constructs. In Hutu-nising the force, the key was that the shorter and stockier the better the military material.[33] This system of recruitment would continue long after independence.

The *Garde Teritoriale* in Rwanda was supposed to have the strength of 1,200 officers and men. In deployment each *territoire* (district), ten at the time, would have a platoon of 50 soldiers and a battalion intervention force comprising 700 officers and men. While this was the intention, it was only short-lived, as the *Garde Teritoriale* in Rwanda was nationalized three months after its creation in August 1960 to become the *Garde Nationale*. This was under the command of the Belgian Major François Vanderstraeten in the impeding status of Rwanda and Burundi being independent states.

Efforts were also being undertaken to Africanize the officer corps. On 4 October 1960, the Rwandan section of *Ecole des Sous-Officiers* (ESO) was transferred from Usumbura in Burundi to Astrida in Rwanda with the mission to train Rwandan Non-Commissioned-Officers. A month later on 10 November 1960 the *Ecole Supérieure Militaire* (ESM), opened its doors in Kigali. Its first intake of seven pioneer students included a young Juvénal Habyalimana, who would become a future president of Rwanda.

The new officer recruits spent their first year at ESM and their second at the Ecole Royale Militaire in Brussels, before undergoing another eight months in Arlon, Belgium, of further training. Of the six Second-Lieutenants to graduate on 23 December 1961, five were Hutus and only one Tutsi, Epimaque Ruhashya. He would remain the only highly- ranked Tutsi soldier throughout the two post-independence Hutu regimes.

These were the elite officers that Lt. Col. Vanderstraeten had to start with as the Commander of the *Garde Nationale*. Vanderstraeten later handed over the command of the new Rwandan force to Juvenal Habyalimana a year after independence in 1963.

Notes

1   Michel Kayihura (PM UNAR-in-exile), his father was Manzi, grandfather, Segore.
2   De Forges (1972), op.cit., pp.205-216.
3   Idem.
4   Idem.
5   Idem.
6   Rumiya, op. cit., p.62-71.
7   De Forges (1983), p.273.

8   J.P. Harroy., *Rwanda,* 1984, Bruxelles, Haye, p.97.

9   Linden, (1977), op. cit., 206.

10   De Forges (1983), pp.262-275.

11   Ibid., p.265.

12   The 85 year-old Gaudensia Mukamazimpaka describing how her father, Chief Ruzamba rwa Sharangabo, used to suffer arbitrary beatings at the hands of the Colonial Administrator.

13   Pagès to Philippart, 6 November 1933.

14   Ian Linden, op.cit, pp.208-209.

15   Adam Hochschild, op.cit.

16   Lemarchand (1970: 106-7) says that "[t]he attitude of the European clergy underwent a major reorientation in the mid-'fifties, partly as a result of impending changes in the policies of the administration, and also because these changes tended to coincide with the arrival of a new category of missionaries. Unlike their predecessors, these newcomers were of relatively humble social origins and hence generally predisposed to identify with the plight of the Hutu masses. They belonged to what is known as 'le petit clergé' (minor clergy), and in many cases their previous experience of social and political conditions in the French-speaking provinces of Wallonia enhanced their solicitude for the 'underdog'.

17   B. Lugan (2004), op.cit., pp.55-56.

18   J. Semujanga (2003), op.cit, p.145.

19   Andrew Wallis, *Silent Accomplice: The Untold Story of France's Role in Rwandan Genocide,* I.B. Tauris, 2006, p.13.

20   G. Logiest 1988 : 62-75.

21   G. Périès and D. Servenay, *Une guerre noire: Enquête sur les origines du génocide Rwandais (1959-1994).* La Decouverte, Paris, 2007.

22   G. Logiest 1988: 75.

23   G. Logiest, op. cit, p.17.

24   Ibid, p.45.

25   Ibid.

26   De Forges, op.cit, p.210.

27   G. Logiest empowered by the emergency decree of the Governor General of Congo-Belge (General Janssens) of October 20, 1959, whose Article 2 states that the Governor General can: a) Entrust to the military authorities all or certain services of the civil administration; b) Substitute the civil authorities with the military authorities as he may deem appropriate; d) Modify the territorial

and administrative organization, in particular the powers and attributions of the various authorities; e) Commission any civil or military staff to exert any civil or military function. Further, Article 4 states that: The military authority substituted the civil authority pursuant to the Article 2b takes, according to his wish, the title of governor, police chief or military administrator; It directly exerts the powers allotted or reserved for the civil authority for which it is substituted by the legislation on the state of exception [...] In times of war or in the event of threat of war the governor general can create military zones of operation which extend to the provinces and districts or city that he determines and appoints the commanders. The commanders of military zones of operation can declare the state of exception in their zone; if it is impossible for them to refer to the general governor in good time about it, they inform him as soon as possible. In the part of the territory that they declare in a state of emergency, the commanders of zone are substituted for the governors of concerned province in the capacity of military governors. NB: When the commander of the FP in Congo, General Janssens, sends lieutenant-colonel Logiest to take up his functions in Rwanda, things become very clear: "Logiest can prohibit any meeting, he can imprison, he can hang anyone he wants" - (E. JANSSENS, I was the General Janssens, Brussels, Charles Dessart, 1961, p. 128.).

28   G. Logiest, op.cit. p.158.
29   Special Resident, Colonel Bem Logiest, during 'reunion de cadres' on January 1960, Lemarchand, p.175.
30   *London Sunday Times,* November 1961.
31   G. Logiest, op. cit, p.159.
32   Discussion with Colonel Lizinde Théoneste who was recruited through the system and was at one time the Chief of Military Intelligence in FAR.
33   Bernard Lugan, *Histoire du Rwanda, de la préhistoire à nos jours,* Bartillat, 1997, pp 547-557.

8

Rudahigwa: Towards Nationalism

Rwanda's resilience may ironically be seen in the reign of King Mutara III Rudahigwa, who was enthroned after the disgraceful banishment and forced exile of his father, Yuhi V Musinga. Musinga's deposition signalled the total subjugation of an already besieged nation.

Of Rwanda's resilience, however, the poet Sekarama, in *Ndabukire Imana yunamuye u Rwanda*[1] (My thanks to God for having rescued Rwanda) had "foreseen" the strength and continuity of the glory of Rwanda in the enthronement of Rudahigwa.

Mutara uru Rwanda	Mutara, the liberator,
warwunamuye rucyunamye	came at the right time
Wabonye rwatangirijwe,	Rwanda was under siege
Urutangirira kure	And you intervened in the knick of time
(....)	*(....)*
Warukenkemuye rukendereye	Re-invigorating a beseiged nation
Warumanuye aho rwari rwamanitswe	Tactfully, spoiling not for a fight
Woroshya ijabo urukura ijuru	And gave vision in the shadow
inyuma.[2]	of the enemy.

127

Though Rudahigwa had let down Rwanda "giving" it to the Christian King (see Chapter VII) by surrendering Kalinga and converting to the alien religion, it was tactful of him to choose "submission" by converting to Christianity ("tactfully, not spoiling for a fight") instead of engaging in an antagonistic "confrontation"[3] with the colonialists, as alluded to in the poem — *Woroshya ijabo* – a confrontation that had led to the deposition of his father, Musinga.

True to the poet's "insight", Rudahigwa, after visiting Belgium, Denmark and West Germany in 1948 and '49, found cause to doubt the credibility of his colonial masters,[4] who included the Catholic Church he had so enthusiastically embraced. In Europe he was influenced by African nationalists whose only voice, in asserting the dignity of their people, was one of defiance against colonialism in the quest for their nations' independence.

It was significant also that after the Second World War Ruanda-Urundi, along with other mandated territories, became trusteeship territories under the United Nations, which started urging for their independence from colonial occupiers. The first UN mission of the Trusteeship Council to Ruanda-Urundi was in 1948, which played a significant role in the political awakening of the Rwandan elite.

Thus encouraged by the UN initiative, Rudahigwa took the mantle to agitate for Rwanda's independence in tandem with other African nationalists near home and abroad, including those he met in Europe. In effect, therefore, as the poet suggests, through Rudahigwa Rwanda moved from darkness into light (*urukura ijuru inyuma*) and was emboldened by a new vision for Rwanda.

In this new vision, one of the most enduring of Rudahigwa's legacies was the Rwanda he saw emerging, with education for all its citizens at the core, if the nation was to unshackle the yoke of colonialism. As a first step during his visit to Belgium he had gotten in touch with the Catholic Jesuits Order, reputed for their insistence on liberal education, and solicited for the establishment of Jesuit Schools in Rwanda.[5]

King Rudahigwa wanted to educate young Rwandans for future leadership, irrespective of their constructed Hutu or Tutsi identities, and had gone on to earmark a site for the school at Gatagara. This was in divergence from the colonial model that emphasized Catholic Church-oriented education for the Tutsi nobles at the expense of the ordinary Rwandans.

To his surprise, however, the Jesuits turned down the request and instead put up the Mwami's coveted school, *Collège Interracial du Saint Esprit,* in Bujumbura.

With this let-down, King Rudahigwa resolved to go it alone seeing that the real solution must lie with the Rwandans themselves. It was then, in 1954, that he initiated the Fonds Mutara (Mutara Foundation) to carry out the mission of educating young Rwandans as future leaders. With this resolve he invited the mainly Tutsi chiefs to contribute to the fund.

Many of the chiefs, already wealthy as heirs of noble families, in addition to their acquired wealth in salaries of up to 12,000 Belgian Francs per month, including customary levies on their subjects as colonial administrators, could have afforded to fund Rudahigwa's initiative.

Their wealth was such that the *sous-chefs* could afford the Studbaker (at 28,000 BFrancs) and the *Chefs* the Buick, a prestigious American limousine popular at the time, at a fortune of 36,000 Belgian Francs. So popular was it that for its swiftness and elegance, the limousine had earned the name *impala* among the Banyarwanda, naming it after the antelope. Their big fortunes notwithstanding, the chiefs did not buy into the idea of the Mutara Foundation and simply refused to contribute.

The Mwami, however, clung to his vision of education for all and decided to go it alone by single-handedly setting up an education fund under the Mutara Foundation. Through scholarships to study in Belgium, some of the Foundation's beneficiaries included Birara Jean Berchmans, Donat Murego,

Nicodemus Ruhashyankiko, Fulgence Seminega, Dr Didas Binagwaho, Dr. Nyirinkwaya, and Gaspard Cyimana. Others such as Anastase Makuza and Isidore Nzeyimana went to Kisantu Mbanza Ngungu in the Congo, while Juvénal Habyarimana and Claver Iyamuremye were in Lovanium University in Kinshasa.

Rudahigwa's conviction was such that he would conscript Rwandan educationists such as Silas Majoro,[6] a Makerere University graduate, and Ezra Mpyisi, an Adventist educationist, on his council of advisors to enhance the education of the Rwandan youth. He would be vindicated when, later, in 1957 during the visit of the Kabaka of Buganda, Omugabe of Ankole and Omukama of Toro at the Mwami's silver jubilee celebration of his enthronement, he learnt that under the British colonial system, education was usefully run by the local authorities under the visiting Ugandan kings for the good of their people.

The Mwami went on to support the establishment of a muslim school *(Intwari)* open to all Rwandans, as well as non-denominational schools known as *écoles laïques,* much to the disenchantment of the Roman Catholic Church. This disenchantment may illustrate the Mwami's falling out with the Church and the colonial administration, but it starkly also bears out his ideal that Rwandans deserved the same.

It is famously recalled how in 1956 the Mwami observed that "there were no objective criteria whereby one can distinguish Hutu from Tutsi,"[7] when reacting to a European settler by the name of A. Maus, a member of the Council of the Vice Governor General. In an impending reorganization of membership, Maus had proposed a separate representation of Hutu in the Council, the rejection of which with the Mwami's influence forced the settler to resign from the Vice Governor General's Council in protest.

Yet the Mwami's was not a universal opinion on the sameness of the Hutu and Tutsi among Rwandans. For instance, as spelt out nearly a year later after the Maus incident in the 1957 Hutu

Manifesto a major grievance was the "political monopoly of one race, the Tutsi race, which, given the present structural framework, becomes a social and economic monopoly".[8]

On the other hand, the example may be drawn of the *"abagaragu b'ibwami bakuru"* (Mwami's elder clients) who in a 1958 statement proclaimed the Tutsi supremacy saying that the Banyiginya ruling clan conquered the indigenous Hutu "tribes" to a state of servitude, and that that was the way it should be.[9] There is no gainsaying that the seemingly irreconcilable sectarianism had taken root within a people long imbued with the ideology that preached racism.

With all the foregoing, by 1958 it was clear that Rudahigwa's ideal of unity and independence of Rwanda was in disfavour in the current status quo. This was not just with settlers like Maus or with some of the Hutu and Tutsi, but also with the Belgian government, as it was made obvious with the official reception the Mwami got on his second trip to Belgium.

A UN report observes that, "it was rumoured that the Mwami had been displeased by the way he had been treated in Brussels in 1958, which was alleged to be so different from the cordial reception he had been given on previous visits. Whatever the reasons, relations with the administration became very strained."[10]

The king, however, did not seem overly bothered by this, confident that the march for Rwandans dignity and self-determination was on course. Already, to his credit on the dignity of Rwandans, was the 1954[11] abolition of the abused traditional institution of *Ubuhake* and *Uburetwa*.

Ubuhake as a traditional institution involved not only cattle clientage but also social rapport among Rwandans that fostered mutual benefit in which a patron benefited from his client as the client did his patron. Both sides were actually gaining more in wealth, protection, social status, etc. Besides, terms of contract were clear: a cow in exchange of manual services after some time. It was voluntary and not coercive, and any contracting party could terminate the contract any time he deemed it necessary. But the fact that *ubuhake* could be hereditary and that one's patron could find a wife for his *umugaragu (kumukwerera)* and, in some cases, give him his own daughter, attest to the cordial relations between the two parties, relations that would often be subject of invocation *(kwirahira)* almost instinctively as a way of boasting about one's patron's or client's positive influence.[12]

The traditional *ubuhake* was also flexible in that it allowed the possibility of a *mugaragu* or his descendants to become patrons. This flexibility can also be seen in the example of Rudahigwa. For instance, while still a prince, he was a *mugaragu* of Chief Rwabutogo rwa Kabale and continued to recognize this relationship through continually citing his patron's name (traditionally known as *kwirahira*) even after becoming king. In the traditional military, ubuhake also implied the relationship between a commander and his men. Thus the commander *ipso facto* became the patron *(shebuja)* of his men *(abagaragu)*, which denoted personal loyalty to the commander. In that sense, all Rwandans were *abagaragu* of the king as their commander-in-chief.

Despite its traditional usefulness *Ubuhake* was turned around by the colonialists and used to entrench the Belgian enterprise by *"Tutsifying"* the administration and marginalizing the rest of Rwanda; for instance, when Tutsi chiefs became colonial *shebuja* (patron) as a result of Mortehan Reform and the rest of Rwandans became their *abagaragu* (clients or subjects). In this way the Belgian enterprise rigidified the traditional ubuhake arrangement through legislation and education of the Tutsi nobility, so that no Hutu or petit Tutsi became a *shebuja* (patron).

This ended up benefiting only the Tutsi chiefs without the concept of reciprocity; thus lacking in mutual benefit and being exploitative. Thus the Tutsi chiefs became associated with the colonial exploitative system. To the Belgian mind, *Ubahake* evoked the European concept of medieval feudalism which was mainly exploitative, where the lords exploited the labour and services of their serfs and peasants who entirely depended upon them.

Therefore, while bearing a semblance to the traditional *Ubahake* it now became a tool of oppression where the chiefs' subjects suffered. That Belgian enterprise turned *ubuhake* into the duality of feudalism with its attendant exploitative overtones and therefore a source of social conflict pitting the "oppressor" Tutsi minority against the "oppressed" Hutu majority.[13] This oppression, though used to serve the colonialists, was turned against all the Tutsi – as defined by the 1933 new mode of identification – in a blanket condemnation as the call for independence mounted, and became the major rallying point fueling the violence during the 1959 Hutu Revolution.

The Hutu Revolution purported to have abolished *Ubuhake* (cattle clientage), mainly practised in central and southern Rwanda, and left its parallel system, *Ubukonde* (land clientage) practised in the north intact, which still survives to-date. The former was allegedly between the Hutu and Tutsi, with the latter being between the Hutu. The revolution thus claimed to have overthrown the "Tutsi" clientage system and left the "Hutu" system intact, in itself negating the excuse of the revolution against any injustice.

Indeed, 1959 was a momentous year. Not only would it see the death of the king in July[14] of that year, but would also see the face and fabric of Rwandan society completely change in a series of political events. Indeed, the king died under dubious circumstances while in Bujumbura en route to New York to present Rwanda's case for the country's immediate independence at the United Nations. He died unexpectedly while in hospital allegedly for a medical check up without the colonial authorities instituting an autopsy to establish the cause of death, making many observers suspect assassination.

As already noted, independence for Rwanda with the king at the helm meant that the Belgians would relinquish their colonial prerogatives including the country's proximity to Congo; yet there existed the alternative of backing the Hutu with their fabricated grievances against their Tutsi "oppressors".

With the king gone, however, and having left no child of his own as heir to the throne, it would be his step-brother, Ndahindurwa, chosen by the *abiru* with the reluctant agreement of the Belgian administration, to succeed him. The new Mwami would be enthroned as a warrior king under the dynastic name of King Kigeri the Fifth. Yet the new Kigeri would not be the warrior-king the name hopefully suggested.

Aged only 21, he was no match for Rudahigwa's "adeptness at reconciling divergent viewpoints and tendencies, [or] at giving a measure of harmony and unity to his following".[15] Kigeri's youthful ineptitude risked being a liability in the heated and daily escalating passions of divided Rwandans, as the clamour for independence intensified with the soon to be formed political parties.

The first in this dispensation was the formation of the political party Association pour la Promotion Sociale de la Masse (APROSOMA) led by Joseph Habyalimana (alias Gitera) on 15 February 1959 followed by Union Nationale Rwandaise (UNAR) on 3 September 1959, only a couple of months after the demise of Rudahigwa.[16] It was clear with UNAR's leading members, who included Francois Rukeba, Michel Rwagasana, Cosma Rebero and Chiefs Kayihura, Rwangobwa and Mungalurire that while the fate of the dead king may have been sealed, not so should be his legacy for Rwandans as one people. To them it was this conviction that led to the formation of UNAR.

Under the leadership of François Rukeba and Michel Rwagasana, both of them Hutu, UNAR's stated main objective was to ensure "the union of all Rwandese for the purpose of achieving true progress in all spheres".[17] This was the nationalist party that, in the name of the Mwami, would purport to hold the Rwandan torch of uniting a people in the darkness that would engulf the country in a few months to come, leading to the first incursions of Inyenzi.

Meanwhile, the formation of a host of other political parties soon followed suit. Chronologically, the first party to follow suit was Rassemblement Démocratique Rwandais (RADER), which came into being on 14 September 1959 under the leadership of Prosper Bwanakweli and Lazaro Ndazaro, but would turn out to be a small party with little impact. Logiest says that, with its formation, RADER "espoused the views of the *Résidence*"[18] which supports the allegation by UNAR that it was created by the *Résidence* in order to weaken UNAR by recruiting a large part of the Tutsi.

On 19 October 1959, Grégoire Kayibanda, a future president of Rwanda, formed the populist Parti du Mouvement de l'Emancipation Hutu (PARMEHUTU) with undisguised support[19] of the Belgians, converting it from the Mouvement Social Muhutu (MSM), an organization he had set up in 1957 in line with the Bahutu Manifesto[20] to look after the interests of the Hutu. Leaders of the new party included Dominique Mbonyumutwa, a Hutu chief from Gitarama, Calliope Mulindahabi and Balthazar Bicamumpaka.[21]

However, as political jostling for eventual national leadership in the coming local and national legislative elections intensified, it would be PARMEHUTU and UNAR that would emerge at the top—the one supported by the colonial administration and claiming to represent the Hutu majority and the other claiming to represent Rwandans, though perceived as Tutsi and vilified by the Belgians for its persistent demand for immediate independence of Rwanda.[22]

In the vilification, for instance, Bishop Perraudin in a confidential circular[23] addressed to all Catholic priests, he denounces UNAR as being under pro-Communist and pro-

Islamist influences citing "irrefutable" evidence alluding to the all-inclusive muslim school whose establishment at Nyamirambo in Kigali was supported by Rudahigwa.

Also echoing the late Mwami's conviction that schools would better be in hands other than the Catholic Church, the circular went on to criticize the party "for its attempts to insulate the schools from the influence of the Catholic Missions 'on the pretext they can better be administered by the state'".[24]

And for its calling upon all "the children of Rwanda" to join together as one in the on-going political process, the church cautioned its audience against UNAR's tendency to "seek a monopoly of patriotism, [as] a tendency which closely [resembled] national socialism".[25]

Yet matters had to come to a head with the Belgian authorities' decision to take disciplinary sanctions against Chiefs Kayihura, Rwangobwa and Mungalurire, as employees of the administration, for participating in a UNAR public rally on 13 September 1959 "in flagrant violation of instructions issued by the Resident".

While the Resident was of a mind to dismiss the three chiefs outright, he nevertheless transferred them to other *chefferies*, provoking criticism that the disciplinary sanction was unfair as the said Resident's instructions were issued after the rally. The chiefs chose to agitate for immediate independence abroad.

The violence that would break out in the first days of November marking a turning point in Rwanda's history was not necessarily linked with the fate the three chiefs, but began in Gitarama and engulfed the entire country as far as Ruhengeri and Gisenyi. PARMEHUTU activists alleged that the violence that started on 1 November 1959 was sparked by a band of young UNAR militants who had attacked Sous-chef Dominique Mbonyumutwa, the PARMEHUTU leader of Ndiza. From then on it spread like wildfire across the country, pitting the more numerous Hutu against the Tutsi in revenge. The result was killing, banishment and arson on Tutsi homes across the country. A UN Visiting Mission Report observes that

> Incendiaries set off in bands of ten. Armed with matches and paraffin, which the indigenous inhabitants use in large quantities for their lamps, they pillaged the Tutsi houses they passed on their way and set fire to them. On their way they would enlist other incendiaries to follow the procession while the first recruits, too exhausted to continue, would give up and return home. Thus, day after day, fires spread from hill to hill.[26]

As the number of casualties mounted,[27] with little or no apparent effort by the Belgian administration to stop the violence, the Mwami was compelled to act to save lives and subsequently dispatched an omnibus cable to the Vice-Governor, the Belgian Parliament and the King of Belgium asking for leeway to intervene as was morally dutiful of his leadership.

Without waiting for a reply to the request, which was denied with a declaration of a state of emergency and the dispatch of Colonel Logiest and his troops from the Congo, the Mwami's court mobilized the "traditional" military regiments, still existing at the pleasure of the court for its protection as custom required, to intervene in countering the Hutu aggression by targeting its leaders.

Ironically vindicating the UNAR insistence of the unity of Rwandans, which was traditionally best expressed in the *Ingabo*, the UN Visiting Mission Report talks of how, along with traditional army chiefs and border guards, "Each commando party amounted to some hundreds of persons or more, and included a majority of Hutu, but the leaders were generally Tutsi or Twa."[28]

Though the traditional commando units made little dent in ending the violence, especially in the onslaught[29] of Logiest's battalions *(Iza Kamina)*, it marked a new chapter. The very existence of the "traditional commandos" became the basis of the formation of the Inyenzi in the struggle that inevitably lay ahead of the new Rwandan exiles.

The United Nations estimated that refugees who fled into exile to escape the violence were about 7,000 at the end of November 1959, with the total number climbing to 22,000 by April 1960. Most of the refugees resettled in neighbouring countries of Tanzania, Uganda, Congo and Burundi with the total number of those living abroad reaching 130,000 by 1963.[30] Among these refugees were the members of the UNAR, who would provide political leadership to the refugees with the hope of one day returning to Rwanda, for as Francios Presiozi[31] is quoted to have intimated, "outside their [refugee] country they will always be subject to pressures, vexations and hostility on the part of the populations where they have sought refuge". The UNAR leadership-in-exile overseen by the Mwami Kigeri V included Rukeba, Mungalurire, Rwagasana and Kayihura.[32] Among the refugees were Hutu,

> ...some of whom [went] in exile with their former lords. It is symptomatic of the persistence of traditional ties within the Hutu community that so many of them would rather go into exile than shift their allegiance to the new regime. Their exact number is impossible to determine. By way of an illustration, however, one could cite the case of Chief Bideri [bya Kanyemera], admittedly one of the most popular of the young chiefs, who, in an interview with the writer, claimed to have been followed into exile by a retinue of about forty Hutu. Similarly, Rachel Yeld reports the presence of a 'group of about fifty Twa families among the main groups of refugees in Tanganyika, who had been dancers and court servants of the Mwami.[33]

The dream of one day going back home went with them, however, and if it was to be realized, it seemed inevitable that one of the core strategies should be a military option of which there were the Mwami's "commando units", members of whom, in all certainty, inspired or perpetrated the first incursions into Rwanda by the refugees and would form the backbone of a guerilla movement that came to be known as *Inyenzi*.

Notes

1   *Cahiers,* No 26, March 2004, pp.82-97'.

2   Ibid., p.94.

3   Lemarchand (1970: 69-70) observes that "Although, in general Rudahigwa displayed no more sympathy towards Europeans than his predecessor, his methods were very different. Where Musinga openly challenged missionaries and administrators, Rudahigwa had a special talent for working within the confine of the established superstructure, rather than against it. He had come of age at time when European rule was already firmly established, and was better able to accommodate himself to the norms of the new system. More importantly still, being himself the product of mission schools, he shared with the up-and-coming generations of Tutsi elites the Western training and education which his predecessor so conspicuously lacked."

4   Upon arriving in Belgium, King Rudahigwa realized that he had limited sovereignty as he was traveling on a Belgian passport, and required Belgian clearance to travel to America with the Intore cultural troupe.

5   Interview with Rwandan historian, José Kagabo.

6   Majoro had been educated in the prestigious King's College, Budo, in Uganda and was a close confidant of Kabaka Mutesa II of Buganda. He was at the time the Principal of Gahini Primary School and headed all protestant schools under Gahini Diocese. One of his students was François "Saiba" Uwiragiye, who became a well known commander in the Inyenzi movement of the 1960s.

7   Lemarchand, (1970), op. cit., p.147.

8   Ibid, p.149; also see the 1957 Hutu Manifesto in (Logiest 1988:51-54).

9   *Ruanda Politique,* 1958-1960, pp. 35-6, cited in Lemarchand (1970:154); Chief Rwangobwa Chrisostome in an interview however purports that those *Abagaragu b'ibwami bakuru* were illiterate and were hoodwinked by "Kirsch", then Assistant Administrator General to sign the document that he had authored).

10   *UN Visiting Mission to Trust Territories in East Africa, 1960; Report on Ruanda-Urundi,* T/1551.

11   The Colonial Administration's Decree of 14 July 1952 established the Conseil de Sous-chefferie and the Conseil du Roi which enabled

the King to enact limited changes on the affairs of Rwandans as he deemed fit.

12   P. Gourevitch (1998), p.47.

13   Ian Linden (1977), op. cit., pp.2-4.

14   Died at one o'clock on Saturday, 25 July, 1959, at Usumbura in Burundi and was buried on Tuesday, 28 July in Nyanza on Mwima Hill. The very day of the burial the new king was proclaimed at the cemetery by Alexander Kayumba, Chief of the Abiru Council.

15   Lemarchand, (1970), p.158, also see Lugan (2004), p.59.

16   Harroy (1984), *Rwanda*. p. 284.

17   UNAR (Union Nationale Rwandaise): Interviews with former chiefs Rwangombwa [Kigali, 28 Jan, 2006] and Kayihura [24 March 2004]), see also Gakuba L. (2007), op. cit., pp. 49-52.

18   G. Logiest, (1988), op. cit., p.101.

19   G. Logiest, 1988, op. cit., p.52.

20   P. Gourevitch 1998:58 (In March of 1957, a group of nine Hutu intellectuals [Grégoire Kayibanda, Calliope Mulindahabi, Maximilien Niyonzima, Claver Ndahayo, Isidore Nzeyimana, Godefroid Sentama, Sylvestre Munyambonera, Joseph Sibomana, and Joseph Habyalimana alias 'Gitera'] published a tract known as the Hutu Manifesto, arguing for "democracy" – not by rejecting the Hamitic myth but by embracing it. If Tutsis were invaders, the argument went, then Rwanda was by rights a nation of the Hutu majority).

21   G. Logiest, op.cit., p.119.

22   Ibid, p.104.

23   Lemarchand, p.161.

24   Ibid.

25   Ibid.

26   UN Visiting Mission, 1960, op.cit, p.28.

27   Laurent Gakuba, *Rwanda 1959-1994*, Coetquen Editions, 2007, p.52 (Among the prominent people killed were sous-chefs Rwamuningi, Katabarwa and Matsiko).

28   Ibid. p.29.

29   As the Special Resident, Colonel Logiest stated in January 1960: 'By virtue of the situation we are obliged to take sides. We cannot stay neutral and sit'. See 'Reunion des Administrateurs de Territoire', Kigali, January 11, 1960, p.2.

30 Ibid. p.32.

31 Presiozi was a delegate of the United Nations High Commission for Refugees (UNHCR) in Kivu until his assassination by a band of Congolese rebels in 1964, while on an inspection tour in the region of Lemera.

32 A government-in-exile would be formed on the eve of independence in 1962 with Rukeba as Prime Minister, Mungalurire as Minister of Finance, Gabriel Sabyeza as Minister of Information and Hamoud Ben Salim as Minister of Defence.

33 Lemarchand, op.cit., p.172 (Indeed, many of the refugees in Uganda (i.e., in Nakivale, Rwamwanja and Kyaka camps), especially from Umutara were abagaragu (clients) of Chef Lyumugabe rya Rusekampunzi, Kabagema ka Sebisaho, Mundende, etc., who were both Hutu and Tutsi.

9

The Mixed Fortunes of *Inyenzi*

As the Mwami and his large entourage settled to their new life in exile, his informal traditional "regiments" in the name of all patriotic Rwandans[1] were in the meantime in disarray. This was not least because there first needed to be political organization, whose structure the UNAR had provided with its earlier exiled leaders — Kayihura, Mungalurire and Rukeba.

The informal traditional army existed, but not in the concrete sense of visible military units. As will be recalled, every munyarwanda belonged to the military and would be called upon to rally behind his king and country in time of need. For many able-bodied Banyarwanda, this seemed such a time. All that was needed was some organization to make their way back home.

In the unfamiliar surroundings of the refugee camps, the new exiles were more than motivated to get back their country. Being in exile to a Rwandan was considered "as good as dead".[2] Most of the exiles saw their stay as temporary and "not exceeding six months". They even refused to plant annual subsistence crops believing that, "by harvest time", they would long be home.

In this wishful thinking, the first year in exile went by. Then the incursions into Rwanda, though isolated, started. The incursions were at first conducted by individuals against specific people and families in Rwanda, including European settlers and Parmehutu activists. These incursions emboldened not only the individuals involved, but the exiled political leadership as it became clear that it was possible to be more organized and make more systematic incursions in the overall ambition of regaining Rwanda. Hence come 1962, the *Inyenzi* guerrilla movement started by organizing small bands of combatants with leaders such as Rukeba, Ngurumbe, Jovit, Mudandi, Numa and Nyabujangwe playing a leading organizational role.

Rukeba and his son, Kayitare alias Masudi, operating from Burundi, which held the largest number of refugees, were especially instrumental and made it possible for the organization of *Inyenzi*. They established links with the newly independent Congo-Kinshasa, with support coming from the Lumumbist *Mouvement Nationale Congolais* (MNC) which offered financial and military assistance to focus and strengthen the insurgent Rwandan exiles.[3] This alliance continued to the mid-sixties, and only served to alarm the French and Belgians as a dangerous and destabilizing menace to their interests in the region, and therefore as something to be emphatically routed.

The exiles' efforts were doomed, therefore, with the numerous incursions of the budding *Inyenzi* in 1962 and early 1963 having not much impact in bringing closer the goal of liberating Rwanda from the Hutu sectarians in government. In their forays, however, there were little "triumphs" such as overrunning a police station in Ngara in Tanzania where they seized arms in early 1963.[4]

In Rwanda the incursions would prove a more difficult task, not least because of Logiest's Garde Nationale's counter-measures against the guerrilla activities as prescribed by the French Revolutionary Doctrine.

It may be recalled that an aspect of the doctrine emphasized generalized violence in a population to rout out any sympathizers or any larking insurgents among them. This applied extreme brutality and extermination that aimed at discouraging the unfortunate population from harbouring any sympathy for the *Inyenzi*. And thus, with each incursion by the exiles, the Tutsi in

Rwanda continued to be persecuted and harassed to attain this objective.[5]

In this light may be seen one of the first extreme applications of the French strategy that happened in Byumba in March 1962, where between 1,000 and 2,000 Tutsi were massacred, following a series of *Inyenzi* attacks that left some policemen and civil servants dead in the communes of Nkana, Mugira and Gatuna.[6]

Meanwhile, the Mwami was gaining a lot of international attention, mainly by Communist China which was just beginning to show its interest in Africa in the evolving global hegemony. With the possibility of the Mwami gaining back power, China, with Soviet Union's approval, saw its chance by offering support to gain a foothold in the region with the pull of the ever enticing promise of the mineral-rich Congo. It helped that the communist-leaning Lumumbists were tied up in the Rwandan cause as it only made it easier for the Chinese entry, if only by proxy for the Soviet Union as the Cold War was reaching its height.

On these prospects of a communist foothold in the region Kigeri was invited to China in 1963, with an offer to provide the Mwami with technical and financial support to further UNAR's ambitions of one day reigning in Rwanda. By this time it was obvious, however, that the UNAR leadership-in-exile that included the Mwami, was badly fractured with ideological and tactical differences about how things should move forward.

The reality of the situation was that the Mwami, or whoever, could not hope to gain victory over the Belgian-backed Kigali government without a well organized and trained group of fighters; thus the Chinese offer for finance and technical support to train a carefully selected group of Inyenzi fighters. Though thirty *inyenzi* were selected, only ten ended up gaining some skills in population mobilization and guerrilla warfare on the Chinese model.[7]

In the meantime, the Mwami had received a package of US$120,000 from Peking for general upkeep of the exiled leadership, and especially to sustain the faltering insurgency. It was thus that in October 1963 the king sent $23,000 of the amount with his personal secretary, Papias Gatwa, to Rukeba for the insurgency effort, and especially the purchase of much needed arms.[8]

This led to what turned out to be the most significant of *Inyenzi* incursions in December 1963. After receiving the financial support, Rukeba and the leadership in exile in Burundi and elsewhere in the region had by November reached a decision to "strike a decisive blow" against the sectarian government in Kigali. This is how Lemarchand describes the December 1963 incursion:

> According to reliable sources, the inyenzi leaders had hoped to organize simultaneous attacks from at least four different quarters: from the regions of Kabale (Uganda), Ngara (Tanzania), Goma (Congo), and Ngozi and Kayanza (Burundi). One group of assailants from Uganda, led by a certain Kibibiro, were reportedly intercepted by the Uganda authorities on December 25, before they reached the border; another, numbering about 600 men, entered Rwanda at Kizinga, on the Uganda border, on December 27, but was almost immediately repulsed by Garde Nationale Rwandais, after suffering heavy loses. About 300 invaders were killed and the rest turned over to the King's African Rifles. Similarly, on December 21 and 22 a series of small-scale border raids were launched from the Kivu in the direction of the town of Cyangugu, across the Rusizi, resulting in the intervention of the GNR and the subsequent execution of about 90 prisoners captured during the attacks. Although the projected raids from Tanzania somehow failed to materialize, during the same period a major attack was attempted from Burundi. The invading force, numbering approximately 200 or 300 men...crossed the Burundi border at Nemba at 4.30 AM on December 21. An hour or so later they attacked and over-ran the Rwandese military camp at Gako. After stocking up on arms and ammunition they went straight to the refugee camp at Nyamata,

where they received an enthusiastic welcome from local Tutsi population. ...Although their ranks had swollen towell over a thousand, by the time they reached the Nyabarongo river, at the Kanzenze bridge, about twelve miles south of Kigali, they were suddenly confronted with several units of the GNR armed with mortars and semi-automatic weapons and under the command of Belgian officers. Overwhelmed by the superior firepower of their opponents, the invaders were quickly repulsed. In the course of the engagement several hundred Tutsi lost their lives, including a handful of Congolese 'rebels'.[9]

In all certainty, this defeat of *inyenzi* would spell the beginning of the end of the guerrilla movement. But the incursion would also provoke a French-inspired government measure that would lead to massacres that would amount to the first Rwanda "genocide".[10]

As a counter measure to the *inyenzi* incursion, older Rwandans still recall how the country became some sort of "IDP camp" where they could not move from place to place without a pass.[11]

To implement this measure, Logiest and his GNR may seem to have literally borrowed from a French article titled, "Effective Self-Defense of the Population Against Guerrilla Attacks" in the Review of National Defense (RDN) of June 1956. The article explains that:

> The affected area is divided into regions or sectors and then sub-sectors between fixed points of control such as road-blocks at military encampments created for the purpose. Between these points of control, commandos go and come in their hunting of the rebels and gathering information about them. They are supported by local self-defense militia who are a source of information for the commandos, though the militia can act on their own in a preventive manner. The methods of action aredifferent according to whether one is in a rural or urban area.

Almost to the letter as in the above quoted article, with the advice of Logiest to the government:

[S]teps were taken to organize civilian 'self-defense' groups among the Hutu population, to counter possible attempts at internal subversion. For this task primary reliance was placed upon the burgomasters and prefects. In addition, one minister was assigned to each of the ten prefectures (now converted into 'emergency regions') to supervise the organization of self-defense units. These arrangements were made within a few hours, in an atmosphere of panic, and therefore with little attention to procedural details or coordination. Meanwhile, Kigali Radio beamed emergency warnings, asking the population to be 'constantly on alert' for Tutsi terrorists. In the atmosphere of intense fear, saturated with rumour and suspicion, the worst was bound to happen. The killings began on December 23, 1963, in the prefecture of Gikongoro, at the instigation of the local prefect, a certain André Nkeramugaba. Addressing an improvised meeting of burgomasters and PARMEHUTU propagandists, keramugaba is reported to have said: We are expected to defend ourselves. The only way to go about it is to paralyse the Tutsi. How? They must be killed. This was the signal for the slaughter.[12]

A total of between 10,000 and 14,000 Tutsi were killed during the reprisals, and would mark the height of government orchestrated pogroms against the Tutsi throughout the decade and beyond. As the above passage attests, it was the precursor to the radio RTLM and the 1994 genocide.

As for the *inyenzi,* it was not the *Garde Nationale* to tame them, but the *inyenzi t*hemselves. The defeat of December 1963 they would never recover from, but mostly for lack of a united front.

The reasons for this were many, uppermost amongst which were ideological and strategic differences among the leadership in exile, as fronted by the UNAR. This was mainly brought about by the dispersal of the UNAR leadership in different countries in the region which left them little opportunity to form a united front. With King Kigeri V much of the time on transit from one country to another in the region and elsewhere in the world, the result of the geographical dispersion of the leadership in Kenya, Uganda, Tanzania, Congo and Burundi was factionalism within the leadership in the different countries.

Consequently, by 1965 and '66 there were several competing factions, namely, Front de Libération Rwandaise (FLR) led by Gabriel Sebyeza, which included Munana and Faustin Gakwaya; Movement Populaire Rwandais (MPR) of Mudandi; Jeunesse Nationaliste Kigeri V (JNK) led by Léopold Nkurikiye from the China group; Congrès de la Jeunesse Rwandaise (COJER) led by Kanobayire with a group of Bujumbura intellectuals including Céléstin; and, Jeunesse de l'UNAR (JUNAR) led by Rucyeba and Kayitare.[13] By this time UNAR was virtually dead.

Each of these factions had a military wing and, aside from the ideological political reason of "conservatism" for the monarchy and the "progressivism" to do away with it in the insurgency efforts, the most debilitating were differences of attitude between those who took part in guerilla activities and the leadership that provided political guidance and material support to the Inyenzi. Moreover, after the December 1963 disaster of the inyenzi loss and the Tutsi massacre, amid the resulting international hue and cry, the funds had considerably dwindled.

By late 1965 some factions such as Mudandi's and Kayitare's, each with battalion-size members, had allied themselves with Congolese rebel movements in their insurgency within Congo with the hope that they would in turn reciprocate when the Rwandese mounted theirs to seize power. It was during this period that the Rwandans received some military training from the Cuban guerrilla tacticians that had been brought by Che Guevara and Raul Castro during their "internationalista campaign".

The Rwandese military flirtations with the Cubans amounted to little, despite a promise of weapons by 1967, and also despite talk of some Rwandans having been recruited to train in Cuba.

Meanwhile, the goodwill the *inyenzi* might have had in Burundi, their main country of operation, had considerably diminished due to Belgian influence and the stipulation by the Organization of African Unity that none of its members should harbour armed elements that could destabilise their neigbours. Rukeba's efforts were being thwarted with weapons being confiscated, including having him occasionally being jailed. Other leaders such as Mudandi suffered the same fate with their arms being forcefully confiscated.

It was around this time that Kayitare met his death at the hands of a Burundian police captain, who many suspected had been sent by Burundian authorities. This dealt a great blow to the *inyenzi*, as Kayitare was one of its leading lights.

All told, by 1968, the *inyenzi* spirit had significantly waned among many of its veterans, with the spirit of others broken. The Rwandan spirit in the *inyenzi* would never completely die, however, as the future awaited where it would inform the struggle to finally liberate Rwanda from sectarianism that would lead to the 1994 genocide.

If the *inyenzi* struggle was a failure, however, an argument has been proffered that this could not be helped, as the guerrilla war was a struggle before its time. According to this argument, the inyenzi were fighting the first inklings of "neo-colonialism" as exemplified by the Belgian influence in the sectarian government. If the *inyenzi* therefore had a grievance, nobody could recognize it as the Organization of African Unity at the time was fighting for the independence of "colonized" Africa in countries such as Zimbabwe, Angola and Mozambique. Without international, and especially African, support, the struggle was doomed to fail.[14]

Mwami Kigeri V and Inyenzi Saiba and Munyurangabo

In the *inyenzi's* fortunes, Mwami Kigeri was very much part of the problem – as much for his inexperience as for his lack of acumen and vision as a leader with ability to unite the Rwandan diaspora in the region. He also maintained a lifestyle that, to many of his subjects, and not least the *inyenzi*, seemed a little too indulgent and extravagant. At the same time, long had the goodwill of his international supporters such as the Chinese dwindled, and along with it the source of funds to finance the *inyenzi* struggle. Meanwhile, remittances of customary "taxes" in the form of monetary contributions of the royalists, both in the diaspora and in Rwanda, could hardly support the monarch's lifestyle.

The contradictions of Kigeri's leadership during the *inyenzi* struggle can best be symbolised in the examples of François Uwiragiye alias Saiba and David Munyurangabo. Saiba was a firm royalist who believed the king's word as the ultimate in all matters regarding his subjects. Formerly a respected school teacher in Gahini and later in Kajaho refugees' primary school, he was among the group of ten *inyenzi* trainees who went to China where he learnt revolutionary war theory and military tactics.

For some reason, Saiba was taken in by what he learnt in revolutionary war theory, which emphasized mass mobilization as an important foundation before military action to attain a political objective. When he was suddenly recalled in early 1964 along with his China colleagues following the disastrous December 1963 inyenzi attacks, he immediately embarked on mass mobilization basing his activities in Burundi, Uganda and, to some extent,Tanzania.

On the other hand, David Munyurangabo was a strapping eighteen year-old in 1963 when Saiba was leaving for China. However, Munyurangabo was already battle-hardened and was part of the expedition that had successfully raided Ngara Police Station for arms earlier that year. Under the direct command of Kayitare in the Rukeba camp operating from Burundi, he ended up being a veteran of many battles including the famous one of December 1963. Despite the defeat, Munyurangabo and his group continued with the incursions and he found himself fighting in Congo by 1965 along the Congolese rebels, where he also received some Cuban training in guerrilla tactics.

Meanwhile, Saiba upon his return busied himself with mass mobilization, always liaising with the king while awaiting Mwami's word to "move". At one time he had mobilized a group of up to 1000 in Bwera in Kasese District in Uganda, bordering Congo.[15] These were nearly two battalions ready for battle, but never once did Saiba engage in an incursion. Whenever he asked the king about when to move to action, the king always cautioned him to wait saying, "I'll tell you when and how and give you the means." Saiba believed this and was always mobilizing the refugee population for their contributions for upkeep of the royal court and duly submitting to the king's aides. But Saiba never received any word from the king.

Saiba and Munyurangabo knew each other in the *inyenzi* struggle, and, in their own admission, never saw eye-to-eye. They were rivals in the factionalism described above that culminated in the fall of *inyenzi.*

Yet Saiba's is a tragic fate, while Munyurangabo's is somewhat a heroic one: the one the unquestioning loyal subject of the king who is let down time and again and the other an accomplished guerrilla who apparently cared not for the monarchy despite being led by Rukeba of UNAR. Saiba never once accomplished a mission, while Munyurangabo was a veteran of many battles right up to the end in 1968 when he admitted, "We had all given up the armed attacks and started the normal struggles of life." Yet when the time came, he joined the RPF struggle and saw it through. Finally, this is how a disillusioned Saiba explains the end of his unremarkable career as *inyenzi:*

> One day in April 1968 I asked my fellows, *"amaherezo ubu ni ayahe"* (what will become of our fate?). Then I told them to see what we could do, for we could no longer rely on Kigeri's lies. I suggested to them that we should no longer send him money,

but see how we could fundraise and rely on our own means. One of my colleagues told it to Kigeri and asked him what they should do to me. Kigeri replied, 'do as you please.' Sirikari, a colleague of mine, revealed to me that they might do away with me. Then I had no other choice than committing suicide, which was either coming back to Rwanda or killing myself. I decided to come back to Rwanda to die, and was apprehended by the security forces and was immediately jailed in Ruhengeri Prison beginning 1968. In court in Kigali, Matayo[16] sentenced me to death, but got life sentence instead. I was released seventeen years later on 15 July 1985, along with eight other prisoners accused of being inyenzi.

The example of Munyurangabo, who went on to become a pivotal point-person[17] during the Rwanda Patriotic Front (RPF) struggle, demonstrates the resilience of the Rwandan spirit. On the other hand, the broken Saiba symbolizes royal decay that was captive in the person of Kigeri and his sense of insecurity in exile, which even led to the persecution of his own subjects in the diaspora.

Kigeri's sense of insecurity is worthy of note. For instance, soon after being invited to Uganda and hosted by Idi Amin in 1971, a story is told of one Thaddée Bihayiga who was brutally arrested in front of his two sons by Amin's soldiers on the allegation of being an anti-monarchist, and was never to be seen again.

Around that period a movement of "anti-Kigerists" was beginning to gain a lot of support with the Rwandan refugees in Uganda through a group that Kigeri insultingly labelled *Imburamajyo* ("the lost ones"). Like Saiba, members of the movement were disillusioned by the monarchy, and mainly comprised Rwandan teachers in exile.[r] The movement would not amount to much, however, as it was crushed by Amin who perceived it a threat at the urging of the Mwami.[18]

Thaddée Bihayiga was condemned of being a member of "*Imburamajyo*", though he saw himself a Rwandan patriot of which he left a legacy. As he was being roughed by Amin's soldiers during the arrest he removed his prized wristwatch and handed it to his sons, Charles Nkurayija and Emmanuel Nkurunziza, saying in Kinyarwanda, *"Jyewe nzize u Rwanda namwe muzarutabarire"* (I am dying for the Rwandan ideal, but you should die for Rwanda).

Those who witnessed it recall it as a moving gesture that was widely percieved as "passing on the baton to carry on the struggle."[20] Both of Thaddée's sons ended up joining the Rwanda Patriotic Army and died heroes of the struggle.[21]

There is more to the family, however, which is of the Abanyiginya clan of the Abenegitore lineage, who trace their roots to the King Kigeri I Mukobanya in the 14th Century. As an example of the undying Rwandan spirit that the family exemplifies, Yohana Gasega, one of Thaddée's uncles left an enduring impression on many refugees when at the age of more than eighty he joined in the December 1963 invasion from Oruchinga Refugee Camp to gain back his homeland that he had been forced to flee. Having been a warrior in his day, as member of the *Abataganzwa* and *Abarima* formations, many recall his humour raising their morale by promising to show the inyenzi fighters "how it was done in the olden days.

Notes

1   Traditionally all Rwandans belonged to the military, *Ingabo z'uRwanda*, with the Mwami being the commander-in-chief.

2   Since the return of Ruganzu Ndoli (from Karagwe) to liberate Rwanda, there was a Kinyarwanda saying *"Nta munyarwanda uhera i mahanga/ishyanga"(i.e. No Rwandese refugee for ever).*

3   Interview in May 2006 with David Munyurangabo, who recalls being trained by and working with Congolese militants. Munyarangabo is a former inyenzi who joined in 1961 at the age of 17 and is a veteran of many incursions into Rwanda throughout the period up to 1968 when the movement fizzled out. He later joined the RPF struggle and is currently a Commissioner in the Rwanda Demobilisation and Reintegration Commission (RDRC)

4   Lemarchand, op. cit., p.219; David Munyurangabo, who participated in the Ngara raid.

5   Lieutenant-Colonel V. Bruneau, *Twenty-third detachment of the 4th Battalion Commando, Rwanda 1962* Brussels, sd, p. 12-13.

6   Report of the United Nations Commission for Ruanda-Urundi, 1962, A/5126, pp.18.

7   Interview with Mzee François Uwiragiye alias Saiba, a monarchist and former teacher in Gahini Primary School (and later in Kajaho Primary School in Uganda) before joining *inyenzi*, who was in the group that received some training before being recalled home following the December 1963 invasions. Saiba recalls learning revolutionary war theory and military tactics including weapon handling. Revolutionary theory comprised the core course with its emphasis on the Chinese model of mass mobilization to attain political ends through military means. Some of Saiba's trainee companions included Ngurumbe Aloys, Sirikare Froduald (who later became a captain in RPA), Munyeragwe Antoine, Nkurikiyimana Leopold, Rwirangira Gerald, Ugirashebuja Anicet, Ruvubi Deogratias, Mudandi Joseph and Bagirishya Emille. April 2006.

8   Lemarchand, op. cit., p.206.

9   Lemarchand, op. cit. pp.222-5.

10   A broadcast of 10 February 1964 of the Vatican Radio expressed the resulting mass killings as "the most terrible and systematic genocide since the genocide of the Jews by the Nazi".

11   José Kagabo, op.cit.

12   Lemarchand, op. cit., pp. 223-4.

13   Interview with David Munyurangabo, op. cit.

14   Discussion with Pierre Karemera, a Rwandan intellectual living in Europe.

15   Ambassador Zenon Mutimura was amongst the 1000 recruits.

16   The judge, Matayo Ngirumbatse, would later become the Secretary General of the MRND up to the early 1990s.

17   Munyurangabo became the Secretary of Security and Mobilisation for "Region D", i.e., Burundi, during the RPF struggle. He would later be appointed a commissioner in the Rwanda Demobilization and Re-integration Commission (RDRC).

18   One of the teachers was Augustine Bapfakurera of Kajaho Primary School, the father of Major Jackson Gatete 2I/C CO in the 9th Battalion.

19   Colin M. Waugh, *Paul Kagame and Rwanda: Power, Genocide and the Rwandan Patriotic Front,* McFarland & Company, Inc., 2004; W. Cyrus Reed, "Exile, Reform and the Rise of the Rwanda Patriotic Front," *Journal of Modern African Studies, 1996.* (Amin was persuaded to act after a failed guerrilla incursion by a young Yoweri Museveni in his early days as a revolutionary, of which it was feared the Rwandans in exile might take sympathy of the rebel, a Hima, and end up becoming a problem in Uganda.)

20   Conversation with the Rwanda Army Chief of Staff, Lt Gen Charles Kayonga who witnessed the event as a young person.

21   Charles Nkurayija died a Provision Junior Officer (PJOII) at Gahinga after the attack of Ruhengeri and Emmanuel Nkurunziza an RPA Captain in Bravo Mobile Combined Force on Mt. Jari in April 1994.

10

Habyarimana and the post-colonial Military

The *inyenzi* may have lost the battle to go home due to the movement's disorganization and factionalism, but the loss was also at the hands of the *Garde Nationale*. The government forces were more organized, borrowing from the French Revolutionary Doctrine, and were far better armed.

The *Garde Nationale,* however, was the epitome of the divisionism that had befallen Rwanda. Sectarianism was not only practised to the highest degree, but, playing the Hutu against the Tutsi, was put to effective use against the *inyenzi.*

To begin with, with the strong Belgian influence, the Garde Nationale was no more Rwandan than when it was the Congolese *Force Publique.* By being exclusive and comprising mainly of the Hutu, the Rwandan military became as segregative as the *Force Publique* had been by not including Rwandans.

In all practical terms, as Logiest had put it, the military had become "nearly 100 percent Hutu." This continued to be ensured through the pignet system and by ministerial decree.[1] As the military writer, Huntington[2], has observed, the military owes its responsibility to its client, the society, and therefore cannot afford to be segregative.

By being sectarian the Rwanda military ceased to be professional. Also, much as it was not nationally Rwandan but a Hutu military, its training, mission and orientation continued

156

to be colonial through *Ecole des Sous-Officiers (ESO)* and *Ecole Supéreure Militaire (ESM)*.

In the years after independence as inyenzi agitation was beginning to stir up, the Belgian officers continued to serve in the military, both in command and training. At the core of it all during the period of transition from the Belgians to the Rwandans was Col Logiest who, in 1960 as the *Special Resident*, had not only seen through the 1959 revolution, but also continued to influence the training of the young Rwandan army. This he continued to oversee, first as Belgian Special *Résident Civil* at independence, then as the first Belgian Ambassador to independent Rwanda, and as mentor of Grégoire Kayibanda[3], the first president of the Republic.

Meanwhile, Lieutenant-Colonel François Vanderstraeten had become the overall Commander of the new army, the *Garde Nationale,* in September of 1962, two months after independence. The Belgian influence on the Rwandan military was designed to continue for a long time. Logiest writes:

> The *Garde Nationale* remained perfectly disciplined vis-à-vis their European commanders and Lt Col Vanderstraeten remained in full command for one year after independence. We had, in fact, adopted the only effective way of ensuring continuity of appropriate command in the units.[4]

By "appropriate", Logiest meant the Belgian training of the handful of Rwandans. But he also meant adoption of the French Revolutionary Doctrine that, as earlier observed, was most effectively used by the Garde Nationale as a counter-measure on the Tutsi to repulse and deter *inyenzi* activity in Rwanda. This would hence define how the *Garde Nationale* related to the population.

In 1963, Lieutenant Juvénal Habyarimana took over command of the *Garde Nationale* from Lieutenant-Colonel Vanderstraeten. It was therefore under the command of Habyarimana that the *inyenzi* would see their rout in the December 1963 invasion that would mark the beginning of the end of the guerrilla movement.

Meanwhile, with the Habyarimana assent to the command of the military, the Hutu socio-political landscape was about to change, even as the *inyenzi* struggle was being overcome. While there may have been Hutu unity under the government of Kayibanda, there now began to appear a crack between the military and the political administration, both of whose leaders came from different regions of Rwanda. How this would play out was to define the country for the next three decades up to the 1994 genocide.

Habyarimana was a northerner from Bushiru, Gisenyi, which was far removed from the south in terms of temperament and history. It was due to their temperament that, at the urging of the now powerful Ambassador Logiest in the face of the rising *inyenzi* agitation, more Hutu northerners began to be recruited into the army for their reputed fearlessness and pugnacity.

Historically, the northerners[5] were associated with violence and "brutality", which could be traced to the death of Father Loupias at the hands of the famous warrior, Rukara rwa Bishingwe.[6] The irony is that Rukara was a national hero for his military exploits, and for daring to kill an adventurous and meddlesome priest. Yet this act of killing the white man would be negatively ascribed to the northerners in general by the colonial authorities as a trait of a reckless and violent people.[7]

This was given credence by their reputation as a stubborn and rebellious[8] lot against external authority, with the many uprisings such as the one led by Basebya and Ndungutse. The northern Hutus were also larger and hardier, adding on to their perceived violent temperament, which persuaded Logiest that they were better suited for the repressive military he was already moulding for Rwanda.

Earlier on, during the 1959 Hutu Revolution, the north had been "cleansed"[9] of the Tutsi constructs — most of whom had forcefully been translocated to Bugesera and Kibungo to create a "Hutuland". Thus recruits from the north perhaps also fitted in Logiest's plan of perpetuating a pure, "100 percent" Hutu military.

With this blatant favouritism of the northerners being practised in the army and not being a secret to anyone, the Hutu of the south (Nduga) decided to do whatever it would take to maintain political power in the country. The Abakiga (northerners), on their part, took it upon themselves to dominate the military under the stewardship of Habyarimana.

There was a further complication, as, administratively, the Hutu of Gitarama held sway in Kayibanda's government sidelining other southerners. For instance, at one time in Kayibanda's cabinet of sixteen government ministers, twelve were said to be from Gitarama Prefecture with eight of these being from the president's home area, Commune Nyamabuye.[10] It was, however, the larger regional division between the northerners and the southerners that would lead to an antagonistic bipolarity amongst the Hutu nationally, with the Gitarama group dominating the politics and therefore the power.

By 1967, there were hints of serious dissent from the military against the political establishment when, in a speech in March of that year, Kayibanda spoke of "the subversive propaganda of those who wish to forment military coups".[11]

Apparently, the military was disaffected by the political leadership for the slow rate of promotions for the army personnel, as opposed to the police. It is arguable that with the military so dominated by the Bakiga, the politicians favoured the police as they saw them as the best option to hold the army at bay in case the army's disaffection militarily turned against them. Lemarchand also observes:

> The existence of a separate police force — the gendarmerie [Police Nationale] — acts as a formidable counterweight to the army. Numbering approximately, 1,200 men and a dozen officers [against the military's approximately 2,500 men, commanded

by a group of some 30 officers, all trained in Belgium], the gendarmerie is looked upon with considerable suspicion by the army, partly because the gendarmerie has been in existence longer, and hence underwent a more rapid Africanisation of its cadres than the army. The promotions that have taken place within the gendarmerie seem somewhat unwarranted to those in the army who are still awaiting theirs, as they feel that the police is on the whole less competent and less disciplined than the army.[12]

In the end, it was not so much the military against the police, but the regional polarity that would swell and animate the power struggle that would lead to the 1973 military coup d'état.

Part of the factors of the power struggle was Kayibanda's naïve conviction that the "Hutu" military naturally owed him allegiance and loyalty as a "Hutu" president. He ensured the loyalty of the military by continuously harping on the Tutsi as the enemy, as evinced by the *inyenzi* incursions.

He was also arrogant enough to believe that the soldiers had no place in politics and government. This led to the Bakiga feeling marginalized and put down as only being as good as canon fodder for the army at the hands of the politicians. As put at one time by Jean Baptiste Musirikare, a Southern Deputy, during a budget debate in parliament on whether to increase military salaries, "there is no point in keeping a well fed dog, because it would be ineffective in its guard duties."[13]

With such arrogance of the Banyanduga politicians and their obvious despising of the Bakiga military, Habyarimana and his comrades in the army leadership started to plot on how to overthrow the Kayibanda government. From the moment of the first hints of military dissent in 1967 it was just a matter of time before the coup.

On 5 July 1973, Habyarimana, leading a coterie of army officers, took over the country in a bloodless coup. Kayibanda was hauled off to internal exile in a house arrest in Rwerere where he was ignominiously starved to death in December 1976.

Meanwhile, Habyarimana and his military junta had come to call themselves *les Amis du cinq juillet* – Friends of Fifth of July, the date of the coup, which they also made a public holiday. The commemoration of the coup with all the military pomp came to overshadow Independence Day, which ought to have been celebrated a few days earlier, on 1 July 1962.

The 1973 takeover of government by Juvénal Habyarimana marked a major milestone in the evolution of the Rwandan military. He began by dissolving the Police Nationale (PN) and co-opted its members in the Garde Nationale as military personnel. With this combination the new institution became the Armée Rwandaise (Rwandese Army). The reason for dissolving the Police Nationale was to centralize the command and exercise a tight grip on the entire security apparatus.

However, in January 1974 Habyarimana introduced the French system of civil policing by creating the Gendarmerie Nationale to accommodate the aggressive French foreign policy under Valéry Giscard d' Estaing.[14] From then on the two forces, Armée Rwandaise and Gendarmerie Nationale, were referred to as Forces Armées Rwandaises (FAR), but retained the same command structure under Habyarimana as the President, Minister of Defence and Chief of General Staff.

The Gendarmerie Nationale, however, did not become fully operational until 1976 when the Franco-Rwanda military cooperation matured with increased French technical and material support in a 1975 Military Cooperation Agreement.[15] The Agreement included the French *Coopérants* (technical personnel) "serving in their French uniform" within the Rwandan army, a requirement that, as we shall shortly see, would be modified years later in 1992 to have the French in Rwandese uniforms.

In the years that followed the 1975 Agreement, so consumed was Habyarimana with the new cooperation that the French doctrine of population control that had so effectively worked in the 1960s against the inyenzi was constitutionalized making Rwanda a "state-garrison". Lugan notes:

> In 1978, a new Constitution affirms the presidential orientation of the regime. The country was completely held by a pyramid of commands controlling the population. Rwanda was divided into ten prefectures literally controlled by ten prefects named by the president, and into 145 communes led by many burgomasters also named by the head of State. These 145 communes were further divided into sectors of 5000 inhabitants, the latter subdivided in five cells of 1000 people, these last in groups even more restricted, which allowed a total control of the population. The councilors of cells were elected and had as their principal task to transmit the instructions of the burgomasters."[16]

Lugan observes that, if one includes this set of strictly controlled social hierarchy to that of the Army, the political party, as well as the hierachical order of the Catholic Church, which was integrated into the ruling party, *Mouvement Révolutionnaire National pour le Développement* (MRND) which came into being in 1975, the country might well have been a state-garrison or military camp.

By the early 1980s, Habyarimana had so entrenched himself in power that his word had literally become law.[17] The only complication, however, was that his family and clan members, led by his wife, Agathe Kanziga, had began to equate their power over him with his rule. Habyarimana seemed to suffer a kind of inferiority complex in front of his wife and her clan. Agathe was of an old Hutu aristocratic family,[18] which intimidated Habyarimana's more humbler and indeterminate roots,[19] thus the influence she asserted on him.

By this time, there began to appear breakdown in the northern power alliance, especially that from Gisenyi Prefecture. There began emerging concerns that military officers from Bugoyi area were being less favoured than those from Habyarimana's home area of Bushiru.

This perception of marginalization would lead to the attempted coup of 1981 by his Chief of Intelligence, Major Théoneste Lizinde and one Commandant Stanislas Biseruka, both of whom were from Bugoyi.[20] The coup was a wake up call not just for Habyarimana, but for the French as well, who immediately saw the threat in the recurrence of a similar happening would pose to their interests in the region.

Consequently, by 1983, a modification to the 1975 Franco-Rwanda Agreement was in place. The Agreement now allowed the French to be "associated with the preparation or execution of military operations and the maintenance of law and order".[21] The same revision allowed the French Cooperants now to wear the Rwandan uniform, as opposed to the earlier provision for French uniforms. This change of uniforms was to mask the now more direct French involvement in the Rwandan military machinery.

To compound the internal threat to the regime that the French were also trying to hedge against, further cracks appeared within the Rwandan military when Habyarimana wanted to appoint Colonel Stanislas Mayuya minister of defense, leading to the Colonel's assassination in 1988 on the flimsy excuse of an attempted military coup.

However, the Franco-Rwanda arrangement would prevail throughout the 1980s until 1992, two years after Rwanda Patriotic Front and Army first attacked in October 1990. To contain the attacks, a further modification was added to the 1975 Franco-Rwanda Agreement that now, to all intents and purposes, integrated the French military to the mission of the Rwandese armed forces.[22]

1992 was a crucial year for the Franco-Rwanda military cooperation, as it is the year in which the RPF/A proved that they were no pushovers and were a force to reckon with, with their determined forays into Rwanda to dislodge the government. This would lead to the June 1992 Ceasefire Agreement and the beginning of the Arusha Peace Negotiations.[23]

For the RPF/A not to be a pushover required that it had to be prepared and motivated for the struggle it had to undertake to right the wrongs and shortcomings that had ensured different generations of exiles and refugees. Throughout the generations, beginning with the first refugees in 1959, they remained determined to return home by whatever means necessary. After the *inyenzi,* it is to the culmination of this struggle that we shall now turn.

Notes

1   Conversation with Colonel Epimaque Ruhashya, the only Tutsi Colonel in the Hutu-nised military between 1960 and 1992, who gives the example of how one Joachim Muramutsa, a Hutu officer of Second Promotion of 1964, had a Tutsi fiancé, and was barred from proceeding for further studies in Belgium by the Minister of Defense, Calliope Murindahabi. Hutu in the army were barred from marrying Tutsi wives by Ministerial Decree. A similar story, it is said, happened to Juvénal Habyarimana whose first fiancé was a *mututsikazi,* but after learning that she is not 'allowed' to marry a military officer, arranged instead the marriage with Agatha Kanziga her secondary schoolmate, and contented herself of becoming just a chaperon. Also see Linda Melvern, op. cit. p.25.

2   Samuel P. Huntington, *The Soldier and the State: The Theory and Politics of Civil Military Relations,* University of Harvard Press, Cambridge, 12th reprint, 1995,p.15.

3   Kayibanda affirms this by autographing his own picture as a present to Logiest, as reproduced in *Mission au Rwanda* (p.120).

4   G. Logiest, op. cit., p.166.

5   Lemarchand (1970: 58) describes them as "Hardier and sturdier than most ordinary Hutu, the Kiga people of northern Rwanda have always been looked upon by their neighbours as a rebellious lot, fiercely, individualistic and contemptuous of established authority".

6   See Chapter 5.

7   The notorious Ruhengeri Prison (built by colonialists) is located at the site where Rukara was hanged.

8   According to Lemarchand northerners are "rebellious" as may also be demonstrated by the Nyabingi sect, with the "climate of messianic unrest experienced by the northern populations made them all the more receptive of subsequent forms of protest against established authority.' See Lemarchand (1970: 100-102).

9   Lemarchand (1970: 173) observes that "By the end of 1960, no less than 5,043 refugees out of a total of 6,732 came from the territoire of Ruhengeri".

10 *Ingingo z'ingenzi mu mateka y'u Rwanda: Imyaka Cumi y'Isabukuru y'Ubwigenge, 1972.*

11 Lemarchand, p.279-83 (writing in that year, Lemarchand notes that "Much of the present uneasiness stems from a conflict of attitude between the army officers and certain politicians whose outlook and policies they find incompatible with their own modernizing aspirations and professional expectations. But it also reflects problems of a more specific order, some having to do with circumstances under which the army came into being, its ethnic composition, and, above all, its seemingly very impressive record as an instrument of national security against [inyenzi] invasions").

12 Ibid.

13 Conversation with a 73 year-old Laurent Mugesera from the Southern Province, July 2003. (The said deputy reportedly committed suicide right after the 1973 coup to evade the vengeance of Bakiga putschists).

14 Franco-Rwanda relations go as far back as October 1962 when the first Agreement of Economic, Cultural and Technical Cooperation was signed. It was under this agreement that Radio France International started airing in Rwanda. In May 1964 the French Embassy was opened and in 1969 a French Mission for aid was created in Kigali. Beginning 1972 the Rwandan military officers started gaining specialised military training in France.

15 The military cooperation agreement with the Rwandan gendarmerie was signed on 18 July 1975 by President Valéry Giscard d' Estaing and General-president Habyarimana. Article One of the Agreement provides that, "The Government of Republic of France avails to the Government of the Republic of Rwanda the French Military personnel needed for the organization and training of the Rwandese Gendarmerie". Article

Two stipulates that "The French military personnel availed to the Government of the Republic of Rwanda [...] are under the authority of the most senior French officer attached to Rwanda, but who reports to the French Ambassador in Rwanda." Article Three specifies that the French military personnel "cannot in any case be associated with the preparation or execution of military operations, the maintenance or restoration of order and legality" and will serve in French uniform. NB: The above agreement would be modified in 1983 and 1992 paving the way for more direct French involvement in the preparation and execution of the 1994 genocide. The Agreement lasted right up until the United Nations arms embargo against the country in 1993. Official French military support for the Kigali regime had reached a level of over 50 million francs (around $8m) per annum by the time.

16   B. Lugan, *François Mitterrand, the French Army and Rwanda.* Editions of the Rock, 2005, p. 38.

17   Colin M. Waugh, *Paul Kagame and Rwanda: Power, Genocide and the Rwandan Patriotic Front* (McFarland & Company, Inc., Publishers, London, 2004), p.185 ("For the most part, Rwanda had no experience of government by constitution, however. [Habyarimana's] administration had largely exercised power in arbitrary fashion, with little reference to any underlying principles of law, whether civil, criminal or constitutional. Under Juvenal Habyarimana, things were done mostly according to the will of the president and so the concept of constitutional democracy which was above and beyond the modification of the executive branch was largely a new one for the Rwandan population.")

18   Agathe Kanziga was from a ruling family in Bushiru (in current Nyabihu District) from the Abagesera clan.

19   Habyarimana's father, M. Ntibazirikana, was a catechist at Rambura Parish in Gisenyi and was originally from Kabale in Uganda. He was brought to Rwaza Parish in Ruhengeri as a houseboy for the White Fathers.

20   Andrew Wallis, *Silent Accomplice, 2006,* p.18.

21   Revision of the Franco-Rwanda Agreement of 12 April 1983 (Alluding to this revision in 1995 in the BBC programme, Panorama, the French mercenary, Paul Barril, commenting on the Francafrique's military inadequacy, including Rwanda's FAR, observes, "When you take a peasant, you take a pupil. You can put him in a military uniform, but that doesn't make him a

soldier. You understand what I am saying? These guys have got absolutely no training, no motivation. No special commandoes, no special action guys, they are a balloon full of wind.")

22   Revision of the Franco-Rwanda Agreement of 26 August 1992, replacing Articles Two and Six of the 1975 Franco-Rwanda Agreement. Also see Andrew Wallis, *Silent Accomplice,* for an indepth look at French involvement in Rwanda.

23   Linda Melvern, *A People Betrayed: The role of the West in Rwanda's Genocide,* Zed Books, 2000.

11

Inkotanyi:
The Genesis and Struggle of the Rwanda Patriotic Front

A story is told of a father and son – the father, a former *inyenzi* and the son, *Inkotanyi* or RPF soldier. The son asks the father, "What happened to you to give up the struggle so soon, buckling to defeat so easily? Isn't that cowardly and a sign of serious weakness unbecoming of *imfura?*" (gentleman of Rwanda).

The father does not reply immediately, but ponders the humiliating affront by the son. "No," he replies after some thought. "We were not defeated, and we certainly did not give up the struggle. Our putting down arms was a temporary setback—a loss of the battle, not the war. What we did was regroup and change tactics: We went back to your mothers, as much part of the struggle as we ever could have been, and made you. And now here you are, the victorious *Inkotanyi*. How wrong could we have been?"[1]

The anecdote is popularly told amongst Rwandans[2] to explain the delay in the Rwandan liberation from sectarianism. However, recalling the story of the likes of Biyahiga "passing the torch" to his two sons who would later join the RPF, perhaps the anecdote may not be so far off the mark. And, given the father's reasons in the above story, there are those who would prefer to think of the defeat of the *inyenzi* as a kind of Rwandan version of the Fabian tactic, which describes a method of wearing out an opponent by delay and evasion rather than confrontation as was accomplished by the Roman General Fabius.[3]

While Fabius adopted a scotched-earth policy destroying enemy resources, which led to the Roman triumph, it does not seem unreasonable to the proponents of the tactic to see a corollary with the Rwandan struggle. If the struggle was to be won, it was going to be one of long-term battles, avoiding foolish defeats, and, other than destroying enemy resources, let the enemy morally destroy himself with his colonial sectarian "ideals", which would eventually bring about his downfall. If this was the realization, all that remained was using time and patience to the struggle's advantage.

It probably could have worked that way, but the struggle was all set in "the long-term battles" and the forms they would take towards the creation of the Rwanda Patriotic Front and Army, the torch-bearer not only of the inyenzi, but also of the Rwandan ideal of an undivided people.

The shape the struggle began to take may be seen with what befell Biyahiga with the coming to power of Idi Amin in 1971, and the arranging of the return to Uganda of the exiled King Kigeri V from Nairobi. It may appear that this gesture by Amin to accommodate the monarch made life easier for the Rwandan refugees in Uganda, but it was never to be. As refugees they were harassed by the locals, always being reminded of their outsider status, while Rwandans such as Biyahiga became scapegoats after Obote attempted an armed return from Tanzania in 1972.

Thus for the sons and daughters of the Biyahigas it would not be a life of ease, but one of seeking the way home. Not just in the refugee camps, in the towns or in the schools the refugee sons and daughters attended they could not be afforded a sense of identity and self-worth in the persecution they endured as outsiders. Writing about President Paul Kagame, Waugh observes that,

[t]he psychological impact on many of the young students was heavy, as the enforced denial of identity under threat of persecution only compounded their feelings of vulnerability and a rootless existence. Even those who joined the army or the civil service after school were never granted Ugandan passports. It was this continuing disenfranchisement, …, that contributed so strongly to the lingering desire of many to make a stable return to Rwanda.

[L]ife in Uganda was hard and nothing was ever permanent for the refugees, thereby pushing them to want to return. On the other hand, and because of their chronically temporary existence, the inaccessible homeland became idealized in the minds of many, creating a pull factor attracting them towards a land which most of them had never even known.[4]

These homeward stirrings gnawed at many throughout the 70s and are best illustrated by President Kagame when, during a newspaper interview, he spoke of the "Rwanda [that] was always at the back of our mind"[5] at a time when no refugee could dare enter the country for the horrors that awaited one if caught.

He recalls his visits to the country in 1978 and '79: "I was involved in a number of things, mostly I managed to sneak into Rwanda, spent some time with relatives in Butare. I was looking around and learning a few things. I was a student. I looked young, so no one suspected me. I went to Zaïre, travelled through Goma, Rutshuro so that I had more or less a picture of the situation around."[6]

It was around this time that he joined Yoweri Museveni's Front for National Salvation (FRONASA), along with a few other of his Rwandan compatriots, including Fred Rwigema. FRONASA, formed in 1971, would see the overthrow of Idi Amin, supporting the Tanzanian military force that invaded Uganda in 1979 and the subsequent reinstatement of Obote back to power after the contentious December 1980 elections.[7] It is during this experience that the seeds of how Rwanda would later be won back were first sown. If the Ugandans could, why not Rwandans? Rwandans constituted Africa's largest refugee problem at the time,[8] and the second oldest after the Southern Sudanese.

Meanwhile, the informal Rwandese Refugee Welfare Foundation (RRWF) was established in 1979 to better consolidate and address the needs and concerns of the exiled community in Uganda. As the organization became formalized into the Rwandese Alliance for National Unity (RANU) later that year, Rwandan refugees were able for the first time to have, outside the irrelevant and emasculated monarchy of Kigeri V, a sense of direction and a vehicle to guide their wills. Indeed, RANU proved the binding force of nationalism in the difficult challenges of disenfranchisement that immediately lay ahead with the Amin ouster. As Waugh explains it,

> [f]ollowing Amin's expulsion, an interim government was formed in which Yoweri Museveni became Minister of Defense, giving him a foothold on the ladder of power in Ugandan national politics for the first time. However, Obote had also returned to power in what was widely recognized as a sham ballot. One of the maneuvers of Obote's UPC during the run-up to the elections had been its campaign to ban all Banyarwanda from voting. Ultimately, large groups of ethnic Rwandans, including many who had been in Uganda since before independence and who had voted in 1961 and subsequent ballots, were prevented from participating in the December poll. In reaction to the rigged vote, many of Obote's defeated opponents in the election, most notably Yoweri Museveni, soon began to prepare for a continuation of the struggle by arms.
>
> Thus by early 1981, Museveni had gone into the bush to fight against Obote's UPC regime and the anti-Kampala campaigns of his National Resistance Army (NRA) was launched. His first raid against the government took place at Kabamba [sic] in Luwero District on February 6, 1981, and among his small band of dissidents numbered Paul Kagame and another Rwandan exile, Fred Rwigema, Kagame's only compatriot in Museveni's attacking force on that day. [...] The northern Ugandans who made up the core of Obote's power base lumped all his

enemies together, for propaganda purposes, referring to them as 'nyarwanda, a derogatory term with racist overtones which served as a combined insult for Banyarwanda, whether old or new, as well as Banyankole or Bairu, and which could include Ugandan citizens in their eyes just as easily as true Rwandan refugees.[9]

It was during the second Obote regime that the harassment[10] of Rwandans reached a new height, leading to the now infamous expulsions of the hapless exiles and Ugandans of Rwandan descent.[11] As famously put by Obote's Minister of Security, Chris Rwakasisi, emphasizing how Rwandans, even those born in Uganda could never claim to be Ugandans, "If a dog gives birth in a cowshed, it does not turn into a cow!"[12]

All tainted with the Rwandan blood had to go. With the expulsion, and nowhere to go, a new sense of nationalism was born by not only the Rwandan refugees, but also Ugandans of Rwandan descent as they fled to Kenya and Tanzania and elsewhere in the world. The Rwandan government on its part would hear nothing of accommodating the exiles. "Habyarimana's official stance regarding the accommodation of returnees was that the country was 'full up' — that there was simply not enough land to support the existing population, let alone to sustain tens of thousands of 'new' arrivals".[13]

Meanwhile, with the war intensifying in the Luwero Triangle, and the government response in harassing the communities there, the reaction was a banding together of the victimized Rwandan settlers and Ugandan neighbours to join the National Resistance Army. It is thus that "the Obote regime, baptized the 'Museveni soldiers' as 'Banyarwanda'. The more the repression of the Banyarwanda was stepped up, the more Banyarwanda joined Museveni and the NRA in the bush. The regime's claim was fast turning into a reality."[14]

Come 1985, however, Museveni's campaign had begun to yield some results and peace was being brokered by President Daniel Arap Moi in Nairobi between Museveni and General Tito

Okelo. During one of the meetings, asked about "this Rwandan business", Museveni wondered aloud, "What is wrong with being a Rwandese?" By this he implied that these were a people vilified for no good reason and had every right to fight for their dignity having grown up in Uganda.[15]

By the end of the Museveni campaign in 1986 that saw the final overthrow of Obote, nearly a quarter (3,000) of the NRA's force of 14,000 was Rwandan.[16] It is this group of battle hardened Rwandans that was soon poised to continue the *inyenzi* struggle of their fathers where it had stopped.

Those who did not join Museveni in the bush sought their fortunes in the diaspora, and with them went RANU. Though it could not work openly in the early years of the 1980s during the Rwandans' second stint in exile, RANU managed to operate clandestinely in Nairobi, while establishing a network of autonomous cells throughout the diaspora through various sorts of associations. In Nairobi, RANU kept aflame through the Intore Society[17] (this included Nyampinga association, a female offshoot) that was registered as a welfare group with the Government of Kenya.

> With membership all over the diaspora, including North America, Europe and several African states outside the Great Lakes Region, a regional structure was established, with an annual RANU Congress [beginning August, 1988] including regional chairmen, representatives of interest groups and the professions, as well as a political bureau with a 26-person executive committee [composed of 11 Tutsi and 15 Hutu] and later, a military high command.[18]

By the end of the NRA struggle in 1986, RANU had grown in moral might among the Rwandans and set about to consolidate its reach through mass mobilization in the diaspora to be inclusive of every shade of Rwandan. It was 1987, however, that would mark the major turning point when, during the Congress of that year, RANU "adopted a new name to reflect its nascent militancy and mobilization: from that time onwards the movement became the Rwandan Patriotic Front (RPF)"[19] and hence came to also be known as *"Inkotanyi"*, naming itself after the tirelessly conquering 19th Century monarch, King Kigeri IV Rwabugiri, whose nickname or "sword-name" was *"Inkotanyi-cyane* (the tireless combatant or indefatigable warrior)".

This shift from a merely socio-political organization, RANU, to a polico-military organization, the Rwanda Patriotic Front and Army (RPF/A), was also against the "backdrop of Habyarimana's declaration in 1986 that there could be no further discussion of a right of return for Rwandan refugees".[20] In other words, the RPF/A struggle would be a liberation struggle to fight for their right to go back home.

In 1987 also, the organization's headquarters moved from Nairobi to Kampala, where the RPF commenced on planning its future activities in earnest. The same year, Fred Rwigema was elected RPF president.

With the experience gained during the NRA war, realizing the "Rwanda at the back of our mind" no longer seemed a dream but a reality that could be made true. There, however, was no illusion that it would be a difficult armed struggle. What was important was the realization of the resources that could immediately be tapped for the difficult endeavour. Chief among these resources were the exiled Rwandans themselves and a millennium-worth of cultural heritage that daily lived in them. It is these that would prove RPF's strength.

By 1988, with the settling of the RPF in Kampala, the process was already in motion. There was need to mobilize the available resources, and culture was the ready vehicle for this purpose. Not only would it provide the way, but the basis for the struggle borrowing from the heroic history of Rwanda's past. This was drawing from a long-standing tradition of "narrativization"[21] through such as poetry *(ibisigo)* and the art of oratorical rhetoric *(ibyivugo)*.

Narrativization was used by the RPF to acquire its own legitimacy and vision. RPF outlined Rwandan history in a bid to cast it in what it considered a realistic perspective. The narrativization of the past glory of Rwanda was passed around in order to create a sense of belonging to a community and history that transcended the experience of conflict.[22]

It is thus that, for instance, the mobilization entailed rallying Rwandans in the diaspora through dances and other cultural activities. For example, *Indahemuka,* a cultural troop formed by the RPF in 1987, deriving its name from one of Cyilima II Rujugira's military formation, *Abadahemuka* in the 18th Century, played an important role in galvanizing Rwandans in the diaspora to finance the war effort.

Another cultural troupe, serving a similar purpose was the *Imitali* based in Brussels, Belgium. It derives its name from the military formation of the same name during the reign of Mibambwe II Gisanura also in the 18th Century.

Mobilization also included artists and musicians in the diaspora, such as Ms Cécile Kayirebwa based in Brussels. Her popular song, *Inganzo y'umunezero,*[23] which served as a signature tune for RPF Radio *Muhabura,*[24] was something akin to a national anthem in the RPF military training schools. The song captured the essence of Rwanda as though in a painting, detailing the landscape, the people, the heroes, the culture and values and rooting them in Rwanda. It inspired a deep sense of patriotism and longing for the homeland.

The struggle was also be informed by the traditional institutions and practices in the pre-colonial period that sustained the state of Rwanda. The practice of *Abacengeli,* for instance, which demanded spilling blood in self-sacrifice for the country, expressed the highest level of patriotism that was demanded of every Rwandan, including the king.

Mamdani speaks of meeting a senior RPF commander in Kigali in 1995. This is what the commander put to him: "You stake your life and at the end of the day you recognise that no amount of contribution can make you what you are not. You can't buy it, not even with your blood."[25]

What the RPF commander implied was that it was only Rwanda that was worth his blood, reflecting the Kinyarwanda saying embedded in the institution of *Ubucengeli* that goes, *wima igihugu amarazo, imbwa sikayanywera ubusa* (if you deny the homeland your blood, the dogs will take it for free).

To many Rwandans, Major General Fred Gisa Rwigema, is *umucengeli*. As the Commander-in-Chief of the Rwanda Patriotic Army (RPA), he not only initiated the struggle but died on the frontline on the second day of the invasion of Rwanda from Uganda in October 1990. He is recognized as a national hero for his vision and leadership, and the act of selflessly putting his life at risk for his country leading from the front. In this sense he is likened to the *abacengeli* of old and his remains are interred at Heroes Acre in Remera ya Kigali ville, in apt resonance with the other sites named Remera[26] in Rwandan history.

The RPA soldiers, initially those Rwigema formerly led in the NRA, were no less invested with their heritage. On their young shoulders they carried an entire history of a military tradition that was handed down from father to son through the generations and *imfura's* (gentleman of Rwanda) incumbency to defending it or win it back as happened during the reign of King Ruganzu II Ndoli in the 16th Century.

It may serve to recall the example of Biyahiga's family, beginning with King Rujugira's military formation, *Abalima*, that was later combined with *Intaganzwa*, to which we trace Biyahiga's uncle down to the sons who were now invested with the charge of getting back their Rwanda. What drove them was not just the xenophobic Ugandans, but also the stories of heroism that had made Rwanda the only place in the region to remain untouched by slavery.

Given the commitment and determination which patriotism demands, even extending beyond the battlefield, deserting from the frontline during the RPF struggle was an abhorable crime. Traditionally, a soldier who was discovered to be a deserter would not be accepted back into society. Thus, an example is given of a deserter who escaped from the frontline in 1991 and returned to Southern Africa to join his family. He was shocked when his Rwandan wife disowned him and collaborated with her local RPF cell to return him to the front.[27]

Such was the binding spirit of the RPF struggle, that it was inclusive of every shade of Rwandan right from the start. Most of the RPA recruits were volunteers, and anybody who chose to join was welcomed regardless of his or her background. It was, after all, a battle for dignity and sovereignty — a Rwandan fight than a sectarian, or, as some writers and international commentators erroneously continue to refer to it, an ethnic civil war.

At the beginning of the struggle, some officers and men did not know a word of Kinyarwanda, while others had Ugandan names. This is typified by the late Lieutenant-Colonel Adam Wasswa, who grew up a Ugandan, given his typical Kiganda name, in the Luwero Triangle, but who rose through the ranks in the NRA struggle to become a brigade commander. When the Rwandan struggle started in 1990, Lt. Col. Wasswa joined the RPA to the surprise of his colleagues in the NRA who never suspected that he was Rwandan. In his admission during the RPA struggle, he was aware of his very roots in Rwanda.[28]

Other than the Rwandans who joined from the NRA, during the period 1990 to early 1992, most of the RPA recruits were drawn from the Rwandans in the diaspora in Uganda, Burundi, Tanzania and the Congo. However, a turn of events to recruit more Rwandans came with the 1991 RPA attack on Ruhengeri Prison, releasing Habyarimana's political prisoners who included Major Lizinde, Commander Biseruka, Captain Muvunanyambo, among others. These former prisoners joined the RPF and were instrumental in persuading Hutu recruits inside Rwanda to join the RPA cause.

However, it was only after June 1992 that the RPA started getting many recruits from inside Rwanda. This was during the ceasefire with the Rwanda Government Forces (FAR) as the Arusha Peace Negotiations gained momentum. During the negotiations it was possible to recruit inside Rwanda taking advantage of the window of opportunity for RPA activity in the calm of the temporary truce that ensued.

In the period between 1992 and 1994 an overwhelming number of recruits from inside Rwanda further joined the RPF, as they could move a little more freely to the RPA zones within Rwanda. It was these recruits who would end up forming the majority in the RPA in the run-up to the 1994 genocide.

Notes

1   A discussion with Pierre Karemera, op.cit.
2   Aloys Ngurumbe, who was amongst the ten China trainees, used to say that they bequeathed the struggle to their children. Being a well known inyenzi, he was arrested in Goma (DRC) by the Habyarimana Security apparatus and jailed in 1975 in Central Prison ("1930") in Kigali and released in 1992 as part of exchange of POWs following the Arusha Peace Negotiations. His son, Lt Victor Ndahiro Nzigiye, would die in the struggle during the attack of Rwempasha in January 1991.
3   The Punic wars (264 B.C. to 146 B.C.) between the Romans and the Carthagians where Roman General Quintus Fabius Maximus won the war by evasion and destroying vital enemy resources and came to be known as "the Cunctator" or "the delayer." Thus the term "Fabian tactics." Fabius avoided direct confrontation with Hannibal and thus avoided allowing himself and his army to be 'the delicate feasting of dogs, and all birds.' - Ernle Bradford, Hannibal. (New York: McGraw-Hill Company, 1981), p. 208.
4   Colin M. Waugh, op.cit. p. 14.
5   Interview with Charles Onyango-Obbo, *The Monitor*, Kampala, 19 December 1997.
6   Ibid.
7   Yoweri Kaguta Museveni, *Sowing the Mustard Seed: The Struggle for Freedom and Democracy in Uganda*, Macmillan, 1997.
8   Linda Melvern, op. cit., p.25.
9   Colin M. Waugh, op.cit. pp. 20-22.
10   Waugh points to the Uganda Times, the official government newspaper, in its issue of January 11, 1982, that set out the

government stance against the Rwandans: "Most atrocities during Amin's era were committed by refugees... refugees have been found to flirt with terrorists in Luwero District and are sponsible for the unrest there....If refugees, particularly those from Rwanda do not reciprocate our hospitality, Uganda may order their government to build camps for them...alternatively we shall tell them to go."

11 Mahmood Mamdani, *When Victims Become Killers,* op.cit. p.168.

12 The Banyankole would tell their Rwandese neighbour that they had no place in Uganda irrespective of their dates of arrival, derogatorily in Runyankole, *"Abizire kare bagende kare"* [first in, first out – FIFO, something akin to stock in Inventory Management].

13 Collin M. Waugh, p. 23; Also see L.Melvern, op. cit., pp.25-6.

14 Ibid.

15 Discussion with Prof José Kagabo, Rwandan historian, op. cit.

16 Mahmood Mamdani, op. cit., p.174.

17 The Society drew its name from the Intore, the name of the elite traditional Rwandan warriors. Among the prominent leaders of the Intore Association then were Charles Muhire, who would later become the Chief-of-Staff of the Rwandan Airforce (with a current rank of Lieutenent General), and Cyprian Gatete who was the treasurer of the Association and later became Assistant Commissioner of the Rwanda National Police.

18 Colin M. Waugh, op.cit. pp.36-39; see also Linda Melvern, op. cit., p.26.

19 Collin M. Waugh, op.cit.

20 P. Gourevitch, op.cit, p.214 [P. Guorevitch quotes Kagame as saying: "We had felt the beginnings of this, fighting in Uganda... Fighting there was to serve our purpose, and it was also in line with our thinking – we were fighting injustice – and it was perhaps the safest way to live in Uganda at that time as a Rwandan. But deep in our hearts and minds we knew we belonged in Rwanda, and if they didn't want to resolve the problem politically, armed struggle would be the alternative."

21 M. Katumanga PhD Thesis, Université de Pau et des Pays de l'Adour, 2002.

22 Eric Hobsbawn and Terrence Ranger (ed), *The Inversion of Tradition*, Cambridge University Press, 1993.

23 *Inganzo y'umunezero* loosely translated means "the artful celebration of the Rwandan renaissance".

24 Mount Muhabura got its name from King Kigeri II Nyamuheshera denoting "beacon" or "showing the way", thus the name for the RPF Radio. Mount Muhabura also served as the RPF/A re-organization hub during the struggle.

25 Mahmood Mamdani, *When Victims Become Killers*, op.cit. p. 174.

26 The name Remera is associated with Rwandan heroism, as exemplified by Prince Forongo and Muvunyi wa Karema. These heroes were essentially liberators from alien occupation, first, by the Abanyoro in the 15th Century, then the Abanyabungo in the 16th Century who had briefly taken Rwanda. Prince Forongo's descendandants were awarded Remera y'Abaforongo (Ngabitsinze Hill – echoing the Heroes Acre) in today's Rulindo District, while Remera ya Humure was given to the great warrior Muvunyi wa Karema).

27 Conversation with Major Jill Rutaremara, Kigali, July 2002.

28 Conversation with Lt. Col. Adam Wasswa, Muhabura Volcanic Ranges, 1991. He spoke of his roots being in Rwimishinya Secteur, Rukara, Kayonza District.

Maj. Gen. Fred Rwigema, first chairman of the RPF and commander of the Rwanda Patriotic Army (RPA)

Commander-in-Chief of the RPA Paul Kagame during the struggle in mid-1992 in the RPF liberated zone in northern Rwanda

Colonel Sam Kaka, RPA Chief of Staff, overseeing the integration of ex-FAR (Force Armée Rwandaise) combatants in February 1995

Paul Kagame being interviewed by the press about the role of the military in national integration

Frank Rusagara, left, in April 1992 with Claude Dusaidi, the then RPF Spokesperson in USA and Canada, during the first RPF Congress

RDF women soldiers

Former combatants-cum-nurses during the RPF struggle displaying their awarded Medal of Liberation (Impeta)

RDF Peacekeepers proceeding for a mission abroad

RDF top brass (left to right): Maj. Gen. Patrick Nyamvumba, Lt. Gen. Charles Muhire, Lt. Gen. Charles Kayonga and Gen. James Kabarebe

Brig. Gen. Frank Rusagara (left) and colleagues at the old Lake Kivu Marine Base of Kigeri IV Rwabugiri

The cross erected in honour of Loupias at the spot where he was killed by Manuka, Rukara's son, in Gahunga k'Abarashi

Frank Rusagara interviews the late Mzee Ladislaus Musuhuke, a former colonial chief (1925-1959) in Bukamba, Ruhengeri

12

Rediscovering *Ingabo z'u Rwanda*

Abatabazi bagira ubatemera[1] (Laying the Ground for The RDF)

The events leading up to the 1994 Rwandan tragedy, the taking of Kigali and the stopping of the genocide by the Rwanda Patriotic Front and Army (RPF/A) have been numerously recorded. In many instances, blow-by-blow accounts have been offered.[2] What is of greater concern to this inquiry is how Rwanda was able to cope with, and prosper, in the aftermath of the genocide and the place of the military in the whole equation. In this, what is definite in what would transpire is that Rwanda would have to have something substantial to draw from if it was to recover.

After the 1987 RANU Congress, an agenda was put in place that came to be known as the Eight-Point-Programme[3]. There were eight points to the newly inaugurated RPF agenda, with the first three forming the core.

The first point in the RPF/A programme was to keep "Rwandans united as one people". The second point was to "ensure peace and security" for Rwandans of every shade. This was necessary, as it would safeguard and re-enforce the importance of national unity, despite the distorted identities on which the Rwandan conflict mainly rested.

Ensuring peace and security further laid the foundation on which the Rwandan society could be propelled towards self-actualization. It is on this realization that "development", which formed the RPF's third point in its eight-point programme, was predicated.

The model of development in the Eight-Point-Programme was based on the precepts of realism in the well known paradigm of power politics. The primary concern of the realist approach is power politics, which asserts that peace, other than a temporary absence of violence, cannot exist.[4]

In this sense, the traditional realist approach to conflict management, therefore, in the aftermath of the genocide, the strategy had to involve compromise and settlement at the social and cultural level.[5] The other traditional, and complementary, approach is based on structural renewal or refurbishment, which concentrates all efforts at conflict management exclusively on economic and political reconstruction.[6]

These complementary approaches may be looked at in two ways, as may have been deemed by the RPF, in what is normally described as "hard" and "soft" power — of which the exploitation of the latter would prove RPF's strength.

"Hard power" is defined by material elements of power such as the size of a population in a given country, military equipment and machinery, the economy, territory and its resources. "Soft power", on the other hand, rests on the intangible, such as culture, language, legends and myths, fashions and customs.[7]

It is in a population's acceptance of norms, values and conceptions that it may bend to another "power's" will, or be attracted to it, other than feel coerced to the new "power's" obligations. For the population in Rwanda to perceive this was absolutely necessary for the RPF as the new power that had taken over from the genocidal regime.

Soft power, therefore, rests on a culture that illuminates and exerts an influence, while acting like a magnet to attract others. As seen in earlier chapters, this may be illustrated in the process of *ku-aanda* in which Rwanda was able to illuminate and enrich incoming communities from annexed territories through integration other than mere conquest. The integration into Rwanda's socio-cultural and economic life continued to be smooth with no regional rivalries or cultural animosities. This was what the RPF/A had to aspire to, of which symbolism had to play a central role, if we take the example of the *agaseke*.

For instance, to symbolically put it in the Rwandan context, soft power can be likened to what is encompassed in the feminine and ornamental traditional Rwandan basket — *agaseke* — which is designed for aesthetic and cultural purposes and passed on as a gift. Its value is not merely in its beauty and high artistic attributes, but in its cultural appreciation as an accomplishment of the patience and hard work expressed in the Rwandan talent.

The traditional basket highlights the creativity of the Rwandan woman as the mother of the nation. Thus, when a young lady is getting married, she is presented with *agaseke* by her mother or aunt symbolically containing "all the treasures of womanhood *(ibanga ry'ababyeyi)*". She had to treasure and not abuse the *agaseke*, as it signified the very foundation of the new family she was destined to bring forth.

Like the Russian nesting dolls, the *agaseke* would contain seven or eight *"uduseke"* receding in size, one inside the other. In the Rwandan culture the seventh child, Nyamwasa (Nyandwi) or Nyirarwasa if a girl, signifies a rise in status of the mother to equal that of men in the patriarchal traditional society. Eight *(umunani)* signifies abundance. The gift of such a set of *uduseke* was, therefore, a wish that the new mother-to-be may beget as many children as possible.

In terms of soft power, therefore, the *agaseke* can be a metaphor for all that is Rwandan; all that has been passed from generation to generation preserving all its attributes. It signifies all the traditional mores that kept Rwanda strong, unified and self-regenerative, as expressed in its poetry, myths, and other folklore. The oral tradition gave Rwanda meaning and life, which, in its beauty, can be symbolized by the colours and patterns (such as *nyamuraza* or *kibaba*) that decorate the *agaseke*. This rich oral tradition, in which *Rwandanness* or *Rwandanicity* found its home and origin, constitutes the soft power intrinsic in the *agaseke* that has always seen Rwanda maintain its glory and rise every time it fell.

The centrality of the *agaseke* and what it signifies in Rwandan culture has led to the basket being enshrined as a national emblem, and glorified in the nation's court-of-arms. It signifies the undivided nation of Rwanda and serves as a reminder to the richness of the Rwandan heritage and its being the core of the strength in the traditional institutions that today form the pillars of national development, such as the *Ingabo,* the traditional justice system *(Gacaca)* and the insistence on the sameness of all in Rwanda in national unity *(Ubumwe).*

From the Sectarian to the National: The Making of the Rwanda Defence Forces

In *Ubumwe,* the Government's struggle to make Rwanda Rwandan manifests itself in a common national identity and bondage that characterized the pre-colonial Rwandan society. Whether one was perceived a "Tutsi" or a "Hutu", it was incumbent upon him or her to live the ideals of *imfura*. And this, really, is what gave a common identity to all the Rwandans, which found its full expression in the military as part and parcel of the society.

What, however, would become of the modern Rwandan military as a socially integrative unifier cannot be seen outside the aftermath of the Genocide, nor the history that led to it. For instance, it may be recalled that the *deconstruction* of the Rwandan state, leading to the genocide, began with the advent of colonialism and deteriorated further during the post-colonial period in the First and Second Republics. The destruction of the state of Rwanda during these periods was spearheaded by the military.

Colonial and neo-colonial occupation of Rwanda, which took a century, from 1894 to 1994, ensured the desecration of the original Rwandan state and the military institution. In the colonial period, it was, first, the Congo-Belge *Force Publique* and the *Garde Territoriale du Rwanda-Urundi*. In the post-independence period, it was the sectarian and Hutu-nised *Garde Nationale du Rwanda* in the First Republic, and then the Forces Armées Rwandaises in the Second Republic. None of these armed forces propagated a national ideology or character. They were sectarian and overtly divisive.

With the genocide over in July 1994, therefore, the task that lay ahead was enormous if Rwanda was to find its feet after all the volatile divisiveness that had found its highest expression in the military. Recalling the unity that existed before the colonialists, national unity had to begin with integration, first within the military and then within the wider society. It was going to be a long process, and the integration was to be done against a grim background, which may be worth to recall.

The aftermath of the genocide entailed more than one million people dead and an entire population displaced internally or having fled as refugees. It also entailed a divided society with a collapsed socio-economic infrastructure. Meanwhile, even as the perpetrators of genocide had been defeated, they had relocated in the neighbouring countries from where they would reorganize and attempt armed return to Rwanda to resume where they had stopped with the genocide. An absence of institutions also included a skeptical international community, whose failure to prevent or stop the genocide was also cynical about Rwanda's chance to survive as a nation. Add to this the relentless efforts by those who had supported the genocidal regime to assist the remnants of the latter to regroup and recapture state power so as to complete the genocide. [9]

Against this background, the RPF realized that since the military was an instrument of violence that was monopolised by the state, it also had a higher social responsibility in facilitating social cohesion. This role could not only be done in the protection of social values from external aggression, but also in the enhancement of these values through the prevention of internal destabilization. The famed scholar, Huntington, captures the role of the army more succinctly when he notes that, "the skill of the physician is diagnosis and treatment, his responsibility is the health of his client. The skill of the officer is the management of violence, his responsibility is the military security of his client."[10] This presupposes an officer who understands the collective national interests as opposed to subjective and sectarian interests.

Here, the model used by the pre-colonial Rwandan society, and later to be applied by what would become the Rwanda Defence Forces (RDF), is illustrative. The classic military organization was rooted in the society. With the military rooted in the society, it was a symbiotic relationship of the military being produced and nurtured by the society, and the military in turn storing, propagating and defending the society's values. The tangible elements of the gravity of power (i.e., the military), must be in harmony with the intangible elements, the government and the people's will to that government.[11]

As the shield of the nation *(Ingabo z' u Rwanda)*, the military protected all in pursuit of national interests. Notably, the survival of the state was ingrained in its ability to manage instruments of violence at one level, and, on the other, their development for the general good of the society. This, in principle relevant even today, should lead to the nurturing and development of a nationalistic leadership at the political and military levels. Such leadership must seek to evolve and invest in the development of the necessary institutional frameworks that must consistently renegotiate the leadership's relevance with the aspirations of the society.[12] It is in this context that Rwanda under the RPF found its defining mission to integrate and re-integrate its people, beginning with the military.

In order to move ahead with this mission, the RPF/A first found it necessary to integrate the earliest captured ex-FAR soldiers in its fighting forces. These included, for instance, those in the January 1991 attack of the Ruhengeri prison, when three senior officers, who Habyarimana had imprisoned as his enemies, were released and joined the RPA ranks. Indeed, two of them, Stanislas Biseruka and François Muvunanyambo, soon became members of the RPA High Command. The integration and, later on re-integration of the ex-FAR and militias, soon took pace and continues to-date drawing from the traditional concept of *Ingando.*

Ingando in Kinyarwanda means a military encampment or assembly area *(rendez vous)* where the troops received their final briefing while readying for a military expedition. The briefing included, among others, re-organization of the troops and allotment of missions and tasks. In such gatherings, the individuals were reminded to subject their interests to the national ideal and give Rwanda their all. This meant that whatever differences one may have, the national interests always prevailed since the nation of Rwanda was bigger than any one individual and ensured prosperity for all. That was the idea behind the institution of *Ingando*[13] as a vehicle for re-integration of captured ex-FAR and militia into the RPF/A.

Even as it applies today, participation in *Ingando* recognizes the dignity and humanity of the participants as equal Rwandans. Irrespective of their roles in the Rwandan conflict, the *Ingando* forms the starting point to conflict resolution. As such, it formed a useful tool for re-integrating ex-combatants into the national army and society during and after[14] the RPF/A liberation war.

This entailed mixing the ex-Forces Armées Rwandaises (ex-FAR) and the regular Rwanda Patriotic Army (RPA) officers and men, which gave them an opportunity to talk about the Rwandan conflict. The objective of the *Ingando* is to help the participants, who today also include members of the greater society,[15] i.e., pre-university students, grassroots leaders, opinion leaders, teachers, ex-prisoners, etc., overcome mutual fear and suspicion, and temptation to revenge. They also allow participants to talk about the history and causes of the conflict and in the process heal the wounds of hatred.

The process followed in *Ingandos* enables the participants to accept responsibility for any harm done to each other and demystify negative perceptions of each other. This allows collective ownership of the tragedy that resulted from the conflict and enables participants to agree on what the future holds for them. It should be emphasized that the *Ingando* provides the atmosphere in which the parties meet without accusing each other.

Drawing from this, the interaction within the military between the different identities that formally had been at war with each other continues to offer a role model of reconciliation and national unity to the society at large. The military, which is engendered by teamwork and efforts towards joint goals easily facilitates the attainment of national objectives and aspirations. This is because the military clearly defines the "common enemy" to the national ideal of guaranteed security. In the case of post-genocide Rwanda, the RPF/A was able to demystify the notion of incompatibility between the Hutu and Tutsi identities through the integration process.

Thus the *Ingandos* form a problem solving mechanism. The *Ingando* workshops help the parties redefine their situation, facilitate a mutual understanding of each other, and identify the grievances, perceptions, and values of the parties and disputes. "Creative problem-solving searches for ways of redefining, fractioning, or transcending the conflict so that positive-sum, or win/win solutions, which leave both parties better off, can be discovered."[16] In short, the psychological barriers of suspicion, rejection, fear and deception are changed through the Ingandos by injecting knowledge and experience about conflict, conflict behaviour, and psychology into the socio-political relationships.

Thus, integration through the *Ingandos* entails refocusing the individual from being a manipulated tool of negative forces into an *imfura y'u Rwanda* (from a genocidaire to being an agent of social change and development) actualizing the ideals of a patriotic Rwandan. With this transformation, the RPF/A was able to provide an example and mediate the various conflicts that characterized the deconstruction of pre-genocide Rwanda.

However, how this military example would finally apply and be accepted by the communities country-wide can be seen in what transpired after the genocide and the insurgency that would result in a chronology of events still being experienced. What would draw from this would entrench the *Ingabo z'u Rwanda* into a veritable national force.

Coming to its Own: Consolidation of RDF Through Fire

After the genocide, as will be recalled, the former government with its military machinery comprising of the ex-FAR and the militias fled and relocated in Zaire, beginning July 1994. The genocidaires continued with their mission in the Kivu region causing more turmoil that brought in new dimensions to the conflict. This transformation of the conflict in the region was animated by various factors.

Firstly, the ex-FAR and the militia forces relocated to the refugee camps with their arms and ammunition, including other military hardware, intact without being disarmed by the host government of Zaïre (now Democratic Republic of Congo) under Mobutu.

Secondly, the host government allowed them to continue military training and organization within the refugee camps.

Third, the international community provided massive humanitarian assistance to the refugees that was transformed to military use.[17]

The fourth factor was that the genocidaires formed alliances with the local Banyarwanda Hutu in Congo to harass the Tutsi including the *Banyamulenge* (Congolese Tutsi), and later other known Tutsi communities in the Kivus.

To cap it all, the Zaïre Government took sides with the ex-FAR and *Interahamwe* and massacred the Tutsi, including the Banyamulenge, many of whom were also forcefully expelled out of the country.

All these factors conspired to enable the ex-FAR and Interahamwe to begin making armed incursions into Rwanda from Kivu in late 1994, with the campaign intensifying in 1995.

To begin with, the genocidaires transformed humanitarian assistance to the Rwandan refugees in the Congo into military hardware and embarked on what came to be known as *Opération Insecticide.* The *Opération* entailed genocidal incursions in Northwest and Southwest of Rwanda between 1995 and 1996.

Note the term "insecticide", which symbolised their continued extermination of the *Inyenzi* (Tutsi cockroaches). Nevertheless, *Opération Insecticide* internationalised the Rwandan conflict, and would form the basis for the forced return of the Rwandan refugees in late 1996 with the RPF/A pre-emptive attacks on the armed genocidaires in the refugee camps, that would be followed by the overthrow of their ally, President Mobutu, in May 1997.

However, even as this regime change was taking place in Zaïre, the first priority for Rwanda was the repatriation and resettlement of the refugees back in their country – an important step in the conflict management process in post-genocide Rwanda. Significantly, the very act of repatriation provided safe passage of the refugees to their original homes and villages. It also built confidence and rapport between the refugees and the RPF/A, who had earlier fled the country in the belief that the RPF was the enemy.[18]

Another important aspect was the RPF/A overseeing their peaceful resettlement and re-insertion back into their communities. This entailed an assurance of security and mediation in disputes over property and other scarce resources.

All was not smooth, however, as isolated incidents of insurgency began after the mass repatriation and resettlement in November 1996. They developed into a full-blown, organized insurgency in May and June 1997 after the fall of Mobutu. The growth of the insurgencies can be traced back to the massive repatriation, that incidentally also included armed ex-FAR and militia.[19]

In October 1997, insurgency operations started in earnest in Rwanda beginning with what came to be known as *The First Opération Alléluia,* which targeted Congolese Tutsi refugees in Gisenyi and climaxed with the Mudende massacres.[20] *The Second Opération Alléluia* in September 1998 targeted Goma and Gisenyi, and was partly "successful" with the capture of arms in Goma.

Meanwhile, counter-insurgency measures taken by the government forces, which included the integrated military, were yet another conflict management strategy. By this time, the integrated forces and their Hutu and Tutsi identities gave more assurance to the population that had earlier been fed on the divisive Hutu extremist propaganda.

The intensification of the insurgency in 1997 entailed the spread of insecurity from the northwest to some parts of western and central Rwanda. The government response was to intensify counter-insurgency operations that saw the ex-FAR and the militia withdrawing back to Congo in 1998. In August of the same year, the RPA re-launched its campaigns in the Democratic Republic of Congo (DRC) in pursuit of the fled insurgents as a continuation of the conflict management strategy.

Nevertheless, the rebels were determined. *Opération Alléluia* was followed by *Opérations Amen* and *Odyssey* in the DRC in June and July of 1999 and 2000, respectively. But both failed due to the RPF/A counter-insurgency operations in the country.

This would mark the beginning of the end of insurgency in Rwanda that saw its conclusion in May 2000.

The end of insurgency in Rwanda coincided with the increased integration and re-integration of 30,000-plus ex-FARs and militia by the year 2000. The insurgency was mostly in northwestern Rwanda and most of the integrated militias came from the region – a process that resulted in pacification in the area. This underscores the efficacy of the integration process as a tool for conflict management.

When the RPF/A re-launched into Congo after August 1998, it necessitated an increased deployment of officers and men. The foreign milieu provided a conducive environment for further bonding among the integrated forces serving a common cause for Rwanda. It also re-inforced their sense of patriotism and nationalism. The working together among the soldiers from different identities and backgrounds further cemented their solidarity and comradeship. On returning home after their tour of duty in the Congo, they influenced change within their respective communities and demystified the hitherto perceived animosities between the different identities of Hutu and Tutsi.

The comedy of rebel incursions continued, however. And, in May and December 2001, *Opération Oracle du Seigneur* got underway in Rwanda, only to be crushed by the RPF/A counter-insurgency operations under the command of the then Brigadier General James Kabarebe[21] that resulted in the capture of the *Armée de Libération du Rwanda* (ALIR) Commander, Colonel Evariste Bemera and his Chief of Intelligence. This capture, which included over 1,700 insurgents, effectively marked the end of insurgency inside Rwanda.

It would be of interest to note that during this period, women, both mothers and wives of the insurgents, played a crucial role in ending the insurgency. The women persuaded, or even volunteered information on their sons and husbands to the local authorities, in a bid to end the rebellion and the suffering it wrought on their families. This is testimony to the crucial role played by women in ending the insurgency, but also in transcending the dilemma of the polarity between the Hutu and Tutsi identities. Incidentally, in broader cultural terms, Rwandan women were traditionally regarded as mothers of "Rwandans" and not mothers of "Hutu" or "Tutsi". Therefore, gender-wise, the women were Rwandans first, whereas what would later be taken as the divisive "Hutu" and "Tutsi" identities were taken after the fathers in the traditional patriarchal society.[22]

What the women in the north during the insurgency illustrated was the necessity of unity and doing away with the negative notions of "we" against "them" in the Hutu and Tutsi polarity. In 2002, this notion of national unity would be underscored in the military through the renaming of the Rwanda Patriotic Army to the current name Rwanda Defence Forces (RDF), which better reflects a more national character.

By changing the name to RDF, this was a classic example of logical problem-solving transcending the conflict that formerly characterized the Rwandan military so that positive-sum, or a win-win solution, left both parties better off. By this, the RDF had rediscovered its historical national character and reflected the *Ingabo z'u Rwanda* of old. It has since gained international recognition with its peace support operations in Darfur in the Sudan and elsewhere.

Despite the changes, the ex-FAR and Interahamwe continued to pose a threat to Rwanda. However, in September and October 2003, *Opérations Trompête* and *Tabara* launched from South Kivu failed and saw the return to Rwanda of the top FDLR commanders, who included Major General Rwarakabije.[23] And beginning 2004 to date, *Opération la Fronde* (sling) has been going on and is doomed to fail with the continued return of other top commanders, such as Seraphin "Mahoro" Bizimungu and Nsanzabera.

In the ideological absurdity of the insurgents, note the Christian insinuation of the genocidal attacks with the names given to the murderous insurgency operations; i.e., *Alleluia,*

Amen, Oracle du Seigneur (Oracle of the Lord), *Trompête* (suggesting Joshua's trumpet as he entered Jericho in the Old Testament),[24] and *la Fronde* (evoking David's defeat of Goliath with the deadly sling).[25] These insinuations suggest the Christian God's blessings, thus giving weight and credence to their continued ideology of hate.

It is fateful irony that, just like the Catholic Church would abet the tragic 1959 "Hutu Revolution"[26], the *Opérations* suggest that Christianity is for the genocidal tendencies and the purification of "Christian" Rwanda from the Tutsi "infidels" who are also *"inyenzi"* (cockroaches). Such naming of the insurgency activities demonstrates how Christianity and religion in general can be perverted and used to condone genocidal acts and other crimes against humanity.

But the Rwanda Defence Forces have since moved on. Though keeping tabs on the remnants of rebel forces in the DRC and Great Lakes Region, today the RDF has gained its reputation as a professional military force that has proved its mettle in peace-keeping operations in post-conflict Africa.

The changing faces of the *Ingabo z'u Rwanda* — from the traditional military formations of the warrior kings to the colonial Congo-Belge *Force Publique* and the *Garde Territoriale du Rwanda-Urundi,* the sectarian and Hutu-nised *Garde Nationale du Rwanda* in the First Republic, and the *Forces Armées Rwandaises* in the Second Republic — it is these that will forever mark the character of the Rwanda Defence Forces. The history that led to the formation of today's RDF can never be divorced from the negative and divisive forces that preceded it, and will always serve as a challenge to overcome. It also remains a challenge for the RDF, therefore, to be a role model of national unity to the rest of Rwanda.

Even as the RDF continues to professionalise its forces to the highest level, it is from the foregoing, and particularly the turbulent history of *Ingabo z'u Rwanda,* that today thrusts it as a force of the 21st Century.

Notes

1   The *Indahemuka* song, *Gira ubuntu* by Maria Yohana Mukankuranga, which was a rallying point in the RPF/A mobilization campaigns for material and human resources giving the selfless example of Fred Rwigema and others.

2   Linda Melvern (2000), Dallaire (2003), Gourevitch (1998), etc; also see Immaculée Ilibagiza, *Left To Tell*, Hay House, 2007; Anick Kayitesi, *Nous existons encore*, Michel Lafon, 2004; etc

3   http://www.orwelltoday.com/rwandarpfinvade1990.html

4   Joseph Nye, *Bound to Lead: The changing nature of American Power*, New York, Basic Books, 1990; Nye, *Understanding International Conflicts: An introduction to Theory*, Pearson Longman, 2007.

5   J. Burton, *Resolving Deep-rooted Conflict* (Virginia: University Press of America, 1987), p.5; M. Banks, 'The International Relations Discipline: Assets or Liability for Conflict Resolution?,' pp.51-70 and A. Groom, 'Paradigms in Conflict: the Strategist, the Conflict Researcher and the Peace Researcher,' pp.71-74, in J. Burton and F. Dukes (eds.), Conflict: Readings in Management and Resolution (London: Macmillan, 1990).

6   See among others, M. Brown, 'Causes and Implications of Ethnic Conflict' in M. Brown (ed.), *Ethnic Conflict and International Security* (Princeton University Press, 1993), pp. 3-27; 'The Causes and Regional Dimensions of Internal Conflict' in M. Brown (ed.), *The International Dimension of Internal Conflict* (Cambridge, MA: The MIT Press, 1996), pp.571-603; M.Ross, *The Management of Conflict: Interpretations and Interests in Comparative Perspective* (New Haven: Yale University Press, 1993); T. Woodhouse, 'Commentary:NegotiatingaNewMillenium?ProspectsforAfrican Conflict Resolution' in Review of African Political Economy (No 68, 1996), pp. 129-137; S. Van Evera, 'Hypothesis on Nationalism and War' in *International Security* (Vol.18, N°4, Spring 1994), pp. 8-9.

7   Joseph Nye, op.cit.

8   Ibid.

9   Andrew Wallis, *Silent Accomplice*, I.B.Tauris & Co Ltd, New York, 2006, p.186 (Wallis quotes Bruno Delaye, Mitterrand's Africa's special advisor, aware that the ex-FAR were rearming and readying for attack from Zaire tells Prunier: "We won't invite the new Rwandese authorities to the next Franco-Africa Summit.

They are too controversial and besides, they are going to collapse any time.")

10   Samuel P. Huntington, *The Soldier and the State: The Theory and Politics of Civil Military Relations*, University of Harvard Press, Cambridge, twelfth reprint, 1995,p.15.

11   Carl Von Clausewitz, *On War* (edited and translated by Michael Howard and Peter Parret), Princeton, New Jersey, Princeton University Press, 1976. p. 579.

12   "National security does not consist of an army, a navy and an air-force—it depends on a sound economy... on civil liberties and human freedoms." – Harry S. Truman, State of the Union Address, 1947.

13   In Conflict Resolution strategies, the concept of *Ingando* is referred to as Track Two Diplomacy, or problem-solving workshops, which help parties search for constructive outcomes.

14   Between 1995 and 1997, a total of 10,500 ex-FAR officers and men were re-integrated in the RPA. And between 1998 and 2002 a total of 39,200 ex-FAR and militia were integrated in the RPF/A as it went on to become the Rwanda Defense Forces.

15   The concept of *Ingando* has been adopted and applied to the wider society by the National Unity and Reconciliation Commission (NURC), where the Ingando are referred to as Solidarity Camps.

16   H. Kelman, 'Interactive Problem-solving: a Social-psychological Approach to Conflict Resolution,' in J. Burton and F. Dukes (eds.), *Conflict: Readings in Management and Resolution*, Macmillan, London, 1990, p. 201.

17   The report of the International Panel of Eminent Personalities to Investigate the 1994 Genocide in Rwanda and the Surrounding Events/OAU, Paragraph 19.22

18   Maj. Gen. Paul Rwarakabije—a former Commander of Armée de Libération du Rwanda (ALIR) and Forces de Libération du Rwanda (FDLR/FOCA) in the Democratic Republic of Congo—who returned to Rwanda on 15 November   2003 (with 160 FDLR soldiers, among them seven senior and junior officers) and was appointed a Commissioner with the Rwanda Demobilization and Re-integration Commission (RDRC), acknowledges that the Rwandan conflict was spread in the Great Lakes Region when the FAR fled to Congo with a large section of the population. It was during a meeting of leaders of the fleeing genocidaire

regime in July 1994 at Mukamira military camp that the decision to vacate" the country with the "entire" population was taken. The fleeing genocidaire government expected a humanitarian catastrophe, which would prompt the international community to put pressure on the new RPF-led government in Kigali and portray it as illegitimate "without a population" to govern.

19   African Rights, *Rwanda: The Insurgency in the Northwest*, London, 1998, pp.1-5.

20   Congolese Tutsi refugees and their families were camped at the Adventist University of Mudende in Gisenyi, most of whom, especially women and children, were killed.

21   General James Kabarebe, at the time Operations Commander, would go on to become the Chief of General Staff of the Rwanda Defense Forces in 2003.

22   Before the institutionalization of the "Hutu" and "Tutsi" identities with the introduction of identity cards in 1933, the Hutu/Tutsi identities were fluid. A Hutu could become a Tutsi *(kwihutura)* and vice-versa *(gucupira)* as a result of gaining or losing cattle, and ipso facto a social status.

23   Maj. Gen. Rwarakabije, op.cit.

24   Joshua 5:13-27 (The New International Version of the Bible, International Bible Society).

25   1 Samuel 17: 1-58, op.cit.

26   Monsignor Perraudin's 1959 Lent letter *(Super Omnia Caritas)* which abetted the sectarian Hutu Revolution; also see Laurent Gakuba, op.cit., p.35.

Epilogue

The resilience of the pre-colonial state of Rwanda and its institutions, which took close to a millennium to build and internalize through culture and a value system, could not be destroyed within a mere 100 years (1894-1994) of colonialism and neocolonialism. Indeed, the pre-colonial period still serves to inform the present, including the ongoing reconciliation and conflict management processes. For instance, the *Gacaca* judicial system and the military integration processes *(Ingando)* are pre-colonial institutions that are serving the continuing post-genocide socio-political and economic development of Rwanda.

This inquiry being on the military and its historical place in the country affirms the traditional role of the Rwandan military in social harmony and stabilization. The present military has drawn its inspiration from the *Ingabo z'u Rwanda* that fully expressed *Rwandanness* or *Rwandanicity*, which continues to provide a measure of ideological foundation to the RDF in post-conflict Rwanda.

The linkage, however, is not only ideological, but also socio-cultural and possibly hereditary. As can be illustrated, the military formations or battalions, such as the *Abanyasanga*, that were formed even earlier than the 13th Century survived up to the advent of colonialism. Perhaps alluding to the hereditary character of the *Ingabo z'u Rwanda*, Chief Nkwaya, the last commander of the *Abanyasanga* towards the end of the 19th Century during the reign of Kigeri IV Rwabugiri has a great grandson in the present Rwanda Defense Forces. Major Bosco Higiro,[1] the great-grandson of Chief Nkwaya, might illustrate the hereditary link.

President Paul Kagame, Commander-in-Chief of the RDF, who is also the great-grandson of Chief Cyigenza cya Rwakagara, the Commander of Uruyange Formation during the reign of King Rwabugiri, would name his son after his illustrious great grandfather. Chief Cyigenza had also commanded the *Nyantango* battalion, which had survived from the 16th Century during the reign of Ruganzu II Ndoli. As we saw elsewhere in the book, similar examples abound in the RDF.[2]

These and many other examples illustrate the hold of Rwandan heritage on posterity and its ability to inspire and forge a new nation learning from the old, while creating new *abacengeli* (Rwandan heroes), both the sung and the unsung. The institution of *Ubucengeli* has always meant investing the destiny of Rwanda in its people through self-sacrifice. The continuity of Rwanda as a state and as a nation, therefore, is guaranteed by the fact of *Ubucengeli,* as there will always be Rwandans who will be willing to sacrifice themselves for the sake of the country and its people. And because of this, Rwanda propels ahead in search of a common and prosperous destiny from the ashes of the 1994 genocide – a product of colonial and neocolonial bigotry that ethnicized and racialized an otherwise one people.

The impact of colonialism was the creation of racism, a system the colonizers and their spiritual partners, the Catholic Church, were evidently not ashamed of. Indeed, the two supported and reinforced each other in mutually beneficial ways. Hundreds of thousands of Rwandans converted, making the church the country's main social institution. Indeed, 90% of Rwandans today are estimated to be Christian. Christianity, however, was not internalized as would be later attested to by the future "Christian" *genocidaires.* Christianity served to replace and marginalize Rwandan socio-cultural ideals, thereby creating a cultural void that was exploited by the colonialists and the Hutu elite to lay a firm foundation for the 1994 genocide.

To the Belgians, and later the post-independence leadership, created the Rwanda they wanted: centralized, easy to control, efficient, intolerant of non-conformity and Catholic. The Belgians transposed on Rwanda their bigotry and historical tendency for socio-political divisiveness. This socio-political divisiveness may be illustrated in a recent case. In September 2007, Filip Dewinter, Leader of Vlaams Belang (Flemish block), the extreme right of the xenophobic Flemish party was quoted by *Reuters* as saying: "We are two different nations, an artificial state created as a buffer between big powers, and we have nothing in common, except a king, chocolate and beer."

The words equate to what President Kayibanda, also disowning his own country, Rwanda, as a nation, once said of the Hutu and Tutsi: "Two nations in a single state – two nations between whom there is no intercourse and no sympathy, who are as ignorant of each other's habits, thoughts and feelings as if they were dwellers of different zones, or inhabitants of different planets."[3]

In the case of Kayibanda, "There [was] a fixation and obsession with the past that hampers the ability to look at the future ... unless people ... look at the future, they are going to continue and relive the past with all the negatives that brings."[4]

Drawing from this, the challenge today remains to create a new outlook that is Rwandan and not "ethnic" and cultivating a culture of inclusive and democratic politics in a decentralized framework that allows people in their respective communities to have a stake in governance. The essence is to guard against wilful manipulation of demographic majorities, such as the Hutu were, for personal gains of political demagogues, the likes of Kayibanda and Habyarimana.

The realization of the Rwandan dream and, indeed, the way forward for African leadership is to resist personalized governance that often results in weak public institutions[5] that are unable to hold individual leaders to account.

Notes

1   Major Bosco Higiro is the son of Nsereko son of Kayibanda son of
    Nyabirungu son of Chief Nkwaya. Major Doctor Guido Rugumire, the
    Commandant of Kanombe Military Hospital is also descended from
    Chief Nkwaya.

2   Col. Tom Byabagamba, Commanding Officer, Republican Guard,
    is the grandson of Rwatangabo and great-grandson of Nzigiye ya
    Rwishyura, both of whom commanded the Ndushabandi Battalion in
    the 19th Century. Major Ruzahaza, Commanding Officer, 41st Battalion,
    is the grandson of Bisangwa bya Rugombituri, the last overall
    Commander of King Rwabugiri's *Ingangurarugo*. Many more
    examples abound.

3   Grégoire Kayibanda during a speech on 27 November 1959.
    President Juvénal Habyarimana is also quoted to have said during
    a MRND Congress on 8 April 1991: "The unity of ethnic [sic]
    groups is not possible without the unity of the majority. Just as we note
    that no Tutsi recognizes regional belonging, it is imperative the
    majority forge unity, so that they are able to wade off any attempt
    to return them into slavery." He was convinced that Hutu and Tutsi
    were distinct ethnic groups that could not be accommodative of each
    other, and of whom by "majority" he meant Hutu in their diversity.

4   Senator George Mitchel, "Soul of India", PBS, 20 September 2002,
    www.pbs.org/wnet/wideangle/shows/media/transcript2.html

5   President Paul Kagame, "Time for Africa to insist on defining
    its own future", *Business Day*, 3 October, 2007; http://www.
    businessday.co.za/articles/opinion. aspx?ID=BD4A577756

Map of *Ku-aanda*

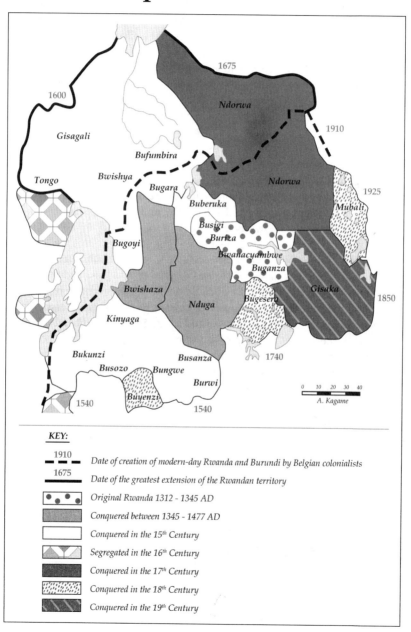

KEY:

1910 *(dashed line)* Date of creation of modern-day Rwanda and Burundi by Belgian colonialists

1675 Date of the greatest extension of the Rwandan territory

Original Rwanda 1312 - 1345 AD

Conquered between 1345 - 1477 AD

Conquered in the 15th Century

Segregated in the 16th Century

Conquered in the 17th Century

Conquered in the 18th Century

Conquered in the 19th Century

Table of Rwandan Kings

YEAR	KING	QUEEN-MOTHER	SOCIAL-ARMIES	CATTLE-ARMIES	CONQUESTS MADE
1091-1124	Gihanga Ngomijana	Nyiraukangaga (zigaba)	Abanyansanga	Insanga	*Rwanda rwa Gihanga*
1124-1157	Kanyarwanda Gahima	Nyamususa (singa)	Abahiza		
1157-1180	Yuhi I Musindi	Nyamata (singa)	Inshyama		
Abami b'umushumi	Yuhi Rumeza	Kirezi (singa)	Abakaraza Gakondo	Imilishyo	
	Yuhi Nyarume	Nyirashyoza (singa)	Inyangakugoma	Ingizi	
	Yuhi Rukuge	Nyirankindi (singa)			
	Yuhi Rubanda	Nkundwa (singa)			
1180-1213	Ndahiro I Ruyange	Cyizigira (singa)			
1213-1246	Ndoba	Monde (ega)			
1246-1279	Samembe	Magondo (ha)			
1279-1312	Nsoro Samukondo	Nyakanga (singa)			
1312-1345	Ruganzu I Bwimba	Nyakanga (singa)			*Rwanda rwa Gasabo*
1345-1378	Cyilima I Rugwe	Nyakiyaga (ega)	Ababarabiri Abariza	Ibirayi	Buriza/Buganza Busarasi/Kigali
1378-1411	Kigeri I Mukobanya	Nyanguge (kono)	Abatsindiyingoma Ibidafungura		Bwanacyambwe Busigi
1411-1444	Mibambwe I Mutabazi Sekarongoro	Nyabadaha (ega)	Uburunga Abadaheranwa	Inshya z'i Remera "	Nduga (of Mashira) (-) Bwanacyambwe *Part* of Bugara (of Muramira) Fight Bunyabungo
1444-1477	Yuhi Gahima	Matama (ha)	Amatanangabo Abazirakubingwa Inyaruguru	Inkondera	N-W (*Budaha, Bwishaza* *Inkiga* *Bugara* (of Nzira) *Mubali* Project against Bungwe
1477-1510	Ndahiro II Cyamatare	Nyirangabo(ega)	Inkindi Ingata Abahunga		Eleven-year *Occupation* of Rwanda by Bunyabungo
1510-1543	Ruganzu II Ndoli	Nyirarumaga(singa)	Ibisumizi	Indolero	*Bunyambiliri, Bwanamukari*

209

YEAR	KING	QUEEN-MOTHER	SOCIAL-ARMIES	CATTLE-ARMIES	CONQUESTS MADE
			Abaruhije Nyakare Nyantango	Ibyiza	Kivu regions, Bugoyi, Bwishya, Bufumbila
1543-1576	Mutara I Semugeshi	Nyiramavugo Nyirakabogo (ega)	Abaganda Impara	Impara	*Bungwe* (Bufundu, Nyakare, Nyaruguru,Bashumba, Buyenzi)
1576-1609	Kigeri II Nyamuheshera	Ncendeli(ega)	Inkingi +Ingangurarugo		*Bukunzi, Busozo,Bishugi, Kamuronsi, Gishali, Tongo Kigezi,Bufumbira, Buberuka*
1609-1642	Mibambwe II Gisanura	Nyabuhoro (ha)	Imitali Inyangakurushwa Abadacumura Abangogo Abarembo		Return of *Bwanacyambwe*
1642-1675	Yuhi III Mazimpaka	Nyamarembo (kono)	Indara (Bunyoro) Abashahuzi (H) Inkuba Abankungu Abatabaga Ababanda Intaremba Inkoramaraso	Amarebe Imitagoma Indoha " " Imitagoma Imitari	Fight with Burundi
	Karemera I Rwaka				
1675-1705	Cyilima II Rujugira	Kirongoro (ha)	Abakemba Indilira Imvejuru Abadahemuka Urwasabahiizi Abadaha Abatanyagwa Abalima	Imisugi Inyangamuteyi Inkabuzima Urutunga Imbaliro " Nyamumbe	Fight with Burundi, Gisaka, Ndorwa

YEAR	KING	QUEEN-MOTHER	SOCIAL-ARMIES	CATTLE-ARMIES	CONQUESTS MADE
			Intalindwa		
			Ibenga		
			Inzirwa		
			Ababito (Abakotanyi)	Inkungu	
			Abatanguha	Mpahwe	
			Igicikiza	Ibikomane	
			Imanga	"	
			Abarota	Iryishe-Rubunda	Rwandized *Mubali, Ndorwa*
1708-1741	Kigeri III Ndabarasa	Rwesero (gesera)	Ibisiga	Umuliro	
			Abashubije	"	
			Abashumba		
			Abanyoro		
1741-1746	Mibambwe III Sentabyo	Nyiratamba (ega)	Abatsinzi	Umunigo	Bugesera-north
			Abagina		
			Abatabashwa		
			Abiyahuzi	Igikwiye	
			Abiru		
1746-?	Yuhi IV Gahindiro	Nyiratunga(ega)	Abadahindwa	Umuhozi	Fight with Burundi, Gisaka, Ndorwa, Buhunde
			Abashakamba		
			Uruyange		
			Abazimya	Ibiheko	
			Intaganzwa	Uruyenzi	
? -1853	Mutara II Rwogera	Nyiramavugo Nyiramongi (ega)	Abakwiye	Amahame	Fight with Burundi
				"	
			Abazirampuhwe	Indilikirwa	*Gisaka*
			Inzirabwoba	"	
			Abazirakugisha		
			Imvuzarubango		
			Imanzi		

YEAR	KING	QUEEN-MOTHER	SOCIAL-ARMIES	CATTLE-ARMIES	CONQUESTS MADE
			Abarasa Abadahigwa	Urugaga	
1853-1895	Kigeri IV Rwabugiri	Murorunkwere (kono)	Ingangurarugo Abahilika Impamakwica Imbanzamihigo Inkaranka Ndushabandi Abashozamihigo Abasharangabo Abamaragishyika Abarinda	Ingaju z'i Sakare Abazatsinda Ndushabandi Ingaju z'i Rwamaraba Ibitare by'i Nyarubuye Imisugi y'i Rubona	Fight with Burundi, Idjwi, Bunyabungo, Buhunde-Butembo, Ndorwa Gikore, Kigezi, Nkole, Bushubi
1895-1896	Mibambwe IV Rutalindwa	Nyirambambwe IV Kanjogera	Abakeramihigo	Ingabe	
1896-1931	Yuhi V Musinga	Nyirayuhi V Kanjogera (ega)	Indengabaganizi Iziruguru Urushashi Imparabanyi Incogozabahizi Imirimba (Rudahigwa's) Intangamuganzanyo Ibihame Ishyaka (T)		
1931-1959	Mutara III Rudahigwa	Kankaze (ega) N/A			
1959-1960	Kigeri V Ndahindurwa				

YEAR	KING	QUEEN-MOTHER	SOCIAL-ARMIES	CATTLE-ARMIES	CONQUESTS MADE
	Abami b'Ibirari (Mythical Kings)	**Abami b'Umushumi (Ahistorical Kings)**	**Abami b'Ibitekerezo (Historical Kings)**		
	Zabizeze	Kanyarwanda Gahima	Ruganzu I Bwimba		
	Kijuru	Yuhi I Musindi	Cyilima I Rugwe		
	Kobo	Nyarume	Kigeli I Mukobanya		
	Merano	Rukuge	Mibambwe I Sekarongoro		
	Nyeranda	Rubanda	Yuhi II Gahima		
	Gisa	Ndahiro	Ndahiro Cyamatare		
	Kizira	Ndoba	Ruganzu II Ndoli		
	Muntu	Samembe	Mutaral Semugeshi		
	Kazi	Nsoro Samukondo	Kigeli II Nyamuheshera		
	Gihanga		Mibambwe II Gisanura		
			Yuhi II Mazimpaka		
			Cyilima II Rujugiro		
			Kigeli III Ndabarasa		
			Mibambwe III Sentabyo		
			Yuhi IV Gahindiro		
			Mutara II Rwogera		
			Kigeli IV Rwabugiri		
			Yuhi V Musinga		
			Mutara III Rudahigwa		

References

"**Achebe:** Africa's genius", *The Daily Monitor,* June 17, 2007; http://www.monitor.co.ug/artman/publish/insights/Achebe_Africa

African Rights – *Rwanda: The Insurgency in the Northwest,* London, 1998

Bishop Classe's letter to Resident Mortehan on 21 Sept 1927

Bradford, Ernle, *Hannibal,* McGraw-Hill Company, New York, 1981

Brown, M. (ed.), *Ethnic Conflict and International Security* (Princeton University Press, 1993

Brown, M. (ed.), *The International Dimension of Internal Conflict* (Cambridge, MA: The MIT Press, 1996)

Bruneau, Lt-col V., *Twenty-third detachment of the 4th battalion Commando,* Rwanda 1962 Brussels, sd

Burton, J. and F. Dukes (eds.), *Conflict: Readings in Management and Resolution* (London: Macmillan, 1990 (M. Banks, 'The International Relations Discipline: Assets or

Burton, J., *Resolving Deep-rooted Conflict,* Virginia: University Press of America, 1987

Chrétien, J.P, *The Great Lakes of Afrika: Two Thousand years of History,* Zone Books, New York, 2003

Clausewitz, Carl Von, *On War* (edited and translated by Michael Howard and Peter Parret), Princeton, New Jersey, Princeton University Press, 1976

Colonial Administration Decree of 14 July 1952

Delmas, L (Père), *Généalogie de la noblesse (les Batutsi) du Rwanda,* Kabgayi vicariat apostolique du Rwanda, 1950

Des Forges, Alison Liebhafsky, *Defeat Is The Only Bad News: Rwanda Under Musiinga,* 1896-1931, Yale University, Ph.D., 1972

Destexhe, Alain, *Rwanda and Genocide in the Twentieth Century,* Pluto Press, London, 1995

Emergency Decree, Governor General of Congo-Belge, October 20, 1959

Eric Hobsbawn and Terrence Ranger (ed) *The Inversion of Tradition,* Cambridge University Press, 1993

Evera, S. Van, 'Hypothesis on Nationalism and War,' in *International Security* Vol.18, N°4, Spring 1994

Franco-Rwanda Agreement of 12th April, 1983

Franco-Rwanda Agreement of 26th August, 1992

Gakuba, Laurent, *Rwanda 1959-1994,* Coetquen Editions, 2007

Gatwa, T., "The Churches and Ethnic Ideology in the Rwandan Crises 1900-1994", (Ph.D. thesis:, University of Edinburgh, 1998)

Gudrun Honke (ed) « Au plus profond de l'Afrique: Européens et Rwandais font connaissance », *Au plus profond de l'Afrique: Le Rwanda et la Colonisation allemande* 1885-1919

Gourevitch, P., *We wish to inform you that tomorrow we will be killed with our families: Stories from Rwanda,* Picador, 1998

Habyarimana, Juvénal, Speech, MRND Congress, 28th April, 1991

Harroy, J.P, *Rwanda: Souvenirs d'un compagnon de la marche du Rwanda vers la démocratie et l'indépendance,* Hayez, Bruxelles, 1984

Henry Morton Stanley, *Through the Dark Continent,* London, 1878, Vol. 1

Hochschild, Adam, *King Leopold's Ghost: A Story of Greed, Terror and Heroism in Colonial Africa,* Pan Books, London, 2002

Huntington, Samuel P., *The Soldier and the State: The Theory and Politics of Civil Military Relations,* University of Havard Press, Cambridge, 12th reprint, 1995

Ilibagiza, Immaculée, *Left To Tell,* Hay House, 2007

Kagabo, Jose, Interview, July 2004

Kagame, Alexis (Abbé), *Les Milices du Rwanda pré-colonial,* Butare, 1962

Kagame, Alexis (Abbé), *Le Code des institutions politiques du Rwanda pré-colonial,* IRCB, vol.xxvi, fasc.I, Bruxelles, 1952

Kagame, Alexis (Abbé), *Un abrégé de l'ethno-histoire du Rwanda,* Editions universitaires du Rwanda, Butare, 1972

Kagame, Alexis (Abbé), *Un abrégé de l'histoire du Rwanda,* de 1853-1972, Editions universitaires du Rwanda, Butare, 1975

Kagame, Alexis (Abbé), *L'histoire de armées-bovines dans l'ancien Rwanda,* IRSAC, 1960

Kagame, President Paul, "Time for Africa to insist on defining its own future", Business Day, 3 October, 2007; http://www.businessday. co.za/articles/opinion.aspx?ID=BD4A577756

Kanyamacumbi, P: *Société, culture et pouvoir politique en Afrique interlacustre. Hutu et Tutsi au Rwanda,* Edition SELECT, A.T.R.I.O, Kinshasa, 1995

Karemera, Pièrre, Discussion, Kigali, 2006

Katumanga, M, Ph.D Thesis, Université de Pau et des Pays de l'Adour, 2002

Kayibanda, Grégoire, Speech, 27th November, 1959

Kayihura, Michel, Interview, Kigali, January 2003

Kayitesi, Anick, *Nous existons encore,* Michel Lafon, 2004

Kayonga, Lt Gen Charles, Discussion, Kigali, 2005

Kelman, H., 'Interactive Problem-Solving: a Social-Psychological Approach to Conflict Resolution,' in J. Burton and F. Dukes (eds.), *Conflict: Readings in Management and Resolution,* Macmillan, London, 1990

Ki-Zerbo, J., (ed), *General History of Africa Part I,* UNESCO, 1981

Lacger, L. De, *Le Ruanda* [Kabgayi: Vicariat apostolique du Ruanda, 1939]

Lacger, L. De, *Le Rwanda ancien,* Kabgayi, 1959

Lacger, L De., *Le Rwanda ancien et moderne,* 2è ed, Kabgayi, 1961

Lemarchand, René, *Rwanda and Burundi,* Praeger Publishers: London, 1970

Liability for Conflict Resolution?,' and A. Groom, 'Paradigms in Conflict: the Strategist, the Conflict Researcher and the Peace Researcher,')

Linden, Ian, *Church and Revolution in Rwanda,* Manchester University Press, Manchester, 1977

Lizinde, Col. Théoneste, Discussion, 1993

Logiest, G., *Mission au Rwanda: Un blanc dans la bagarre Tutsi-Hutu,* Didier Hatier, Bruxelles, 1988

London Sunday Times, November 1961

Lugan, Bernard, *Rwanda: le génocide, l'Église et la démocratie,* Éditions du Rocher, 2004

Lugan, B, *François Mitterrand, the French Army and Rwanda,* Editions of the Rock, 2005

Mamdani, Mahmood, *When Victims Become Killers: Colonialism, Nativism, and the Genocide in Rwanda,* Fountain Publishers, Kampala, 2001

Maquet, J.J., *The Premise of Inequality in Ruanda,* 1961

Mbonimana, G."L'Instauration d'un royaume chretien au Rwanda, 1900-1931", (Ph.D. thesis, Universite catholique de Louvain, 1981)

Melvern, Linda, *A People Betrayed: The role of the West in Rwanda's Genocide,* Zed Books, 2000

Mitchel, Sen. George, "Soul of India", PBS, September 20, 2002; www.pbs.org/wnet/wideangle/shows/media/transcript2.html

Monsignor Perraudin, 1959 Lent letter *(Super Omnia Caritas)*

Mugesera, Laurent, Discussion, Kigali, 2003

Munyurangabo David, Interview, Kigali, May, 2006

Museveni, Yoweri K., *Sowing the Mustard Seed: The Struggle for Freedom and Democracy in Uganda,* Macmillan, 1997

Musuhuke, Mzee Ladislas, Interview, 2005

Mutimura, Ambassador Zeno, Discussion, Kigali, November 2007

Muzungu, B, (ed), *Les Cahiers: Lumière et Société,* Kigali, No.1-36

Muzungu, B, (O.P.), *Histoire du Rwanda Pré-colonial,* L'Harmattan, Paris, 2003

Muzungu, Ph.D. Thesis, « Le Dieu de nos pères », 3 vol., Bujumbura, 1974

Nduwayezu, Chrysologue, « La Force Publique au Rwanda depuis 1916 à 1960 » (Mémoire in ESM, Kigali, July 1987)

Ntezimana, E, "Le Rwanda social, admnistratif et politique à la fin du dix-neuvième siècle", in Gudrun Honke (ed), *Au plus profond de l'Afrique*: *Le Rwanda et la Colonisation allemande 1885-1919*

Nyakatura, J.W., *Abakama (Kings) of Bunyoro-Kitara,* Kisubi, Marianum Press, 1999

Nye, Joseph, *Bound to Lead: The Changing Nature Of American Power,* New York, Basic Books, 1990

Nye, Joseph, *Understanding International Conflicts: An introduction to Theory,* Pearson Longman, 2007

Pagès, Andre. *Un Royaume hamite au centre de l'Afrique,* ERCB, Brussels, 1933, Vol.1

Périès, Gabriel and David Servenay, *Une guerre noire: Enquete sur les origines du genocide rwandais (1959-1994).* La Decouverte, Paris, 2007

Prof Roger Louis, *Ruanda-Urundi 1884-1919,* Clarendon Press, Oxford, 1963

Reed, W. Cyrus, "Exile, Reform and the Rise of the Rwanda Patriotic Front," *Journal of Modern African Studies,* 1996

Report of the United Nations Commission for Ruanda-Urundi, 1962, A/5126

"Reunion des Administrateurs de Territoire », Kigali, January 11, 1960

Rodney, Walter, How Europe Underdeveloped Africa, 1972, EAEP, Nairobi

Ross, M., *The Management of Conflict: Interpretations and Interests in Comparative Perspective,* New Haven: Yale University Press, 1993;

Ruanda Politique, 1958-1960

Ruhashya, Col. Epimaque, Interview, 2005

Rumiya, Jean, *Le Rwanda sous le Régime du Mandat belge (1916-1931),* Paris, 1992

Index